D1577925

LOU HENRY HOOVER

MODERN FIRST LADIES

Lewis L. Gould, Editor

LOU HENRY HOOVER

ACTIVIST FIRST LADY

NANCY BECK YOUNG

UNIVERSITY PRESS OF KANSAS

© 2004 by the University Press of Kansas

All rights reserved

Published by the University Press of Kansas (Lawrence, Kansas 66049),
which was organized by the Kansas Board of Regents and is operated
and funded by Emporia State University, Fort Hays State University,
Kansas State University, Pittsburg State University, the University
of Kansas, and Wichita State University

Library of Congress Cataloging-in-Publication Data

Young, Nancy Beck.

Lou Henry Hoover : activist First Lady / Nancy Beck Young.

p.   cm. — (Modern first ladies)

Includes bibliographical references and index.

ISBN 0-7006-1357-9 (cloth : alk. paper)

1. Hoover, Lou Henry, 1874-1944. 2. Hoover, Herbert, 1874-1964.

3. Presidents' spouses — United States — Biography.

I. Title. II. Series.

E802.1.H75Y68 2004

973.91'6'092—dc22

2004012543

British Library Cataloguing-in-Publication Data is available.

Printed in the United States of America

10 9 8 7 6 5 4 3 2 1

The paper used in this publication meets the minimum requirements of the
American National Standard for Permanence of Paper for Printed Library
Materials Z39.48-1984.

For Mark

CONTENTS

EDITOR'S FOREWORD

Lou Henry Hoover was a star-crossed first lady. Her four years in the White House came between the tenure of the stylish Grace Coolidge and the extended stay of the controversial Eleanor Roosevelt. As a result, Hoover's record has faded in the popular mind to the point where she has become only a name on the list of twentieth-century presidential wives. Such a judgment is misleading. When Lou Hoover moved into the White House in 1929, she had a long history of involvement with the Girl Scouts and women's athletics to prepare her for her new duties. During her husband's presidency, she continued her commitment to the Girl Scouts and used that connection in reacting to the Great Depression. In her work as first lady, she spoke on the radio, gave interviews to the press, and pursued social causes. She represented an important transition between the presidential wives who played merely social and ceremonial roles and those who were committed to various causes and developed their own staffs to help them achieve their goals.

Bringing Lou Henry Hoover into clearer historical focus and locating her in the record of modern first ladies are Nancy Beck Young's goals in her informative and lively study of this complex woman. Access to the rich collection of Mrs. Hoover's personal and policy papers has allowed Young to construct a narrative that explores the Hoover marriage in fuller detail than any previous scholarly work. Young also explains the first lady's views on race, her efforts to use voluntarism to fight the economic crisis that shaped the Hoover presidency, and her growing conservatism. With the abundance of information and insights that Young supplies, the reasons for Lou Hoover's accomplishments and failures in her challenging role become clear. More than just a pale forerunner to Eleanor Roosevelt, Hoover was an innovator as a presidential spouse, as well as a victim of the assumptions that she did so much to change.

Thanks to Young's illuminating narrative, Lou Henry Hoover's service between 1929 and 1933 can now be seen as an important turning point in how first ladies fulfilled their special role in American politics and society.

Lewis L. Gould

ACKNOWLEDGMENTS

This book resulted from a conversation I had with Lewis L. Gould in the summer of 1998. It is to Lew that I owe my largest intellectual debt in terms of conceptualizing and completing this project. I also benefited from stimulating conversations with and comments from several historians who aided my efforts: Deborah Blackwell, Bill Childs, Kendrick Clements, David Hamilton, Sarah Harper Case, Joan Hoff, John Inscoe, Kristie Miller, Martha Swain, and Leigh Ann Wheeler. Fred Woodward performed above and beyond the call of duty in his role as editor at the University Press of Kansas.

Equally important was the assistance I received from the dedicated staff of the Herbert Hoover Presidential Library. I was made welcome on each of my trips, and the archivists never failed to answer my many queries or fetch the numerous boxes I requested. I am indebted to Tim Walch, the director of the library, and his staff, particularly Brad Bauer, Jim Detlefsen, Dale Mayer, Dwight Miller, Matt Schaefer, Lynn Smith, Pat Wildenberg, and Cindy Worrell. The librarians at McKendree College cheerfully filled my many interlibrary loan requests and provided great friendship as a bonus. My deepest thanks go to Rebecca Bostian, Bill Harroff, Debbie Houk, and Liz Vogt.

Financial intervention at key junctures sustained my efforts. I gained an important grant from the Herbert Hoover Presidential Library Association in the beginning stages of my research. Throughout the course of my investigation, McKendree College was most generous, providing small grants to support additional research and travel expenses so that I could attend conferences and present papers about Lou Henry Hoover. Associate deans David Brailow and Dennis Ryan welcomed each of my grant applications and shared their insights into my work. Gerald Duff, the provost of the college, deserves a special word of thanks. He has nurtured my career since I arrived at McKendree and has created an intellectual environment that supports and encourages scholarship. Finally, John Riley and the White House Historical Association provided a grant that allowed me to complete my research in a timely fashion.

Being a college professor provides a scholar with a captive audience on whom she can test new ideas. I reaped all the benefits of that situation and none of the complaints. Countless McKendree students listened to and tested my ideas about Lou Henry Hoover. My students also played a critical role outside the classroom. A special word of thanks goes to the student research assistants who have worked in my office over the years: Rachel Brandmeyer, Carl Florczyk, John Jurgensmeyer, Erin McKenna, Dawn Pedersen, Matt Sherman, and Dana Vetterhoffer.

Finally, I would like to acknowledge my friends and family for their support. John K. and Kenna Beck, John Keitt and Shari Beck, Thomas Clarkin, Tom and Margie Foster, Karen Gould, and Jon Lee all provided love and friendship when they were most needed. My most important debt is owed to Mark E. Young, who has been with me each step of the way and has sacrificed his own work to the benefit of mine. Although I could not have completed this book without the assistance of the aforementioned individuals and institutions, any flaws that remain are mine alone.

LOU HENRY HOOVER

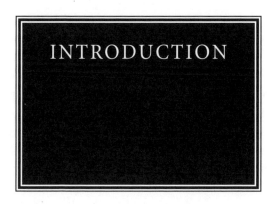

INTRODUCTION

Lou Henry Hoover filled many roles over the course of her vibrant life. She was an activist, a wife, a mother, a philanthropist, a geologist, an outdoorswoman, a clubwoman, a writer, a progressive, and a conservative. Because she undertook these diverse activities on her own terms, she cannot be compressed into a single category. The word *activist*, though, describes both her demeanor and her various pursuits. During her life, including her four years as first lady, she took on many causes and garnered significant public acclaim. Americans in the first four decades of the twentieth century admired this popular and skillful woman.

Lou Henry Hoover accomplished much before, during, and after her White House tenure. Although she respected the trappings of the past, Hoover revolutionized the office of first lady, turning it away from its traditional, nineteenth-century moorings toward a more modern, activist direction. Her role was unlike that of the women who preceded her, whose function had been little more than to entertain White House guests. Hoover refused to be merely an appendage of her husband, and she adopted a number of social causes. She did substantial work for women and children, the arts, humanitarian concerns, relief of the unemployed, and conservative political organizing. Yet, in the decades that followed, the public forgot her innovations. As the unelected spouse of the man whom most Americans blamed for the Great Depression, her celebrity faded after 4 March 1933.

Lou Henry Hoover instituted several key innovations—reliance on a women's advisory network, and expansion of the East Wing secretarial staff into policy work, for example—that have faded from memory with the passage of time. Part of the reason for this forgetfulness is the lack of sufficient scholarship about Hoover. More important, she fell victim to contemporary Democratic partisans who wrongly suggested that she lacked social skills and that she was ignoring the misery of the Great Depression. In fact, this complicated woman was a talented and popular hostess who helped revitalize the White House social program. Her vision, however, threatened the staid mores of the Washington, D.C., social elite and invited criticism. The gulf between the perception and the reality of Lou Henry Hoover's depression relief work also proved significant. She established an extensive relief structure through her contacts with women's voluntary associations, but for a variety of reasons—including deference to public expectations about the first lady's role and a belief in self-help and community relief—she never fully explained her White House work to the American people. As a result, much of her activism remains hidden.

What made Lou Henry Hoover the first modern first lady? The easy answer involves her many groundbreaking precedents. She spoke on the radio, tackled civil rights, fought the depression, and helped impoverished mountaineers—all first-lady firsts. The conditions that made this work possible are more complicated, involving both personal and societal circumstances: her marriage to Herbert Hoover, and the social revolution in gender roles that occurred in the late nineteenth and early twentieth centuries.

Marriage to Herbert Hoover, the man she called Bert when businesslike and Daddy when loving, helped facilitate Lou Henry Hoover's activism. Prior to his election to the presidency in 1928, the Hoovers had constructed an effective public marriage. She used their private relationship as a springboard to her public career in the volunteer community. Shared values about social priorities characterized their work, which sometimes overlapped and sometimes ran on parallel tracks. In the years between the Great War and the Great Depression, the Hoovers grew concerned about what they viewed as the destructive tendencies of modernity. Although they appreciated the benefits of efficiency and scientific management, for example, they worried about the impact of urban values on the social fabric. They framed their political ideology and their activism to counter the potential destruction of community support networks. For the Hoovers, a rural, small-town model of rugged individualism and community service was more humane than urban alienation from traditional morals. Issues ranging from Belgian relief to the Girl Scouts to the Great Depression became opportunities to tout these values.

Between 1914 and 1918, the Hoovers tackled common problems, such as fund-raising to alleviate Belgian starvation and managing American food resources during wartime. Such conditions made it easy for the two to work in partnership. Additionally, Herbert Hoover's encouragement of Lou's public activism made her transition from wife and mother to public figure seamless. By the 1920s, however, their specific interests had diverged. He focused on his duties as secretary of commerce and his presidential ambitions, while she became entrenched with voluntary organizations such as the Girl Scouts and the Women's Division of the National Amateur Athletic Federation. More important, Lou had learned during the Great War that she could act independently. In short, she grew during that period, whereas her husband, who already functioned well in the public sphere, had no need to change in any fundamental way. Thus, Lou Henry Hoover had less reason for sustained public cooperation with her husband by the late 1920s.

With the onset of the Great Depression in 1931, the nation's economic privation might have brought the Hoovers back into shared activism, but it did not. Herbert Hoover's obsessive overwork prevented him from seeing his wife as an ally. Additionally, more than a decade of independent action made it difficult for them to recreate their wartime cooperation. They were, after all, fifteen years older and already set on their separate courses. Lou Henry Hoover nonetheless transcended these circumstances to become the first modern first lady, developing depression-fighting strategies analogous to her husband's West Wing efforts. After 1933, both Hoovers embraced conservative, partisan politics.

Lou Henry Hoover's career first emerged because of a wartime public partnership with her husband, but with the passage of time, that partnership became more fictive than real. Lou became an activist in her own right, although the causes she advocated were always congruous with her husband's interests. She carefully manipulated her public acclaim, giving public talks, appearing as the honored guest at countless dinners and other public gatherings, and lobbying behind the scenes for the advancement of her agenda. Such undertakings melded well with her adventurous spirit and her belief in community involvement, traits that dated to her childhood. Indeed, throughout her married life, Hoover combined her private responsibilities as a wife and mother with her public interests, much in the style of upper-middle-class and elite women from privileged backgrounds.

Lou Henry Hoover arose as a public figure alongside significant changes in the way women lived their lives. Because these shifts helped make her activism possible, they bear further consideration. Rooted in nineteenth-century reform, the woman's rights movement (constructed in the singular) spanned into the early twentieth century. The most well-known demand was voting rights, but women also sought reforms related to education, property rights, and jury service. By the 1910s, the woman's rights movement had given rise to feminism. The feminist ideology was both more expansive, in that its supporters wanted to change all aspects of male-female relations, and more restrictive, in that its adherents did not speak for all women.

Even though she was not tied to the woman's movement or to feminism, Hoover benefited from both of them. The enlargement of opportunity, especially for white, middle-class women, meant that individuals of Hoover's generation occupied a very different world from that of their mothers. By the choices she made in college and the work she did with voluntary organizations, Hoover implicitly accepted the changed landscape in which women and men lived. She never spent much time as an adult thinking or writing about feminism specifically, but the manner in which she constructed her life and the causes she advocated were intrinsically tied to the new social mores. Indeed, when queried by young women whether they could combine scientific careers with marriage and motherhood, she answered in the affirmative. Likewise, her work with the Girl Scouts and women's athletics reflected her belief that women could enter the public sphere.

As the options available to middle-class women expanded, Hoover forged a separate, activist career for herself in the 1920s and 1930s. In the larger society, feminist leaders campaigned on behalf of the equal rights amendment or child labor laws; radical feminists, such as Alice Paul, insisted that women and men be treated the same; and social feminists urged protective legislation for women because of their inherent differences from men. But many more women, like Hoover, responded to this changing world without contemplating the source of their enhanced opportunities. Thus, Hoover is an important figure for understanding the complexity of gender roles in the interwar years.

By the 1920s, the range of behaviors open to women had expanded, allowing them more options than previous generations had enjoyed. More important, these new roles came without specific labels, and the women who adopted them did so without thinking of themselves as rebels. Thus, Hoover's life offers an alternative and provocative assessment of women's activism in the decades immediately after suffrage was won. She ignored the ideological wars within the feminist movement in favor of practical work that helped the next generation of American women learn how to negotiate their various options. Her legacy, too long overlooked by scholars and the public, transcends the arcane debates about the origins of feminism. Study of her life reveals a dynamic woman who used her activism to refashion the office of the first lady into a modern institution that reflected societal changes in the way American women lived their lives.

CHAPTER 1

FROM TOMBOY TO FIRST LADY

Lou Henry Hoover remained rooted in the experiences of her rural Waterloo, Iowa, childhood and her formative years in California. Born on 29 March 1874 to Florence Weed and Charles D. Henry, she was the first of two daughters. Her youthful activities, many of them atypical for Gilded Age girls, prepared an adult Lou Henry Hoover for an intriguing life that melded traditional household work with public philanthropy. Her family instilled a variety of traits, including the love of knowledge, travel, and the outdoors. She learned that life, when approached with curiosity, provided unlimited opportunities for adventure. A belief in practicality and a desire for privacy moderated her otherwise boundless exploration. Lou's sense of self ensured her a successful career in women's voluntary organizations and an unprecedented range of activism as first lady.

Her parents provided Lou and her sister Jean with a modest lifestyle. Charles D. Henry worked as a country banker but never settled long in one location. Florence Henry's chronic asthma prompted the family to seek a warmer and drier climate. They moved several times during Lou's childhood—to Texas, to Kansas, and finally to California, first Whittier and then Monterey. Childhood experience with financial need shaped the way Lou Henry responded to her husband's acquired wealth, creating a sense of entitlement felt only by the new rich who had known youthful want.

Charles D. Henry (left) fishing with his daughter Lou Henry, c. 1895. (Herbert Hoover Presidential Library-Museum)

As a child, Lou relished the time she spent with her father, who taught her to fish by her fifth birthday and to ride bareback by age six. These leisure activities were rare for girls, whose play was usually designed to instill maternal and housekeeping skills. She especially enjoyed their camping trips and described one in a college essay: "All is still. The flames have departed. The coals smolder and grow dim among the ashes and the vision vanishes amid the vague smoke of the campfire. The stars still keep their solitary vigil from the narrow belt of heaven that is outlined by the cañon walls." After one overnight trip, she told her mother that she would prefer to sleep outside. Such tendencies troubled Florence Henry, who tried to interest her daughter in domestic arts such as sewing and mothering. Young Lou, coming of age at a time of change in women's roles, merged nineteenth-century notions of the woman's sphere with evolving educational and voluntary opportunities.[1] Nonetheless, her love of outdoors and adventure dictated much of her adult life—she majored in geology in college, had a lifelong commitment to the Girl Scouts, and willingly charted new territory for first ladies.

Lou's family imposed few limits on her activities. As a popular schoolgirl, Lou organized literary and scientific clubs, had African American friends in California, and challenged traditional gender roles. A classmate recalled that despite Lou's "refinement and grace," she was "known to have taken a long rope, climbed a tree at a school picnic, tied the rope to a strong branch and thus provided a swing for the party." Because she was the only girl willing to engage in masculine play, some classmates viewed her with suspicion, while others cheered her accomplishments.[2] Criticism curbed Lou's irreverence toward expected female behavior and taught her to accommodate traditional virtues. The spirited girl chafed at limitations based on gender but had little taste for rebellion.

Lou's parents moved the family to Corsicana, Texas, in early 1879 and remained there until mid-1880. In an essay that she later wrote for a high school composition class, Lou recalled: "It was after midnight when the train pulled up, and the only recollection I have is of a darkie (the hotel porter) picking me up and sitting me on his shoulder and with a satchel in the other hand, carrying me across the square to the hotel." The year in Texas was a culture shock. Lou found her new neighbors to be quite welcoming as long as she accepted their racial customs and mores, some of which she absorbed. She noted in her essay the proximity of whites and African Americans, and she adopted the language of the white South when speaking of black southerners.[3] This brief sojourn into the former Confederacy revealed much to the relatively young Lou about sectional politics, an issue that would later affect her White House tenure. Although as an adult she occasionally pushed for fair treatment of elite and middle-class blacks, she never completely overcame the prejudices prevalent among white Americans of her era.

In high school, Lou thought and wrote about women's quest for equality. In an essay on universal suffrage in 1889, she opposed as unfair the classing of women with "idiots, maniacs and 'jailbirds' far below the roughest, least intelligent scamp." Though she acknowledged that women cared little for political offices such as county clerk, road overseer, or sheriff, Lou insisted that temperance and public education demanded female attention. Her views reflected contemporary public concerns. The movement for women's suffrage, which originated in 1848, was showing signs of strength in the western United States. Likewise, middle-class women had organized against excessive alcohol use. Her interests as a teenager in what were perhaps the most significant public policy questions for women caused Lou to speculate more widely about women's rights.[4]

At age sixteen she wrote "The Independent Girl," which reflected her desire for liberation from the staid expectations of female conformity to the woman's sphere. The views articulated in this piece were quite personal. Lou relished freedoms that were incomprehensible to earlier generations of women. She argued: "The independent girl is truly of quite modern origin and usually is a most bewitching little piece of humanity. . . . [She is an] ambitious little personage who never asks for and seldom receives advice of any kind." Such a definition of womanhood meshed well with the emergence of a public sphere of activity for middle-class white women in the nineteenth century. Interestingly, Lou's implicit views about marriage foretold the partnership she would build with Herbert Hoover nine years later: "But sooner or later she is sure to meet a spirit equally as independent as her own, and then—there is a clash of arms ending in mortal combat, or they unite forces and with combined strength go forth to meet the world."[5]

After graduation in 1891, Lou Henry entered the state normal school in Los Angeles, where she studied before transferring to San Jose Normal School. Her college years revealed an affinity for the Republican party. She saw it as the forward-thinking, progressive political organization of her generation, and she adopted a commitment to female equality because it was the right thing to do. The essays and reports that Lou wrote while a student at San Jose revealed her careful study of a range of contemporary social problems, including nationalism and politics, the labor question, temperance, and the proper function of education. As was consistent with emerging GOP doctrine, she viewed working-class complaints in simplistic terms: "If the laboring classes have such a vast majority," she queried, "why should they, and will they, not use their power at the polls?"[6] Such a perspective, which she retained throughout her adult life, overlooked the history of farmers' and workers' protests in California.

As graduation approached in May 1893, Lou Henry considered her life after college. Between the summer of 1893 and the fall of 1894, she worked both as an assistant cashier at her father's Monterey bank and as a third-grade teacher. In the summer of 1894, Lou heard a lecture by John Casper Branner, the chair of the Geology, Mining, and Engineering Department at Stanford University. Lou relished combining a scientific major with her orientation toward the natural world. She matriculated at Stanford, where she studied geology with additional coursework in Latin.[7]

Lou's life was transformed when she met Herbert Hoover in a geology lab class at Stanford. A shy and earnest young man of twenty-one, Hoover possessed a shock of hair atop his square-jawed face. Thin and of average height, he was alternately described as boyish, aggressive, and taciturn. Orphaned as a child, he had worked his way through Stanford, where he was a senior when he met Lou Henry. He found her self-sufficiency and spirit of adventure to be unlike that of any other woman he had known. That she also studied geology proved her intellectual and physical readiness to join with him on his globe-trotting career as a mining engineer. Hoover, who was Professor Branner's "handy boy" in the geology department, took it upon himself to "aid the young lady in her studies both in the laboratory and in the field." He viewed "this call to duty" with much delight and later reflected that he had been "stimulated by her whimsical mind, her blue eyes, and a broad grinnish smile." Lou Henry's background, especially her enjoyment of "the out-of-door life of a boy," further attracted Hoover.[8]

Just as Bert found much to admire in Lou, likewise, she developed warm feelings toward him. Bert reminded Lou of her father. He enjoyed the outdoors, and he appreciated women's intellectual abilities. Here was a man, she thought, who would encourage her various interests and who possessed a sense of playfulness. Indeed, he took her to her first party on campus, where they discussed their common backgrounds and beliefs: an Iowa birth and a California childhood, the importance of studying the science of the earth and appreciating the natural world, and the advantages of a free Stanford education, which enabled students such as Lou and Bert to study at a university that they otherwise could not afford.

Bert graduated at the end of Lou's first year at Stanford, but by that point, the two shared an emotional commitment. While away on a mining job, Bert found himself "desperate" that he might not be able to sustain his relationship with Lou Henry. They decided to write to each other, which implied a commitment for couples in the late nineteenth century. An agreement to marry when their circumstances permitted it sustained Lou and Bert for the remainder of her studies at Stanford and during the early and difficult years of his career. Little of their correspondence from these years survives, but one twelve-page letter from Lou to Bert contained not the typical declarations of love and longing that might be expected; rather, it presented a treatise about the difficulties of arranging an athletic field day for Stanford students in the spring of 1898. Lou told Bert, "I think that one good view of us at an exciting, a critical, moment, might "bridge the physical distance between us more" than any amount of chit chat gossip. That's why I told it at such length dear. And I was right at the heart of it all."[9]

Lou's years at Stanford overlapped with the second generation of American women who sought higher education. The earliest generation of college women had matriculated between the 1860s and the 1880s, and the third generation attended between the 1910s and 1920s. College women in the mid-nineteenth century, though crucial pioneers in the expansion of women's right to an education, maintained their identification with traditional, domestic ideals. Women of Lou Henry's generation did not. Self-described as Gibson girls and "New Women," female college students in the 1890s and 1900s were more engaged with the world and its problems than were the women who preceded them. Through their shared experiences in and out of the classroom, these coeds developed a significant attachment to the culture of women's voluntary organizations, which they populated in droves. They also developed an appreciation for women's athleticism. In these ways, Lou typified her generation.[10]

While Bert worked, Lou thrived as a young coed in the 1890s. She attended sporting events and classical and contemporary plays, joined the board of directors of the Women's Athletic Association, pledged the Kappa Kappa Gamma sorority, and enjoyed numerous

Lou Henry posing on the porch rail of the Kappa Kappa Gamma House at Stanford University. (Herbert Hoover Presidential Library-Museum)

college dances. Lou went to several campus debates about contemporary political issues. Even though Lou was among the first women in America to study geology, there was no evidence in her many letters home of discrimination from male professors or students. To the contrary, a male geology student declared, "Oh, Lou Henry— why we would rather have her than not."[11] Lou chose to concentrate on the positive meaning of this casual but cryptic comment and drew much-needed confidence, which in turn fueled her ability to take a public role in the world. Her Stanford studies did not give her an understanding of the challenges that less economically and socially advantaged women faced in their pursuit of equality, however.

After graduation, the search for employment brought Lou face-to-face with gender bias. Despite earning a geology degree from Stanford on 25 May 1898, Lou had little hope of finding a job in her field. For women to be hired in scientific jobs, several conditions were necessary: there had to be a lack of available male workers, job descriptions needed to be "downgraded" or "feminized," and employers had to be willing to hire women. In a long letter to her friend and former roommate Evelyn Wight, Lou discussed the differences between being male and being female. She complained that her degree, an A.B., "unfortunately does not stand . . . for 'A Boy'—ah, what wouldn't I give just about now to be one! They would not want me to stay meekly at home—I would not still have to face that old question of how far obedience is dutiful and I would have something to work for." Instead of rebelling against male privilege, however, Lou moved toward marriage and an unpaid public career. Yet her accommodation of traditional expectations should not be read as capitulation, for Lou never abandoned her individuality or personal autonomy. Her conception of marriage varied greatly from the nineteenth-century worldview of her mother's generation, in that she expected a coequal partnership with her husband and used her marriage to expand her public, political rights.[12]

With no job in her field, Lou sought part-time activities. Soon after graduating from Stanford, she joined her mother in volunteer work for the Red Cross to support the U.S. troops in the Spanish-American War. First she rolled bandages, but she soon became the secretary-treasurer of her local chapter. Then the war ended and the need for bandages eased. What would Lou do with the rest of her life? Fortuitously, Bert Hoover, who had been corresponding with Lou throughout his early mining adventures in Australia, wired her a marriage proposal. His firm, Bewick, Moreing and Company, was sending him to China, but first he wanted to come home to the United States and marry Lou.

Lou and Bert were married 10 February 1899 in the Henry home. A Catholic priest performed the brief civil ceremony. The Henry family had not met the groom before his arrival for the wedding, but, as Lou's mother recalled, "after he had been here a few days . . . I think we all liked him about as much as Lou did." In time, Lou became a Quaker like her husband. Her mother explained, "As Lou is so fond of traveling and going among strangers the proposed life seemed her ideal one."[13]

The newlyweds had a fun-loving and warm rapport. During their early years together, Lou maintained her childhood habit of keeping

Lou Henry and Herbert Hoover on their wedding day, 10 February 1899. Charles D. Henry, Jean Henry, and Florence Weed Henry are standing in back of them. (Herbert Hoover Presidential Library-Museum)

a diary. Apparently, Bert viewed the diary as an opportunity to demonstrate both his wit and his love for Lou, because many years later when rereading her diary, Lou found some "fantastic, absurd, facetious imitations of my own supposed emotions—in Bert's handwriting!" Some of Bert's insertions in Lou's diary revealed his social inadequacies; for example, whereas Lou "created her own atmosphere" at parties, Bert "felt like a wet crow." In the same passage, Bert wrote of Lou: "Note! She was dressed fully on time!!" Not to be outdone in her own diary, Lou retorted on the bottom of the page that her previous tardiness had resulted because "the tailor brought her gown just 15 minutes before she was to appear in it a mile away."[14] Although the competing diary entries suggest the playfulness between the couple, there is also an undercurrent of Bert's need to control his marriage. Lou defended herself, but always within the bounds of her vows, a bargain she upheld for the remainder of her life. Even when she later emerged as an important activist in the world of women's voluntary associations, she calibrated her public career with Bert's so that her work would accommodate his.

Love did not compensate for the culture shock the Hoovers encountered in China. Lou abhorred the "*wretched*" food choices when she and Bert first arrived in Shanghai, a port city on the East China Sea located at the mouth of the Yangtze River. Nor was she pleased with the shopping opportunities. Nevertheless, Lou proved herself capable of adopting the demeanor of a corporate wife. She studied Chinese and visited mines with her husband. Bert told friends, "She reads Chinese readily, and constantly keeps me open to insult because my English speaking Chinaman in town always addresses her in Chinese and me in English." Lou referred to Bert's employment almost as if it were a position they shared: "if we stay on here, and are going to want to go to work again in the spring, we would want the winter here."[15] Indeed, her use of the word *we* to describe Bert's career path suggests that their partnership extended beyond the confines of a traditional marriage to include an active role for Lou in Bert's work.

The year 1900 brought the Boxer Rebellion to China, where a patriotic and nativist faction of the population attacked foreigners, Chinese Christians, and missionary schools. The uprising was a reaction to European efforts to carve up China, much as had been done in Africa. The Russians, British, and Germans each had a sphere of influence. Despite a history of hostility between them, Chinese secret societies allied with the imperial court to expel the Europeans. The Boxer Rebellion was part of that process, and although several hundred people had been killed by June, such efforts were ultimately ineffective. China's regional governors opposed the imperial government and offered protection to the foreigners. The majority of the hostilities took place near Beijing, and Western forces gained control within a few months.[16]

Lou rose to the occasion during the upheaval. She observed in her diary that 1 June 1900 was the date of the Chinese Dragon Festival, when "we were all to be massacred by 8,000,000 heavenly soldiers, but the day passed quietly here." The Boxers surrounded the European compound where Lou and Bert lived along with about 800 others in Tientsin (now known as Tianjin), a coastal city eighty miles south-southeast of Beijing. The fighting in Tientsin was intense until Western forces dislodged the Boxers and destroyed their position behind the old fortresses. Prior to the rescue, the Hoovers used their bicycles to survey the firing lines, riding along the barricades to avoid injury. Lou disregarded warnings for women and children to seek shelter, calling the alerts "pure nonsense." Nevertheless, danger surrounded her. "Many [shells] fell about our house, none in it. One broke high-up, and pieces fell down on [the] house," she recalled. She carried but never fired a Mauser automatic .38-caliber pistol and assumed night-watch duties. Lou treated patients at the local hospital and helped outfit a dairy for the Tientsin population. Bert recalled, "I saw little of her during the first period of the siege."[17]

The rebellion encouraged both her tendency toward self-deprecation and her dislike of the media. Lou Hoover later explained that accounts of her heroism were overstated: "My share of protection lay much more toward the region of a kitchen and dining room."[18] Equally significant, she grew to distrust newspapers for their inaccurate reporting. When she read her own premature obituary during the Boxer Rebellion, Hoover worried about how the false reports would affect her parents.

At the conclusion of the Boxer Rebellion in the summer of 1900, the Hoovers journeyed to London to negotiate control of the Chinese mines. They returned to China by way of California and Japan, where Lou remained for the winter. A year later, Herbert Hoover, at the age of twenty-seven, accepted a junior partnership with Bewick, Moreing, and the couple departed China on a tramp steamer headed for London, by way of Nagasaki.[19] Hoover's rise within the mining world made his family rich and generated a slow shift in Lou's approach to public involvement. Entrée into British society and active membership in the Society of American Women in London occupied much of her time. She worked with the club's educational and philanthropic efforts but later downplayed or dismissed such aristocratic leanings.

Lou Henry Hoover inspects the armaments during the siege of Tientsin, 1900.
(Herbert Hoover Presidential Library-Museum)

When the couple moved to London, they abandoned the playfulness of newlyweds and adopted the responsibilities of the adult world. As early as 1901, Lou asked her father to help her establish "a little educational fund . . . as a nucleus and loan it out to people who need just a little more to finish their education. Preferably to those who have made their own way thro' a good deal in the past." She had been inspired to take such a course of action by one of her husband's cousins, who provided domestic and agricultural labor in exchange for room and board and tuition.[20] This small act of charity was just the first of thousands that occurred over her life. Indeed, Lou Hoover mixed individualized assistance, such as that given to Bert's cousin, with more bureaucratized charity through organizations such as the Red Cross and the Salvation Army.

Although Lou's correspondence with her family contained detailed narratives about the mundane—London housekeeping dilemmas—and the serious—how to finance the entertaining necessary to support Bert's career advancement—there was almost no reference to her first pregnancy. In June 1903, Lou sent her parents a somewhat cryptic letter in which she referred to their possible anger with her for "the secret" and explained, "I am sure when you think it over you will feel I did right. For I felt Mama would only worry so much about us all if she staid [*sic*] there. Or else she would come on over here,—and I would really rather she came at any other time." Lou assured her parents that she had "the best of doctors and nurses and everything within a moment's notice." She also described the various problems that had kept her and Bert from being able to pay her parents' passage to London. She closed with more positive thoughts: "the doctor says I have been quite perfect,—both as to conduct and condition,—so on the whole, you think I was right in not worrying you beforehand, don't you?"[21]

Lou gave birth to Herbert Charles Hoover Jr. on 4 August 1903. Although she named her son after both her husband and her father, she still called him Jr. Years later, Herbert Jr. dropped his middle name, just as his father had done. Bert soon arranged for his growing family to journey to Australia, and by the middle of September, the family had set sail, with the baby "in a basket." Bert noted, "traveling with babies is easier than with most grownups." He continued on a steamship to China while Lou and the baby remained in Kalgoorlie. Lou helped her son send a telegram to Bert informing him that "I weigh fourteen pounds ten ounces" and that "Mother's well too."[22] Bert assumed preeminence within the family, and he was oblivious to the difficulties of parenthood. Lou chose to support her husband first, herself second, and her children third. This ordering of her priorities suggests the imperfect nature of Lou's independence at that stage of her life. Indeed, although the first fifteen years of her married life were traditional, she still cultivated the leadership characteristics that dominated her activist career.

Between Herbert's birth in 1903 and the end of the decade, Lou Hoover was occupied with motherhood, a second pregnancy in 1907, and the world travel necessary to support her husband's position as a successful mining engineer. Two trips around the world took the Hoovers to many exotic destinations, including Egypt, India, Australia, New Zealand, Burma, Japan, and Russia. Upon learning of a second grandson's birth on 17 July 1907, Florence Henry wrote to her daughter: "We send our best love to the dear little one and his mother and his relatives in London. We are so glad to

Lou Henry Hoover with her sons, Allan and Herbert Jr., in Burma, 1907.
(Herbert Hoover Presidential Library-Museum)

hear of Bert's arrival home before the stork arrived." Like his brother, Allan Henry Hoover departed for his first international destination, Burma, at the age of five weeks.[23]

The years between the birth of the children and the outbreak of World War I saw Herbert Hoover build on his business success with more travel, and Lou joined him as often as she could. By the early 1910s, the Hoovers were independently wealthy, and from World War I on, they lived off the interest from his investments. During the war, Hoover placed most of his assets into a trust; he then divided "a certain large portion" of that money into three parts: one each for the boys, and one for Lou. The boys were to receive their money upon the attainment of maturity, while Lou's interest went into the "general family income that we live on."[24] Additionally, Lou drew from these funds to support the causes she cared about and to travel extensively for the Girl Scouts and the Women's Division of the National Amateur Athletic Federation, among other organizations.

Such status allowed the couple to enjoy worldwide vacations with their friends Abbie and Edgar Rickard and to mimic in other, more trivial ways the behavior of those with old money. For instance, they dressed for dinner every night and relied on maids and secretaries. Lou, however, was not consciously aware of the freedom purchased by having servants. Few middle- or working-class women could ever hope to match Lou's advantages, and the deference she received from these women transformed her from an adventuresome out-doorswoman to "the Lady," as her female employees often called her. Indeed, money shaped Hoover's public activism and colored her political philosophy at the outbreak of the Great War.

Money also gave Lou Henry Hoover the luxury to pursue her intellectual interests. She was writing biographical essays on the dowager empress of China and a British scientist. Skilled with languages, she also collaborated with her husband on the translation and English-language publication of *De Re Metallica,* a project that she conceived and directed. *De Re Metallica* was a Latin folio on mining published in 1556 by Georgius Agricola, a German physician who had been born Georg Bauer. Back in their student days at Stanford, the treatise had fascinated both Bert and Lou. While exploring the British Museum Library, Lou rediscovered the volume; she procured a copy and began translating it into English.[25]

It took the couple four years to translate the Latin text, which was the first work to combine "knowledge on mining, metallurgy, and industrial chemistry." Their task involved "scientific detective work," because Agricola had invented Latin phrasing to describe technical procedures, rendering his work inaccessible to all but trained geologists.[26] The project helped Lou Henry Hoover further her organizational and managerial skills.

The Latin translation project and the frequent travel associated with Bert's work challenged Lou's parenting skills, but she did not believe that her husband's career demands hurt her children. Sometimes the children accompanied them, and sometimes they stayed with Lou or with their grandparents in California. Thus began a tradition that continued until the boys became adults: the shifting of their care from their parents to their grandparents, to other family members, and to trusted nannies and servants. As a result, Lou made many decisions about the usual childhood maladies via telegrams

Herbert Hoover, Lou Henry Hoover, Abbie Rickard, and Edgar Rickard in St. Mark's Square, Venice, Italy, February 1912. (Herbert Hoover Presidential Library-Museum)

and mail, rather than dealing with them in person. And Lou missed many of the milestones important to a parent, although her mother (as well as paid caregivers) wrote detailed letters about the children's activities. Little by little, Hoover became a female aristocrat, detached from the mundane concerns of motherhood and endowed with sufficient time for public involvement outside the home.

Lou Henry Hoover structured her life much like other women of her day. She graduated from college, had only two children, and ultimately devoted significant time to the work of women's voluntary organizations. Collectively, women's decisions about family, which included higher divorce rates and a sexual revolution, reflected the contested terrain of marriage as Victorian notions of home life gave way to the companionate family. The latter was much smaller than the typical nineteenth-century family, which consisted of more than seven children, on average, for white women in 1800 and three and a half children in 1900. Lou Henry Hoover gave birth to her two sons at age twenty-nine and thirty-three, adhering to another common trend among modern women. Increasingly, women compacted their childbearing years into their twenties and early thirties so that the last half of their lives would be free from child-care responsibilities. Thus, Lou's departure from Victorian norms paralleled the trends among women of her generation, except with regard to her child-rearing practices. She relied much more heavily on paid caregivers than did the typical middle-class woman. Additionally, she rejected the advice of modern child-care experts who advocated structure and critiqued excessive play, preferring to indulge her sons' curiosity about the natural world. Lou's selective application of modern standards to her life choices cleared the way for her activist career from the mid-1910s onward.[27]

The outbreak of the Great War remade Lou Henry Hoover's relationship with the world. No longer simply a wife and mother, she became a public figure, first involved with relief work in Europe and then with food conservation in the United States. In August 1914, the American ambassador in London, Walter Hines Page, tapped Herbert Hoover to oversee the safe passage home of vacationing Americans. Now responsible for the American Relief Committee, Bert asked Lou to administer a women's relief committee. Although Bert's correspondence indicated his great respect for Lou's administrative skills, he later said that her efforts involved "holding the hands of the frightened."[28] From this seed, however, grew an entire forest, as Lou began to manifest the notions of service and activism that she had written about as a high school and college student. From 1914 until her death in 1944, she worked with countless causes but fit into no single category of women's reform work. Because she listened to her independent muse, sometimes she acted for her own benefit, sometimes for women and children collectively, and sometimes for humanity as a whole.

The 1910s were a significant time in the history of American women's public activism. Suffrage leaders had united behind Carrie Chapman Catt's "winning plan," which joined state-level suffrage campaigns with lobbying for a federal suffrage amendment. Other feminists and activists concentrated on workplace protections for blue-collar and immigrant women, the elimination of child labor, and the establishment of a minimum wage, for example. African American women used the club movement to advocate the end of lynching and access to the vote for blacks. Food safety, good government reform, the creation of public parks, and the kindergarten movement were some other crusades in which women participated. Lou's activism meshed well with these diverse movements.[29]

Lou chaired the Resident American Women's Relief Committee while in London and was the only female member of the men's committee. The committee drew its membership from the Society of American Women in London, an organization with which Lou had a long affiliation. Between August and September 1914, more than 1,200 women traveling alone received aid, and by 1916, the committee had facilitated the return home of more than 26,000 American women and children. The "large numbers of distracted women" who encountered "real distress" due to the sudden outbreak of war disturbed Lou.[30] Her organizational abilities were put to good use providing financial and emotional assistance to stranded American women.

On 3 October 1914, Lou and the boys sailed for home. She took Herbert and Allan to Palo Alto, where they would be far removed from the war. At Bert's behest, Lou applied her bureaucratic skills to the Belgian cause in California. He had been appointed head of the Commission for Relief in Belgium, a neutral organization formed to help the Belgians after the German invasion and occupation. Bert contended that voluntary American aid at the rate of 20,000 tons of food per month was the only solution for the millions of Belgians who depended on breadlines for survival. Lou lobbied Californians to support the cause and, using her husband's San Francisco office, assembled a shipload of food destined for Belgium.

That fall, Hoover asked his wife for "suggestions re publicity campaign" and "when are you coming home?" Bert's focus was on the challenge of humanitarian relief. He inquired about the "general situation" regarding the committee Lou had "instigated" in San Francisco, along with whether she "could be effective in stimulating further action." The Belgian campaign was "the greatest work to which we could be devoted," he said. Lou responded that she had "ceased making Belgian appeals" while awaiting "further instructions." Her greatest fund-raising success came from soliciting "monthly subscriptions." Because of her public speeches, "Stanford raised two thousand," and San Franciscans contributed over $100,000.[31]

Before she sailed back to Great Britain in November 1914, Lou arranged for the care of her children should she and Bert perish in the war. She also wrote a letter "to be given to Herbert Jr. if his Mother should die. And to Allan when he is old enough." Her letter explained the life lessons her sons would need to become successful, caring men, including faith in God and the power of prayer. In keeping with her own philosophy of relief, Lou advised her sons that asking for help was not enough: "we must be trying as hard as we can first with what we have before we ask for anything else,—or any more." While expressing how deeply she would miss her sons, Lou reminded Allan that her first responsibility was to "take care of our dear Daddy, who is so kind to us, and who has to stay over there in England and work so hard." Soon after arriving in London, Lou wrote to Allan, "How I wish this old war were over."[32]

Lou's purpose in returning to London was not simply to be Bert's helpmate but rather to be his full partner in relief work. Her choice between her husband and her sons represented what she hoped was the best solution to an intractable problem—how to care for her husband and his public agenda while also nurturing her children. Lou's frequent letters to the boys contained numerous references to nature and to their collection of animals, themes that had been important in their prewar lives. There were almost no words about the war and Lou's involvement in it. Occasionally she discussed her European travels but included no explanation of their import to either Bert or her humanitarian concerns.

By July 1915, relief work in London consumed Lou Henry Hoover. She brought the boys back to England because Bert did not like being "parted from them for the whole of the war," nor did he like Lou "constantly crossing the Atlantic in war times trying to do two jobs." Because she was unwilling to abandon her own war relief work, she explained that there was "no hope" of resuming a

California residence until the war ended.[33] In addition to her efforts on behalf of stranded Americans, Lou devoted considerable attention to the operation of a 200-bed Red Cross surgical hospital under the auspices of the American Women's War Relief Fund. The hospital treated the English military and operated an ambulance service that convoyed wounded English soldiers from the front lines back to safety.

Lou revealed that her deepest interests in the crisis were related to the personal, human suffering. She investigated cases of abuse in Belgium, and she called her most trusted contacts to discern the location of the Belgian husband and American son of a Belgian American woman trapped behind German lines. Bert, in contrast, focused on the larger problems associated with the overall relief effort. He told a colleague that Belgium was "truly a depressing place to go." Lou's personal approach to the crisis led her to develop a plan that would allow Belgian women to participate in the efforts to save their families. She asked a close associate to assist in the sale of Belgian lace to Americans, and when in the States, she gave numerous speeches about this unique philanthropy. By 1916, Lou described herself as a "forwarding agent" for the sale of Belgian lace in the United States and England.[34]

Because the situation in Belgium was dire, Lou Henry Hoover traveled back to America to raise money, effectively using the media and public appeals. In her American speeches, Lou stressed that the universal "democratic acceptance" of the situation meant that there was "little of the feeling of abject self-effacement attached to the usual receiving of charity." As a result, Lou explained that she felt a "real elation every time I see a Belgian bread-line," because "these brave people were getting a sufficient supply of wholesome clean food." However, she related, "the effect on American men" was "quite the reverse. They are frightfully depressed by it. My own husband will not visit a bread-line unless literally compelled to, and—like most of the other men—has his eyes near full of tears before he leaves."[35]

Lou credited Stanford first and California second for setting the example that led to America's role in the relief of Belgium, but she also criticized her homeland for not doing enough. Calling the problem "too great for private charity to grasp," she acknowledged that "some Government aid" was necessary, even if "none of the Belligerents would touch it." In fact, both Hoovers endorsed a public-private partnership to solve the Belgian crisis. Nevertheless, she coupled her frustrations over America's insular thinking with declarations that the Belgian problem would soon be over.[36] Even after the United States entered the war against Germany and the Hoovers had returned to their home country, Lou Henry Hoover spoke about the problems in Belgium. Her emphasis, though, shifted in tandem with her husband's new career as director of the U.S. Food Administration, a new government agency in charge of the American food supply.

Return to the United States landed Lou Henry Hoover in the middle of a significant demographic shift regarding women's employment. Approximately 1 million women entered the labor force in a wide variety of fields, ranging from heavy industry to office work. Their employment intensified the concerns of Progressive Era feminists and activists who supported women's self-actualization but worried about abusive workplace conditions. Indeed, the war brought to the foreground the changes that industrialization had wrought in average working women's lives, specifically, their exposure to workplace dangers and the contradictions between the assumption of female gentility and the reality of privation and work. Additionally, wartime demands for an enlarged bureaucracy meant an influx of young, often unmarried, middle-class women into the paid workforce for the first time.[37]

In this new phase of her emerging public career, Lou Hoover advocated on behalf of female clerks in the Food Administration. Lou planned and helped institute the Food Administration Club, which contained a gathering place, a restaurant, and a residence for young, single female workers in wartime Washington. Lou became both benefactor and strategist. While secretaries managed the day-to-day affairs of the club, Hoover tackled larger concerns such as procuring space and funds for its operation. Lou estimated that approximately 300 women were employed at the Food Administration, with the overwhelming majority being new to the city. Hoover's belief in wholesome social and leisure activities as a counterbalance to the problems of urban life and industrialization helped explain her commitment to the club. Lou's plans for the club accorded with the efforts of feminists who were interested in protecting women from the excesses of the urban environment.

Her initial efforts proved so successful that Hoover, with the cooperation of her husband and his staff, expanded her endeavors in the fall of 1918. Food Administration officials researched the typical expenses and expectations of their female employees and reported to Lou Hoover, who sought additional housing space for female workers. A memorandum disseminated among Food Administration employees revealed Herbert Hoover's endorsement of his wife's activities, and he requested that they cooperate with Lou. Despite the success of the Food Administration Club, Lou Hoover did not broaden its mission to include all female clerks working for the federal government. Nor did she push for its continuation beyond the end of the war. The departure of war workers after the armistice only partially explained this decision, for when her husband became commerce secretary, Hoover only briefly considered and rejected the idea of creating a similar club for women workers there.

Lou Hoover also publicly joined her husband's campaign regarding food conservation. She followed the U.S. Department of Agriculture's efforts to research and discover new foodstuffs—such as Chinese petsai, chayote, dasheen, and mango—that could be substituted for the items being voluntarily rationed on the home front. An article on the Hoover family diet, which now included sausage and rice cakes, potato fish loaf, and barley sponge cake, appeared in *Ladies' Home Journal:* "Mr. Hoover can go to sleep every night with an absolutely clear conscience so far as his own observance of the principles and practice of wartime food conservation is concerned. . . . In that home is a Food Administrator of even greater authority than he. For Mrs. Hoover is just as much on her job as her husband is on his." The article went on to provide many examples of "Hooverizing" within the Hoover household. The specific details of food conservation, though, fell to their many domestic servants, because Lou Henry Hoover spent much of the war in California.[38] Thus, it was easy for her to tout the virtues of conservation to the public when she did not have to do the work herself.

Lou Hoover gave public speeches on behalf of the Food Administration conservation effort in which she expounded on the power and the rights of individuals. She told the Rockville, Maryland, Women's Council of Defense, "What you did individually seems very little in comparison, but remember if millions of other

Americans had not done the same, nothing would have been done. Calculate how much you saved, and you can calculate therefrom, whether it is one, or two or three, lives who *your* household is directly responsible for being alive today!" Regarding rumors that the Food Administration would confiscate home-canned produce, Lou Hoover insisted that the government "doesn't care to know what any woman has in her pantry." Anyone who asked for an inventory of a woman's pantry should be locked in that same closet until the police came to arrest the culprit, she contended.[39] The Rockville speech conveyed a message of empowerment to an audience of female grassroots activists. It reflected Hoover's belief in the primacy of individuals working at the local level to preserve American society. Her remarks about privacy within a woman's kitchen also revealed her prioritization of individual rights and responsibilities within mass society.

After the armistice, Lou Hoover turned her attention from food conservation toward veterans' issues. This shift reveals the flexibility and the range of her activism. When the war ended, she worked with the Red Cross to ensure the safe return of American veterans. As associate director of the Bureau of Canteen Services, Hoover helped create the Canteen Escort Services, a program in which female Red Cross volunteers accompanied wounded soldiers as they journeyed home from the battlefields. Members of the Canteen Escort Services provided assistance ranging from simple companionship on hospital trains to the provision of all food and medical care on regular trains. Hoover wanted to ensure "maximum comfort" for "the men themselves, and the minimum use of able-bodied, able-minded young men" to do so. Her goal was obtainable because "the Red Cross has a limitless number of women and older men eager and able to do anything necessary in the cause."[40]

By January 1919, the escort program was firmly established, with the majority of patients moving through the mid-Atlantic section of the East Coast. In the first two months of 1919, more than 3,000 Red Cross volunteers tended to more than 25,000 patients. A Red Cross official told Hoover, "the work so ably started by you is progressing rapidly and . . . the value of the canteen escort service is being demonstrated and meeting with enthusiastic reception on the part of the medical officers as well as Red Cross officials."[41]

Lou Henry Hoover's organizational and bureaucratic skills expanded during the war—first with Belgian relief, then with the Food Administration, and finally the Red Cross Canteen Escort Service. The breadth and depth of her activism suggest a sophistication of political engagement that was not common among the typical single-issue female activists of the era. Her range of experience served her well as she solidified her leadership within women's organizational culture in the 1920s.

Growing public involvement did not lessen her commitment to her family, however. With the war over, Lou used the lessons of that conflict to stress the values that she hoped would shape her sons' priorities as they grew to adulthood. Lou told Allan how his father had been named an "honorary citizen of Belgium" for his work on behalf of that nation during the early months of the Great War, and she credited his actions for saving Belgium from German domination and the Belgian people from certain starvation. In describing her husband's accomplishments to Allan, Lou Hoover noted, "You will probably never have the chance to do as great things for the world as your Daddy had,—they don't come very often in a good many hundred years." She also stressed, "*very* often, people don't know that the big thing *is* a big thing until it is past,—so it is well to treat all the little ones with as much consideration as the big ones."[42]

Although her remarks were intended strictly as praise for her husband, they applied equally well to her. Lou Henry Hoover—in addressing the "little things" in individual people's lives affected by the Great War—amassed a record of humanitarian activism on a par with that of her husband. Lou helped stranded American tourists, Belgian women, female government clerks, and returning soldiers, which, in her own words, can only be described collectively as a "big thing."

Following on this record in the 1920s, Lou Henry Hoover matured as a public figure. Her work remained tangentially linked to that of her husband, who served as secretary of commerce for Presidents Warren G. Harding and Calvin Coolidge, in that her causes paralleled his interests, but her activism was no longer simply an adjunct of his career. Before the 1920s, Hoover's activism had been either crisis induced, as in the Boxer Rebellion and the Great War, or individualistic, as in her scholarly efforts. In the 1920s, though, her children were teenagers, and her family's financial circumstances remained secure, giving her the time to develop a sustained agenda of her own.

Lou Henry Hoover's maturation as an activist paralleled the maturation of the women's movement. Although there had been factions within the suffrage movement and other smaller groups of activists that had focused on issues other than the vote, before 1920, winning the franchise for women dominated the political agenda. After the vote was won, however, no unifying issue remained. Politically minded women divided according to the disparate concerns that had caused them to seek the vote in the first place. A small, relatively coherent faction of professional women who emphasized their similarity with men sought an equal rights amendment to protect their careers. The overwhelming majority of female activists, sometimes termed social feminists, advocated social concerns ranging from maternal and infant protection to labor rights and prison reform. A third group moved into the partisan political fray. Although many of these activists shared a commitment to group identity, only a minority accepted all the tenets of feminism.[43]

Hoover's work exhibited both a depth and a breadth of concerns, including a strong penchant for the betterment of women and children. In her hierarchy of activism, Girl Scouting ranked first, women's athletics second, and public affairs third. She also contributed meaningful support to a host of other organizations, among which were the American Association of University Women, the Women's Auxiliary of the American Institute of Mining and Metallurgical Engineers, and the Red Cross. One journalist declared, "it is safe to assume that she has been asked to serve on more committees and commissions than any other woman in the country."[44]

In the first nine years of the decade, Lou Henry Hoover undertook significant training that prepared her to become an innovative, activist first lady in 1929. Unlike the typical clubwoman, Hoover's eclectic membership list reflected not self-aggrandizement but a commitment to hard work on behalf of her public agenda. Indeed, she honed her bureaucratic leadership skills in the 1920s. In an article on the political impact of the cabinet wives, a journalist described Lou Hoover as "the intellectual light of the cabinet" and "the busiest women in it."[45]

Hoover blended public activism with parenting and household management, thus balancing both traditional and modern perspectives. Her public career serves as a poignant reminder of the difficulties encountered by individuals in the intermediate stages of an evolutionary change. Her life unfolded in a vastly different fashion from that which nineteenth-century women valued, yet when compared with the choices women made in the last half of the twentieth century, Hoover's accomplishments seem somehow incomplete. Such an assessment, however, ignores the context in which she lived and the significant hurdles she overcame to become the first modern first lady. That process began in earnest in the 1920s when she emerged as a political figure in her own right. Indeed, although she spent much of that decade—and the remainder of her life, for that matter—denying a political component to her public activism, in reality, Lou Henry Hoover mastered the art of informal politicking. Her modus operandi was not through the partisan party system but through the voluntary organizations that played a key role in women's public political activism.[46]

Even as Lou Henry Hoover established a permanent public space for herself, she remained focused on her family's needs as the primary nurturing parent and as the manager of the family's finances. The 1920s saw her raise her boys to adulthood, become a grandmother, and lose both parents—her mother in 1921 and her father in 1928. She permitted her sons maximum freedom of exploration, which differed starkly from the Victorian notion that children should behave like miniature adults. At one point, the household included pet turtles and alligators. In other ways, she encouraged adult behavior. For example, money given to the boys took the form of an allowance to inculcate responsibility, not an indulgence or a dole that would encourage indolence. She discussed with her son Allan the reasons behind giving him his "salary," which she dispensed "for remembering to do all those little things about right ways of living!"[47]

The combination of Lou's busy schedule and her husband's even more demanding one meant that they were never conventional parents. Still, the rigors of their public careers did not lessen their attachment to their children. Much as she had during the war, Lou requested that her assistant prepare "a little diary of important events."

On one occasion, she told an aide, "[your letters] gave me a better view of my own family than anything that I have heard from them in the past weeks!"[48] Although some observers who were more accustomed to traditional parenting styles later contended that the boys had been spoiled, Herbert Jr. and Allan became productive, successful men.

During this decade, Lou Hoover emerged further into the public spotlight. Happy about the benefits that accrued to her work with voluntary organizations, she nonetheless disapproved when journalists used her acclaim as a conduit for information about her husband. In her contacts with the media, she insisted that her remarks remain focused on her own public activities. For example, when asked, "How does it feel to be the wife of, possibly, the most popular man in the world," Hoover responded with a smile, "I never talk about anything but my own work, that is Girl Scouts." In 1922, one journalist distinguished between the formal "Mrs. Herbert Hoover" and the "real Mrs. Hoover." The reporter explained, "She knew what she had to say, and when that was said no urging would bring more. It might not be amiss to mention that what she had to discuss was her work with the girls of America, and NOT what Herbert Hoover was doing in his bigger way with all the people of America."[49]

She rejected wholeheartedly any implications that her work was unimportant or that her purpose was simply to advance her husband politically. The statement "I want to be a background for Bertie!" was attributed to Lou Henry Hoover in a 1923 book, *Boudoir Mirrors of Washington*, creating a false, traditional image of her. Hoover believed that Mary Austin, a writer who had once been a friend, was the author of the anonymous book, which damned Hoover with faint praise. The author juxtaposed compliments against negative descriptions of Hoover's dinner parties and her interactions with London and Washington society. Lou Hoover disliked the book because the author ignored her independent accomplishments in the world of philanthropy and voluntary association work. Countless journalists, though, picked up the phrase and constructed a skewed portrait of Lou Hoover. She remarked, "If there is one thing that I have gotten sensitive about, it is having anything that I have to do called 'making a background' for any member of my family! . . . There was no truth in it whatsoever. It has been quoted innumerable times and it is worse than the proverbial red rag."[50]

Though Lou Hoover's activism became more independent in the 1920s, it remained in sync with her husband's career. Their common public interests, however, gained a bureaucratic flair as communication between the two sometimes occurred through intermediaries. For example, Lou received a mass mailing that Bert had sent to supporters of the American Relief Administration (ARA). Bert hoped to reconstitute the ARA, which had fulfilled its European relief mission, into the American Relief Administration Children's Fund and to focus on domestic concerns, specifically children. When Lou failed to answer to Bert's missive, she received a second appeal—"we desire to maintain our relationship to you"—and responded with a very apologetic note.[51] Throughout the 1920s and into the 1930s, Lou Henry Hoover became a regular consumer of the ARA Children's Fund's largesse. She often drew on its philanthropy to benefit her work with Girl Scouts and the Women's Division of the National Amateur Athletic Federation.

Work with voluntary organizations that bolstered young girls and women occupied much of Hoover's time. Through the Girl Scouts, women's political associations, and women's sports, Hoover helped broaden notions of a woman's place in society. Later in life, Lou Hoover pondered, "I always feel I was a Girl Scout when I was young, and so many of the girls we know in history or story were really Girl Scouts in spirit."[52] Hoover's great love of nature and the outdoors had helped shape her personality and her philosophy of life, and she hoped that, through Girl Scouting, she could reach countless other girls in a similar fashion and empower them to blend old and new mores for women, as she had done in her own life.

That Girl Scouting developed alongside the industrialization and urbanization of the United States was no accident. Girl Scouts, Boy Scouts, and other youth organizations with a focus on nature sought to inculcate the next generation of Americans with an appreciation for the disappearing aspects of rural culture. For Americans born in the late nineteenth century, who remembered life before the advent of mass marketing and the urban consumer culture, the Girl Scouts provided its members with the scientific knowledge to appreciate the flora and fauna of nature. Additionally, the Girl Scouts balanced women's outdoor activism with more traditional domestic arts. This combination of old ways and the modern spirit of adventure matched the social flux of women in the 1920s. According to the census taken at the beginning of the decade, more Americans lived in urban areas, defined as places with at least 2,500 residents, than in rural areas. The advent of automobiles, the radio, and motion pictures fundamentally changed youth culture. For Lou Henry Hoover, then, Scouting mediated between the rural culture of the past and the emerging urban culture of the future, and she spent the rest of her life looking for ways to combine the best of the old and the new.[53]

Lou Hoover was invited to speak before a Girl Scout group in Washington, D.C., on the subject of wartime food conservation on 21 November 1917. At the time, Juliette Gordon Low's organization was five years old, and by 1920, it had 70,000 members. Its organization was touted as democratic, but control had gravitated to a cohort of East Coast women well known to one another, resulting in powerful cliques and divisive feuds. Hoover nonetheless viewed Girl Scouts as the best character-building organization available to young women. Established Scouting leaders drew Hoover further into the orbit of Girl Scouts, and she organized a troop of her own. She told a Girl Scout colleague, "I think that one does not know much about Girl Scouting until she has played about with some little girls for a while. And I really have great fun with mine." Although Lou Hoover worked with Troop 8 for ten years, hosting Girl Scout meetings at her 2300 S Street home and then at the White House, in her typical bureaucratic style, she turned regular management of the troop over to an assistant.[54]

Hoover's organizational and diplomatic abilities won her positive reviews from the Scouting hierarchy. That, combined with her husband's new post as secretary of commerce, made Lou Hoover an ideal candidate for national Girl Scout president when, in the summer of 1921, the current president decided to step down. Many within the organization lobbied Hoover to assume the position. Lou Hoover's organizational abilities were already legendary, and the Girl Scouts needed strong, effective leadership. The organization faced a split between those who favored "a democratic association, with a representative committee, and an autocratic one run by paid executives," noted one Girl Scout leader, who also suggested that Hoover's "own good sense . . . could influence us all if you were our president."[55] Hoover, who agreed with the advocates of a democratic structure, assumed her first term as president in 1922 and was reelected in April 1924.

Early in her presidency, Lou Hoover improved the governance, the finances, and the public image of the Girl Scouts. Hoover declared the impossibility of constructing "a uniform system of government over the entire country until it has become more 'settled' with Scout troops." Thus, she advocated "guidance," not "government," that respected geographic and demographic differences among the various troops.[56] Perhaps her most important contribution in this regard was support for the Lone Scout program, which allowed isolated rural girls to participate in Scouting without a local troop. She valued the individual over the group but also possessed a strong belief in cooperative, group decision making.

To raise money, she naturally interweaved her talents at drawing out elite women from the voluntary community and her connections with the male corporate world. Edgar Rickard, a close family friend who had worked with Bert as a mining engineer in prewar London and in Belgian war relief, was a reliable aide. She asked the Girl Scouts' executive committee to debate several revenue proposals: whether to make the organization "entirely 'self-supporting,'" whether to make the organization "entirely 'charitable,'" and whether to support it "entirely 'from the Field.'" Because of her objections to a reliance on charitable donations, Hoover advocated a combination of the first and third approaches.[57] Finally, Hoover engineered a national fundraising campaign, announced in November 1924. By the end of the month, almost $400,000 had been pledged, with more than $250,000 coming from New York City alone.

Lou Hoover used her celebrity in a variety of ways to publicize the Scout movement. She often took the message of Girl Scouting to other women's voluntary organizations in her public addresses. In Hoover's mind, the best way to improve the Girl Scouts' public image was through its publications. Thus, she supported the *American Girl* magazine, which had seen an increase in circulation from 6,000 to 50,000. Hoover wrote several articles for it, one on camping and one on Grace Goodhue Coolidge's childhood, in an attempt to boost the magazine's standards. Lou also supported the *American Girl* financially by helping to procure advertisements from the Hoover Vacuum Company and other domestic manufacturers. Finally, Lou encouraged her sister to write children's literature geared toward the Girl Scouts; one result was *Nancy Goes Girl Scouting,* a book for young girls that described the many different activities the organization offered.

Beyond the challenges of governance, financing, and image, Lou Hoover also had to recruit new Girl Scout leaders if the organization was to grow and thrive throughout the United States. Thousands of girls had been turned away from Scouting owing to a lack of adult volunteers to serve as leaders. Because of the popularity of Scouting, Hoover explained, the leadership shortage required a long-term, not a temporary, solution. Ultimately, Hoover addressed the leadership crisis by developing a "snappy" and "fun" curriculum to attract college women to Scouting. It was introduced at Stanford University in 1923, and by the mid-1920s, the curriculum was available in 155 colleges and universities in forty-two states. Typically, education departments offered the classes as part of the summer curriculum, and more than 10,000 women matriculated in these programs. At the 1925 national Girl Scout convention, Hoover laid out her theory of Girl Scout leadership: "Truly we want *to lead,* rather than to *teach,* just as truly, we want *to accompany,* rather than *to lead,* when feasible," she declared. "And just as truly, we want always to have a watchful eye that we do not even *suggest* too much."[58]

In one key way, Lou Hoover aligned with her husband, who was then the secretary of commerce, to promote Girl Scouting alongside a middle-class home-ownership program. In 1923, the General Federation of Women's Clubs, as part of the National Better Homes in America program, constructed a model middle-class home on public parkland in Washington, D.C. Lou Hoover saw the laboratory, training, and outreach potential of such a structure and applied the concept to establish the Girl Scouts' National Little House as an "educational Home Making Center." The National Little House became a destination for visiting troops, and local troops used the Little House to practice cooking, housekeeping, and gardening skills; soon, Little Houses appeared in other cities throughout the country. Arguing that the Little House would be a "halfway house between the playhouse of childhood and the home every girl hopes to achieve some day," Lou Hoover revealed the traditional, domestic component of her activism.[59]

In the early 1920s, Hoover began using her position in the Girl Scouts as a reason not to make formal political speeches. She was less ambivalent about nonpartisan political behavior, however, and was a strong financial supporter of the League of Women Voters in its earliest days, donating $1,000 to the organization in 1921, 1922, and 1923. Hoover brought speakers from the League of Women Voters to the 1923 Girl Scout convention. She also worked with the California Civic League of Women Voters, addressing that group's October 1923 fund-raising campaign. In her remarks, Hoover contended that politically minded women should broaden their focus beyond simple advocacy of "Child Labor laws, and so-called educational development and other child welfare provision[s]" to include "a heritage of simple, sane, effective government and custom" that appealed to the majority of women.[60] She contended that the wide range of women's interests paralleled those of men. The goals of the National Woman's Party and the more numerous social feminists worried Hoover, for she insisted that women, like men, cared about more than an equal rights amendment or issues specific to women and children.

Lou Hoover's political identity in this complex period remained tenuous. Uncomfortable with avowed partisan politics, she played only a scant role in Bert's presidential politicking before 1928. Her Girl Scout work and her commitment to women's athletics had elements in common with the social feminists, but Hoover most enjoyed these activities because they shielded her from the political gender wars of the decade. Yet she remained strong in her defense of a woman's right to an independent career. For example, in response to a coed's inquiry in 1921 about engineering as a career for women, Hoover replied that the prevailing notions of the woman's sphere would have no more or less influence on women engineers than on women in other professions. She advised young women interested in the profession to specialize in whatever branch most interested them. When asked why, she responded, "why not?" She contended, "a woman who has taken correct care of herself all of her life should have *no* so-called 'physical weakness.'" When asked if "the engineering profession [is] a test of her womanliness," Hoover declared the question to be "incomprehensible." She refused to even consider the views of those who believed that such a pursuit would render a woman "masculine." She preferred the use of the word "unusual," which she viewed as a neutral term, over "unconventional," which she saw as a negative characterization, to describe professional women.[61]

The scandals of the 1920s taught Lou Henry Hoover much about American politics that she later drew on as first lady. After revelation of the Teapot Dome scandal within the Warren G. Harding administration, Lou complained to her sons about the fraudulent oil leases. She was frustrated that the Senate insisted on spending its time investigating "all the rubbish" instead of debating "any real legislation!" She contended that Secretary of the Interior Albert Fall "was undoubtedly at least criminally careless in the appearance of wrong-doing," which left her without "any faith in Fall's honesty." Explaining away the corruption, she concluded, "probably once in a while some [dishonest people] get elected to office by their too careless constituents. So hereafter we have to be a little more careful in elections. And we all have to remember, too, that there are a great many thousand people in the government for every one who is found corrupt."[62]

She directed her greatest invective at Thomas J. Walsh, a Democratic senator from Montana, who was among those "men who started this investigation" with "an eye on the democratic success in the coming election" rather "than on straightening out evil." Those motives, she believed, explained why "they made tremendous assaults on the whole administration,—and tried to assume that the whole cabinet and both Presidents and every Republican living and dead was as corrupt as Fall at his worst." To her, Democrats were equally guilty.[63] Such partisan views foreshadow Lou Hoover's defensiveness after Democratic critics blamed her husband for the Great Depression.

Lou Henry Hoover also expressed her frustrations publicly. She worked with the General Federation of Women's Clubs to develop a national campaign to increase law enforcement. The clubwomen hoped to eradicate or reduce a variety of crimes from murder to swindling, and especially Prohibition-related offenses. They wanted their views stressed in both the Republican and the Democratic party platforms. An April 1924 conference in Washington, D.C., drew 500 delegates from thirty-six states and another 1,000 from the immediate area. Calvin Coolidge addressed the 1,500 women, who, by virtue of the membership rosters of the various voluntary organizations they belonged to, represented more than 10 million women.[64]

Hoover's politics in the 1920s, then, took many forms. Belief in the primacy of the individual to affect policy and influence the future linked her work with the League of Women Voters, her advocacy of women's careers, her criticism of Teapot Dome, and her work with the law-enforcement crusade. Not naïve, she recognized the negative role that some political actors played, and often her statements carried a partisan tinge.

Lou Henry Hoover advocated on behalf of women's athletics because she believed that recreation and physical fitness were necessary components of women's health, identity, and equality. She was the primary figure in the creation of the Women's Division of the new National Amateur Athletic Federation (NAAF), which was inspired by the poor physical condition of Americans at the outset of World War I. Additionally, the NAAF was seen as an alternative to the Amateur Athletic Union, whose support of competitive sports and the Olympics angered those, like Hoover, who preferred a more egalitarian and universally inclusive model of sport.[65]

Preparations for the organization began in 1921 when Lou Henry Hoover had several informal conversations with Secretary of War John W. Weeks, Secretary of the Navy Edwin Denby, and Colonel Robert M. Thompson, among others. She contended that for the proposed NAAF to function properly on behalf of young women, a separate women's division was necessary. To facilitate the women's division, she brought the Girl Scouts into the planning process, and Hoover became the only female vice president of the umbrella organization.

Like the majority of feminists in the 1920s, Hoover believed that women and men were fundamentally different. Her philosophy made sense in an era in which working-class women suffered health problems from industrial hazards and for whom the biology of reproduction was too often destiny. Social feminists worked in a variety of ways to protect women's essential nature, ranging from those concerned about the health and safety of immigrant and poor women to those who worried about the propagation of the "white race." In her work on behalf of women's athletics, Hoover fell somewhere in the middle.

The Women's Division, though, was never her primary concern. She hoped that the organization would broaden access to physical education for women who did not attend college, but internecine conflict and financial difficulties limited the scope of the otherwise successful Women's Division, which was more effective than the moribund NAAF. Lou Hoover established some important principles, such as protection from "the wide-spread recent exploitation of women in competitive athletics." She worried that the single-minded pursuit of victory resulted in unhealthy practices for female athletes. When the Women's Division first faced practical difficulties in 1923, Hoover "did absolutely nothing regarding the revival, because . . . it was better to let it die now than to try to resuscitate it and have a more spectacular death later!" A slight recovery by February 1924 encouraged Hoover, but her optimism was premature, and she spent the bulk of the 1920s using her various contacts to raise money. Although her concept for the Women's Division was sound, the organization struggled because the physical education experts who staffed it knew little about fund-raising, unlike the volunteers who ran the Girl Scouts in the 1920s. Despite its financial problems, the Women's Division hosted regional workshops, developed universal play days in schools and colleges, and prepared standards for women's sports.[66] Hoover's fondness for sport and her optimism that a solution could be found led her to support the Women's Division until its demise. It remained extant but was never financially secure, and in 1940, it merged with the American Association for Health, Physical Education, and Recreation.

In her work with the Women's Division, Lou Henry Hoover helped discredit the notion that a woman's physiology prevented her from enjoying physical activity. Hoover hoped that her efforts would attract all women to fitness and leisure activities, but not until the 1970s did average Americans engage in regular exercise. Because Hoover and the Women's Division focused on participation rather than competition, female athletes were not accorded parity with male athletes. Indeed, notions of sports in America became increasingly identified with victories and losses. If Hoover's vision of universal participation attracted few women to athletics, it changed even fewer male minds about the primacy of competition between organized teams. Put simply, Lou Henry Hoover proffered an unpopular view of sports, in that she encouraged greater female athleticism than society preferred while also advocating the elimination of male competitive sports. Her views, though, were entirely in keeping with the anticonsumption ethos she adopted in the 1920s—the antithesis to the modern, competitive mentality that troubled her.

Herbert Hoover's decision to run for the presidency in 1928 proved an important turning point. In the spring of 1927, Lou wrote to both boys about their father's potential candidacy. She said, "Allan, you asked what about it when people asked you about your father running for President in 1928. Well, I'd like to know that myself." Hoover typically "treat[ed] it very lightly . . . and [made] jokes" when she would have preferred to "tell them what I think about people who are so lacking in the essentials of kindliness as to introduce such subjects into general conversation, where of course they can not be discussed." Her hesitancy about entering the White House asserted itself when she complained of Bert's friends making only a partial commitment to his political future. Unaware of the extent of Bert's presidential ambitions, Lou avowed, "I should like it if the friends who started this talk about the Presidency would see it through or drop the subject,—instead of starting it off, and then settling back and expecting us to bring it off,—when we had never wanted it in the first place,—and Daddy had fought it off altogether as long as he had the strength." She was angrier with his critics, "who talk so much about his enormous fortune." Piqued by the gossip, Hoover suggested that they might "provide the fortune for him, before they assail him so for having it."[67]

Such statements denote two important distortions of the truth—that Herbert Hoover did not want to be president, and that the family had no wealth. The fictions Lou told her sons reflected her continued discomfort with both wealth and the publicity that accrued to presidents and their families. She knew much about those matters from her friend, first lady Grace Goodhue Coolidge, with whom she shared an interest in Girl Scouting and gardening. The two fondly referred to each other as "Bleeding Heart" and "Lily of the Valley." Coolidge, though, had remade the image of the first lady into one of a glamorous style setter, something to which Hoover did not aspire and could never achieve, with her bent toward the natural world and her statuesque and matronly bearing.[68]

No matter who raised the question, Lou Hoover contended to her sons, "Daddy is playing ball in a team, and whether anyone ever persuaded him to run for the Presidency or not, he certainly would not do it, directly *or* indirectly while Calvin Coolidge was still apparently thinking of it. For of course he would never plot against the man who was captain of his team." She explained that their father's most difficult problem was keeping his friends and supporters from denigrating Coolidge. Furthermore, she insisted that there was no need to speculate what he would do if Coolidge did not run, because he "does not give it any consideration himself."[69]

She acknowledged that although she had no idea whether Coolidge would run again, his closest associates suggested that "he has not the slightest intention to run again." Such a private stance, Hoover told her sons, would make "it very difficult for whomever is going to follow him,—because that person could be busy with his preparations now." That situation troubled Lou, because the practical result was that Herbert Hoover's "enemies within the party" were left to start the campaign season. Hoover wanted Herbert and Allan to "laugh" at those individuals who "push it to whether Coolidge is going to run or not, and what Daddy would do then," believing that the best response was to "say that is altogether too many ifs to give a prophecy about."[70] This letter to her sons reveals Hoover's own self-deception regarding her husband's political future, but the most significant aspect of the letter is not what Hoover wrote but what was implied. Bert's race for the presidency resulted not because of his public partnership with Lou but because of his own independent political goals. By the time of the 1928 election, Lou and Bert Hoover no longer functioned in perfect harmony with each other. Though there was no ideological or emotional divide between the two, they did not cooperate on the same public projects. Instead, they operated on symmetrical, parallel tracks. Only from this perspective does Lou's uncertainty about Bert's candidacy make sense.

As Bert's behind-the-scenes campaign for the White House progressed, Lou adjusted to the possibility of becoming first lady. On 2 August 1927, Calvin Coolidge declared, "I do not choose to run for president in 1928," without elaborating on his meaning. Some contemporaries speculated that he wanted the Republican party to draft him as a candidate, while others wondered whether personal concerns had caused him to lose interest in politics. Still others speculated that Coolidge disapproved of Hoover's covert campaigning while he was still a member of the cabinet. Nonetheless, Herbert Hoover and his backers used the Coolidge announcement as justification to begin his quest for the nomination in earnest. Lou Hoover's friend and Girl Scout colleague Sarah Arnold asked, "I wonder if with me you would dread the presidency almost as much as you would welcome it." Favorable public commentary on Lou Hoover's qualifications for first lady compensated for her internal conflict over such a prospect. In the spring of 1928, a supporter told Lou Hoover, "not the least of the arguments for the selection is the qualifications of the President's wife!"[71]

In mid-February 1928, Lou Henry Hoover told George Akerson, one of Herbert Hoover's political advisers, "whenever your people want me to do anything more than to be pleasant and affable and firm to the newspaper ladies, you must tell me what to say!" This statement reflects her willingness to cooperate with Bert's campaign and her aversion to the media and partisan politics. Ever watchful of how her statements might affect Bert's political endeavors, Lou hinted how she might structure her formal duties as first lady. She sent Akerson an unidentified newspaper clipping, which she said "only amuses me." Even the manner in which she parsed her sentence revealed her partisan political passivity: "I still think the enclosed very much better than any interview that could have been published of me on my husband or his candidacy!"[72]

In 1928, Americans faced a choice not only between Herbert Hoover and Al Smith but also between Lou Henry Hoover and Catherine (Katie) Smith. The two potential first ladies were as different as the two candidates. Lou Hoover's Stanford University education and her extensive reading made her an erudite and graceful woman, while Katie Smith's demeanor accorded with her Lower East Side heritage. Despite Smith's admitted fondness for an occasional drink of alcohol—then a controversial choice for women from middle- and upper-class backgrounds—Democrats generated articles testifying to her respectability and American roots.[73]

Hoover partisans highlighted the differences between Katie Smith and Lou Hoover in private and public discourse. Smith's critics told unkind jokes suggesting that she was not suited to be first lady.

Campaign literature presented Hoover as the embodiment of Prot-
estant, Prohibitionist virtue so dear to middle-class women. A full-
page advertisement in the *Delineator,* a popular women's magazine,
contained pictures of both Hoovers and proclaimed, "Thirty-seven
Leading Women tell why they will vote for Herbert Hoover." After an
accounting of Herbert Hoover's accomplishments, the advertisement concluded, "Hoover's cause is the cause of the home. Every
woman should feel the deepest pride that her vote can help make
this great man the leader of our country."[74]

Despite such favorable comparisons, Lou avoided active, public
involvement in the race, preferring instead to work behind the
scenes. When Edgar Rickard approached her about assisting the
Hoover for President National Engineers Committee, she declined.
Again evocative of her public modesty and her conception of what
constituted appropriate political behavior on the part of a presidential candidate's wife, Hoover argued, "I really don't think I should be
any member of a Hoover-for-President club of any kind! Do you?"
Her public political modesty did not cause her to block women's
groups that wished to politic for Bert, however. In fact, after much
intervention, Hoover tentatively agreed to be a guest at a political
function staged by the Women's Auxiliary of the American Institute
of Mining and Metallurgical Engineers. Auxiliary officials stressed,
"while the people of course are working for Mr. Hoover, after the
women have seen you they [will] go away and work for *you* to be in
the White House!"[75]

Drawing on her bureaucratic and organizational talents, Hoover
coached her close friends and acquaintances about how to write re-
cruitment letters for her husband's campaign. For example, she advised, "you could make a logical opening by saying that you understand from mutual friends that although a Democrat in principle,
he [a University of Virginia professor] is now concerned about the
future of the party under its present leadership and feels that it is
necessary to support Herbert Hoover at this juncture." She also
wanted her letter writers to encourage women's activism on the part
of the recipients: "[ask] him [the Virginia professor], I suppose, if
he would suggest the names of any women of his family or acquain-
tance with similar inclinations who would be interested in studying
the problem together."[76]

During the campaign, Lou Henry Hoover denied herself a public voice, speaking instead through Ruth Fesler, one of her secretaries. For example, when a member of the American Association of University Women revealed her plan to write to each of the association's state chapters on behalf of the Hoover campaign, Fesler exaggerated Hoover's deference to the tradition of the silent presidential spouse. Fesler replied, "as she is not taking *any* active part in the campaign, I am taking it upon myself to reply *personally*. . . . I should think if you were doing it on your *individual* initiative and not as an officer of the A.A.U.W. there could be no objection."[77] Thus, although Hoover undertook a few private, behind-the-scenes political activities, she refused to do or say anything that might appear publicly in a newspaper. This tactic, combined with GOP advertising about her, suggested to the public that Lou Henry Hoover would continue the tradition of first lady as silent helpmate. Nothing was further from the truth as it unfolded between 1929 and 1933.

Lou Henry Hoover encountered significant media scrutiny during her husband's presidential campaign. On a campaign swing through the Midwest that included a stop in West Branch, Iowa, Herbert Hoover's hometown, Lou Hoover mystified the women journalists covering the contest. Hoping for an interview and some colorful tidbits to round out their stories, they tracked Hoover down to the train, where they found her preparing for the next stop. According to Bess Furman, one of the journalists, "the most significant thing that Mrs. Hoover told us was that women reporters in Washington all knew she was never quoted. . . . We took the hint and departed, wondering audibly, as soon as we had cleared the railroad tracks, what the Hoovers thought they were out there for if it wasn't to get campaign publicity, and how did they think the papers would get the facts straight if they didn't give them the facts."[78]

Most troubling to Hoover, though, was the incessant coverage of what she termed non-issues. For example, the *Washington Post* headlined a story "Mrs. Hoover Escapes Death in Auto Crash," but the actual incident, according to Hoover, was much less dramatic. The car carrying her and her guests slipped on an icy patch and hit a fence. The paper, however, reported that the car had "crashed through the guard rails of a bridge over the Shenandoah River." After explaining her familiarity with automobile trips over extremely challenging terrain, she told one of her companions on the trip: "I think we did exactly what was best and *exactly* what I wanted to in our entire trip. The fact that a few feet of ground happened to be slippery at one particular moment on that particular road, can't in any way warrant us in supposing that the red clay of the other road would not have been very much worse in very many spots!"[79]

Ruth Fesler told her boss that she had said nothing to the press about the accident. Ironically, Hoover exaggerated the *Post*'s reliance on Fesler as a source, suggesting incorrectly that Fesler had been quoted in the text as verifying the false details. Hoover thus commented, "Therefore, when they say in the article that the details were corroborated by her, they were plainly and simply lying,—there is no other word for it." Hoover acknowledged that other Washington papers provided much more accurate coverage but noted, "we will keep the cutting from the *Post* for our grandchildren. My Janet [Lou's niece], however, is spending most of her time giggling over the picture of us all 'leaping' out of the various windows, much as girls seem to be coming feet first out of the swimming pool when the moving picture reel is reversed."[80]

Lou told another correspondent: "you know there wasn't any accident—at least such as has been described by the newspapers. All that happened was that while going at a very slow speed the machine skidded and the car straddled a low stone fence—no bridge in the picture at all! None of us were hurt or even slightly shaken nor has there been any after effects." To yet another correspondent she claimed: "I do hope you did not receive a sensational news item which came from Winchester about our hanging precipitously, jumping from the car, and otherwise having an exciting time. Alas, that did not happen to us. The story was the exaggeration of some garage man or reporter."[81] This unfortunate media attention reinforced Hoover's skepticism about journalists and caused her to avoid them and the public spotlight.

To facilitate her husband's race for the presidency, Lou Hoover realized that she had to either limit her own activities or procure a substitute hostess. Unwilling to consider the former, she engaged Sue Dyer, a friend since their Stanford days, to act as "official hostess" at their Palo Alto home and see to the needs of their many overnight guests. The exigencies of running for president made for an unpredictable household schedule. Lou Hoover noted, "Bert does in such matters what appeals to him at the moment. Last week when there was a big conference going on in Washington he said to be ready to feed from twelve to twenty each lunch or dinner, as he would probably be bringing a lot of men home. No one came." Exhaustion from the day's work explained the empty dinner table, according to Bert. "On the other hand, yesterday morning six men turned up for breakfast whom he had invited and then forgot all about," Lou lamented. As Hoover explained to Dyer, "it occurs to me that it would be a wonderful idea if you had 'your knitting' on the porch or in the living room and said how-do-you-do to them as they arrived," deciding who should be seen and who should be dismissed.[82]

Although Lou had eliminated the potential conflicts between her activism and her husband's political career in the 1920s, the presidential campaign introduced a new set of challenges. Prior to inviting the Daughters of the American Revolution delegates to tea at her Washington home in 1928, Hoover ensured the propriety of the situation so as to avoid political repercussions. She told that organization's president: "I felt that it could so very likely be misconstrued as a political move on my part for my husband! So I have replied that it seemed to me not at all becoming on my part to *offer* such an invitation. However, when the suggestion came from . . . the Chairman of your Invitation Committee, I felt very different about it and was only too glad to be able to help."[83]

The public, political redefinition of her husband's character and record troubled Lou Hoover. In the midst of the campaign, she told a friend, "I often think not only how one 'suffers' at the hands of one's friends but how one really gets to be—at least to the world—what one's friends (or foes!) picture one instead of what one really is or does one's self!" The campaign process left her to "wonder how much resemblance to the real Herbert Hoover will be in the Herbert Hoover who finally emerges from this round of published description by friend, enemy, and dollar-per-inch space writer! And even what his wife is!" Because she distrusted the media, she hoped that family friends would remember the "realities behind both public masks!"[84]

Said Lou Henry Hoover of her campaign efforts in 1928, "Am I tired? Not a bit. Why should I be? All I have done is ride about and meet friendly people and receive beautiful flowers. The candidate has to make all the speeches, but his wife gets all the flowers." To a supporter, Hoover explained her decision to remain aloof from formal campaign activities: "I hope I am not disappointing you too much by saying that I think with almost certainty you will not see any message from me during the campaign." Recognition of her "personal interest" in the election's outcome dictated Hoover's reticence. After the election was over, Hoover thanked a friend for sending her reports of the electioneering process out in the various states: "I always felt that the campaign must have been 'lots of fun' for those who could go out into the thick of it and 'do things,' and I shall greatly enjoy this chronicle of it."[85] Such correspondence provides another glimpse of Hoover's self-revision; although she had not actively campaigned, she had participated in other ways.

Ultimately, the campaign provided Lou Henry Hoover with an introduction to the seamy side of American politics, which she found distasteful and unnecessary. "The loss of my faith in humanity is very much harder upon me than the possible loss of the Presidency," Hoover contended. "I mean that instead of attempting to see justice done an opponent and a fight carried on on honorable lines,—while they would not stab him or another enemy in the back themselves,—[leading Democrats] are standing quietly by and watching it done by those of their colleagues without an audible protest." At other times, she appeared less troubled by the political assignations that accompanied the 1928 campaign, telling one associate, "the things that are said now about my husband . . . do not distress me personally."[86]

The transition from candidate's wife to incoming first lady proved a busy one for Lou Henry Hoover. Just days after the election, Herbert Hoover announced plans for a six-week goodwill trip to eleven South American countries. He hoped to ease tensions resulting from increased American economic activity in the region. Lou's decision to accompany her husband afforded the perfect respite from the partisan bitterness of the recent election, and her Spanish language skills rendered her a significant member of the Hoover team, according to the president-elect. Her participation suggested the manner in which she might influence gender roles as first lady. Never brash or strident in her activism, Lou Henry Hoover nonetheless challenged traditional mores while visiting South

America. Recalled Ruth Fesler, "it was most interesting to me to see how excited the women were in catching a glimpse of Mrs. Hoover. . . . Many times I saw the women's faces light up as they cried 'viva la Senora de Hoover' when we drove past." Additionally, Hoover broke precedent when her picture appeared in local newspapers both as a member of the arrival party and with local elite women, because women were rarely depicted publicly in that fashion.[87] Thus, even before she entered the White House, Lou Henry Hoover previewed the innovative manner in which she would perform her new duties. A key component of her activism was an unstated but fully internalized sense of entitlement to equitable gender roles and public work.

The challenges of the next four years made it impossible for Lou Henry Hoover to overlook partisanship. Ironically, her own activist agenda during her tenure as first lady exacerbated the political challenges that accompanied residence in the White House. Had Stanford University chancellor David Starr Jordan's postelection predictions held true, the story of her years as first lady might have been very different, but by 1932, almost no one in America agreed with Jordan's 1928 statement: "you and your honored husband belong henceforth to the world of humanity, not to Stanford, in any limited or narrow sense, not to the Republican party nor even to the United States. After the mandate of yesterday, I hold our country in higher esteem than I ever felt before."[88] Yet the question remained whether Lou Henry Hoover could apply Jordan's idealism to the daunting responsibilities that confronted her as the new first lady.

CHAPTER 2

AN ACTIVIST FIRST LADY IN TRADITIONAL WASHINGTON

Inauguration day, 4 March 1929, dawned cold and rainy. The Hoovers had dined with the Coolidges at the White House the night before. The following morning, Lou Henry Hoover donned a plum velvet outfit and rode to the Capitol for the ceremonies. At almost fifty-five years old, the incoming first lady retained a healthy vigor but was heavier than in her younger years. She wore her almost white hair neatly coifed close to her head, and her voice was pleasant and dignified. Unconcerned about glamour and style, she nonetheless paid careful attention to her wardrobe. Matters of substance and friendship ranked higher, and she tarried too long talking with Grace Coolidge just before the inauguration began. The two women arrived after the swearing in of Vice President Charles Curtis and almost missed Herbert Hoover's recitation of the oath of office.

"It was hard to determine which looked more contented, the woman who was renouncing the cares of 'First Lady,' or the one who was just about to enter upon those duties," declared one journalist who covered the inauguration. Shortly after 11:00 A.M., as Chief Justice William Howard Taft administered the oath, Lou stood by Bert's side impassively as the rain poured down. Then they enjoyed a White House luncheon with almost 2,000 guests, the inaugural parade, and a tea and reception for 1,500 people later that afternoon. Instead of attending the inaugural ball, a small charitable affair, the Hoovers asked that Curtis be the official host.[1]

After the day's festivities had concluded, Mary Randolph, the social secretary to Grace Coolidge and now to Lou Hoover, was "so tired that my eyes were crossed." But she was summoned to a meeting in the west sitting room with Hoover, where Randolph received instructions to arrange a large musicale a mere five days later. The new first lady did not want the event to appear overly formal, so she requested that Randolph hand-write the invitations. On the drive home, Randolph reflected, "behind me the first day under what was to be, from then on, 'The Big Top,' with plenty of side-shows and lots of ballyhoo."[2]

Friends and colleagues of the Hoovers were confident that the administration would prove to be successful. Soon after the Hoovers entered the White House, David Starr Jordan told the new first lady, "we shall probably experience an era of good feeling, such as came in once with James Monroe, and never since." Philippi Butler declared: "Would that we were to be Secretary of War or Something so that we would just have to be there!! May your reign be a happy one. It will be a successful one without wishing. I only wish further that we might do something some time to lighten your burdens for you."[3] Biased by optimism, Butler overlooked the fragile economy and the problems it might cause the nation's first family.

During her years as first lady, Lou Henry Hoover paid scant attention to such flattery. She was too busy juggling her own activist agenda with her responsibilities as wife and first lady. Although Lou and Bert never quite resurrected their public marriage, Lou found that more of her public time was given over to the care of Bert than had been the case previously. She maintained a standing policy that her engagements were "always . . . tentative," out of deference to her husband's often last-minute need for "assistance," which "must naturally take precedence over any other of her personal engagements."[4]

These declarations do not mean that Lou Hoover approached her duties as first lady from a traditional perspective. Instead, she employed a complex blend of tradition and activism in and out of the White House. She balanced her hostess duties with her outside interests in a seamless fashion, but she shifted her earlier priorities. She diminished the scope of her involvement with voluntary associations, but only to compensate for her new responsibilities. The White House became her laboratory as she modernized all aspects of its social agenda.

Lou Hoover became the first modern first lady with an activist agenda—an entity previously unseen in the East Wing. For Hoover, activism meant addressing the problems—large and small—she encountered in the world. This commitment to public works stemmed from her belief that she should use her talents and her means to improve society, and it shaped all aspects of her tenure as first lady. Since Hoover performed her hostess duties with aplomb, one could interpret her activities as nothing more than busyness, but that would be incorrect. Although Edith Wilson and Grace Coolidge, for example, had executed their hostess duties with elegance and charm, neither woman, nor any other first lady before Hoover, had pursued an actual agenda. That Lou Henry Hoover did so while also fulfilling traditional expectations marked her as a transitional figure with a revolutionary approach to entertaining. Put simply, both the larger meanings and the minutiae of White House social functions became a significant component of Hoover's multilayered activism.

She set precedents on which future presidential spouses expanded. In the spring of 1929, one journalist remarked, "She might well have been chosen on her own merits, for with the exception of Mrs. Washington and Mrs. Madison she is the best known and most widely acquainted woman to whom this historic honor has come." Another publication hailed Hoover as "a strong woman" perfect for the "First Lady's job." The evaluation of Lou Hoover in *Review of Reviews* proved even more significant: "judging by space in popular magazines for March [1929], it was Mrs. Hoover who was installed in the White House last month."[5] She also guarded her privacy and tempered the public face of her activism.

In comparison with her predecessors, Hoover staked significant new territory for the office of first lady. Throughout the nineteenth century, first ladies had done little more than entertain and decorate. As a modern, independent woman, Hoover had few credible models on which to draw as first lady. Indeed, the institution had entered a state of flux before World War I, when first ladies made a few initial but halting forays into the public sphere.

When Edith Bolling Galt Wilson assumed some presidential duties during her husband's recovery from a stroke in 1919–1920, she did so not as an independent woman but as a helpmate caring for her ill spouse. She acted as an executive secretary and gatekeeper for

Woodrow Wilson's visitors, isolating the White House in the process. Furthermore, her behavior generated public and political criticism, and she became a cautionary lesson against future first-lady activism. Florence Kling Harding opened up the White House again and brought in press coverage, but the scandals that marred her husband's administration and his untimely death limited her influence. She appreciated her public role much more than any of her predecessors, but she maintained a provincial view of political affairs. Grace Coolidge, Lou Hoover's close friend and Girl Scout colleague, personified the glamour of the 1920s with drop-waist dresses and short hemlines, but she was not allowed to be interested in her husband's political career. Nevertheless, she was active in cultural matters, operated in the political spotlight in 1924, and redecorated parts of the White House until her husband halted the work. Thus, these three women provided few examples for Hoover's activist demeanor.[6]

In the first year of the Hoover administration, before the Great Depression began, Lou concentrated her energies on White House entertaining. She restructured that traditional role by merging the social with the political, so as to reinforce her husband's policy agenda. In the process, she modernized the White House social calendar. However, her involvement with other issues, ranging from education to "the betterment of women and children," kept her busy every day. One journalist noted that such a rigorous schedule would strain most women, "but with Mrs. Hoover this is not likely to happen, for she knows how to apportion her time and conserve her strength." Indeed, Lou Hoover "outdistanced her predecessor, Mrs. Coolidge," with regard to "friendly meeting[s]" with women seeking White House support for a variety of causes. The first lady's social secretary arranged appointments so that there would be no wasted time in Hoover's day. Instead of greeting large numbers of guests one by one, as had been the accepted practice before the Hoover presidency, Lou Hoover welcomed small groups of guests to make White House affairs more intimate and productive.[7] By 1929, social events in Washington had grown stale and ritualized. Hoover changed existing customs for two reasons: she hoped that her guests would enjoy themselves more if White House events were less stuffy, and she recognized the wisdom of using the White House social calendar for partisan gain. For some years prior to the Hoover presidency, it had not been common practice to invite guests for "political" reasons, but Hoover changed that. As such, her work as hostess must be understood in activist, not just social, terms.

Because management of White House social affairs took time away from her other causes, Hoover applied activist methods to maximize her efficiency. The chief usher, Irwin H. "Ike" Hoover (no relation to the first family), recalled that "Mrs. Hoover held regular cabinet meetings before and after each large social affair at the White House." The attendees included the first lady, her secretaries, and the military aides—all the key personnel responsible for White House social affairs. Like Grace Coolidge, she insisted on approving details of events in advance. Because Lou Hoover did more social entertaining than many of her predecessors had, Ike Hoover described her as being "in a class all by herself in so far as extensive entertaining was concerned."[8]

Lou Henry Hoover imbued the strictly social functions of the White House with political import. This marriage between activism and the traditional expectations of first ladies met with a mixed record of success and failure. The most notorious example was her tentative adoption of a civil rights cause when she entertained an African American woman, who also happened to be a congressional spouse. However, Hoover failed to follow up this bold White House departure from the Jim Crow culture of segregation with more sweeping pleas for racial justice.

The Great Depression intensified the political dynamics of White House social matters, even as it cast a pall over Lou Hoover's entertaining. Bert's social needs—for his own comfort and relaxation, but also for the purpose of enhancing his public policy agenda—dictated Lou's management of the White House social schedule, especially after the depression became the dominant political and economic issue for the Hoovers. Her charm and graciousness as a hostess contrasted with the president's often dour public face and helped explain their very different public images. When revealed to the public, Lou Hoover's social responsibilities helped humanize the Hoover presidency. Unfortunately for her husband's political career, however, such glimpses were rare.

Weeks before the inauguration on 4 March 1929, journalists contended that Lou Hoover "must completely submerge her own private life and become for the next four years in truth a 'servant of the people.'" A writer for the *Washington Herald* suggested that "only the very personal friends of the President or his wife" should be welcomed "into the private living quarters." Hoover ignored this advice, and "woman guests" who were "kindred spirits" and close friends of the first lady were frequent visitors during Lou Hoover's White House tenure. They "help[ed] Lou Henry Hoover be herself, as well as the wife of the President."[9] Lou Hoover also brought the family's extended circle of friends into the White House, much as she had in each of their previous homes. Her break with this tradition of isolation ensured the availability of her women's political advisory network and revealed her merger of first-lady entertainment responsibilities with an activist strategy.

Even before Herbert Hoover's inauguration, Washington journalists critiqued Lou Hoover's appetite and aptitude for managing the White House. "She must be the head of a big business concern—for the White House plant is just that," declared a writer for the *Washington Herald*.[10] White House employees numbered between fifty and sixty, and their salaries ranged from $780 to $1,800 a year. The first family paid the White House grocery bills for all but the "official" parties hosted for domestic and foreign leaders. One observer contended that the first lady would have to be a frugal manager to keep the White House food budget under $2,500 a month, especially considering that state dinners with more than 100 guests cost more than $1,000 per event.

Hoover's preparations for residence in the White House included a careful survey of policies about domestic employees. She learned that eighteen household servants received meals as part of their compensation. The Hoovers retained those servants already employed in the White House and brought in additional domestic help. Despite these efforts, Hoover found it difficult to reorient the White House staff toward her modern expectations. She described the White House as "a funny house downstairs here, not like 2300 [S Street], where . . . almost anyone could stay on and concoct small meals for us in the kitchen! It seems to necessitate three or four cooks here if they get some soup and a steak and dessert."[11]

Large household management was not a new concern for Lou Hoover. During her entire married life, Hoover had depended on an extensive household and secretarial staff, and she demanded excellence from her employees. In addition to their salaries, she provided numerous other forms of assistance, such as college tuition, vacations, health care, and retirement benefits. Most of the staff appreciated the Hoover style and were loyal. Indeed, former staff members typically chose to return to the Hoover household, given the opportunity. One White House maid, however, published a book that criticized Lou Hoover's use of hand signals to communicate with the staff. From Hoover's perspective, the hand signals were nothing more than an efficient mechanism to provide for the comfort of her guests, but critics easily caricatured them.[12]

Moving into the White House necessitated many decisions about furnishings and decorations. Lou and Bert found their residential quarters "as bleak as a New England barn." The president did not pay much attention to the aesthetics involved in decorating, however. As one of the first lady's secretaries reported to a decorator, "Mrs. Hoover says that it was unfortunate that her husband gathered enough sofas and chairs together to make the study livable, and she has just been unable to get him down to a definite discussion of the room since." Herbert Hoover viewed decoration in political and symbolic terms. He had reclaimed the original upstairs study, which had been converted into a bedroom during the Theodore Roosevelt administration, for his own use out of deference to the memory of Presidents Abraham Lincoln and William McKinley. Lou Hoover, according to her husband, studied a painting celebrating the Emancipation Proclamation, which Lincoln had signed in that room; located the furniture that had been in the study then; and recreated the room as Lincoln had used it, including his desk.[13]

Lou Hoover's sharpest criticisms were reserved for the second-floor rooms: "The upstairs, which in the House is in many ways so much more charming than below, is in a much worse condition as to furnishings than the lower floor." During her tenure, Hoover crafted a more relaxed environment that welcomed the first family's numerous guests to the second-floor residence. She provided for informal entertaining, overnight guests, and even play space for her grandchildren and other young White House visitors. "The Hoover White House had the living charm of a home, especially in its family quarters,—a gracious, friendly and individual home yet quite distinct

from the charm of its other eras," recalled Dare Stark McMullin, a
protégé of the first lady. "More than most houses, it converses with
its owners. Mrs. Hoover and the White House kept up, for four years,
charming conversation together!" Another observer said that Lou
Hoover's decoration of the White House "combined the charm of
California informality and that coveted 'lived-in look.'"[14] Although
not everyone in Washington agreed with her choices, Hoover proved
to be a constructive force in the mansion's history, because she respected and studied its past as a prerequisite to redecorating.

Prior to Hoover, only Lucy Webb Hayes, who moved into the
White House in 1877, and Grace Coolidge had shown any sustained
interest in historical furnishings. The mid-nineteenth-century first
ladies had considered the furnishings of the late eighteenth and
early nineteenth centuries to be "decayed" and of no further usefulness. Although Hayes had initiated research into historic White
House furnishings, her findings were not preserved. Hoover arranged for McMullin to study historic White House furnishings as
part of her overall redecoration program, and McMullin's findings
helped Hoover recreate the various White House rooms as they
might have been when the structure was first built.[15]

Redecorating the White House was paramount, because in 1925,
Grace Coolidge had urged Congress to help restore White House
furnishings in accordance with the style of the building. Provisions
had been made for the acceptance of donated furniture and the
creation of a temporary oversight committee, but the work stalled
when Calvin Coolidge criticized the committee. Hoover worked
closely with Harriet Pratt, who was the wife of a wealthy business-
man, a former Girl Scout activist, and a member of that committee.
Hoover and Pratt completed work on the Green Room and the East
Room, procured some Adams china and antique chairs from the
1780s, and duplicated several pieces of Monroe furniture, which
Hoover paid for and donated to the White House for the second-
floor Rose Room. Three decades before Jackie Kennedy, Lou Henry
Hoover had begun restoration of the White House.

Hoover's approach to decorating the White House, which under-
went no substantive construction or renovation of existing rooms,
mirrored her philosophy of comfortable elegance. She recognized
that the White House possessed "three zones of hospitality, though

of course in use they frequently overlap." The ground floor was "open to anyone who cares to stroll through"; formal entertaining occurred on the main floor, which had been redone in 1903; and the last area for entertaining was the private floor. The north hall housed numerous playthings for the Hoover grandchildren. Because Hoover so loved the out-of-doors, she converted the south portico into a "porch living room," replete with many potted plants.[16] Hoover made additional changes designed to improve conditions for the household employees. New dining and sitting rooms were added for the Hoovers' staff. Thus, even as she conformed to expected behavior of first ladies, Hoover did so with a nod toward modern principles.

While struggling with the decoration of White House rooms, Lou Henry Hoover also oversaw the construction of an isolated retreat in the Blue Ridge Mountains of Virginia. The building of Camp Rapidan expanded the precedent of previous chief executives who had sought refuge outside of Washington. For example, Theodore Roosevelt had vacationed in Virginia, Woodrow Wilson had gone to the Jersey shore, and Calvin Coolidge had removed to the Black Hills of South Dakota for relaxation. Although it functioned only during the Hoover presidency, Camp Rapidan became the first retreat built explicitly for the president. Franklin D. Roosevelt institutionalized the idea with his Shangri-La vacations at the site that would become Camp David, the permanent presidential retreat in Maryland, but Lou Henry Hoover introduced the notion with Camp Rapidan.

Hoover's work on the camp indicates another facet of her organizational innovations as first lady. She planned the location and arrangement of the weekend camp, which grew out of a desire for privacy and isolation from the public and an escape from the demands of Washington, D.C. Unlike the women who had preceded her as first lady, she was more than capable of such work. Hoover had drawn many of the plans and had tended to the details of the construction of the family's Palo Alto home in the early 1920s, which now serves as the residence for the president of Stanford University. According to White House physician Joel Boone, she possessed "a very fertile mind" and was well equipped to plan the perfect presidential camp. Despite its isolation, the camp eventually contained many modern conveniences: electric lights, telephones, regular newspaper delivery, and postal service "dropped from an airplane!" The Hoovers initially paid $15,000 for the property and spent another $200,000 in improvements out of their private funds. The twenty-four rustic, pine camp buildings were constructed for just under $14,000. Lou Hoover required the "biggish" facilities to be habitable from early spring through late autumn, with an "occasional snowy Winter camp."[17]

To facilitate the executive functioning of the camp, Lou proposed a building with ample office space for both male bureaucrats and female secretaries, along with sleeping quarters for eight to ten people. Additionally, she included space for domestic help, Secret Service agents, "and very likely a small detachment of some contingent of Uncle Sam's Army or Marine Corps!"[18] Such requirements explain the extensive size of the camp, which covered many mountainous acres and contained numerous buildings.

In many ways, this small village typified Hoover's gift of solitude to her husband, especially during the difficult later years of his presidency. The rustic beauty of the Blue Ridge Mountains inspired the location of the retreat, as well as Hoover's nature-related theme in decorating the buildings. Consistent with her organized and methodical personality, Hoover left ten pages of directions for the maintenance of the gardens at Camp Rapidan. She had planned the landscape not just from an aesthetic perspective but also from a botanical, scientific perspective. She instructed: "The President is very fond of color in gardens so where possible *and appropriate to the species,* arrange the flowering shrubs and flowers so as to give mass effect of color."[19] This scientific use of nature as decoration reflected Hoover's independent, intellectual talents.

As soon as the facilities were equipped for entertaining, both Hoovers used Camp Rapidan as an informal site for conducting business. The first lady frequently entertained Girl Scout colleagues. One Hoover associate commented after her stay at Camp Rapidan, "I am sure you will go down in history without any question as the epitome of a gracious cordial hostess, and I am all for rewriting the alphabet books at once with: 'H is for hostess' followed by your photograph greeting hosts of Girl Scout guests."[20] Such a combination—Hoover's use of the retreat for activist purposes while ensuring the comfort and enjoyment of her guests—exemplifies her ability to balance traditional expectations of political spouses with modern demands on them.

Management of the White House social scene involved more than setting food budgets, overseeing domestic employees, arranging furniture, and building a weekend retreat. To please the social mavens in the capital city, Lou Henry Hoover needed an appreciation of their social prejudices, including hierarchy in entertaining. First lady Edith Roosevelt had been the first to employ a social secretary, Belle Hagner, and subsequent first ladies continued the practice. Despite the contention of one journalist that "Mrs. Hoover, of course, with her cosmopolitan experience, requires no steering past the social errors that threaten the newcomer to Washington," she opted to hire additional secretaries. In fact, Hoover employed more secretaries than "any woman who ha[d] been mistress of the White House" up to that time.[21] However, Hoover never quite meshed with the incumbent social secretary.

The youngish Mary Randolph, who had been born around the turn of the century, had worked previously as Grace Coolidge's social secretary. Randolph retained her post for the first year of Hoover's stint as first lady, but the two women shared little common ground regarding White House entertaining and activism. Described as "popular in Washington society ever since her debut year," Randolph was "small, slight and smartly dressed." She handled her duties "with great efficiency and tact" while proving herself "a companion and friend to the First Lady." Randolph maintained a "businesslike" office and was respectful of its tradition. She oversaw "countless mailbags of letters" and kept the first lady's appointment book, "a delicate matter to avoid embarrassing mistakes."[22]

Joining Randolph were Ruth Fesler and Mildred Hall. Both women had worked previously for Lou Hoover and, unlike Randolph, supported Hoover's activist philosophy. Fesler had studied history at Stanford University with the hope of having a career in the foreign service, and Hall, a Maryland native, had worked at various secretarial jobs in Washington before a stint at the Girl Scouts' Little House brought her to Hoover's attention. The first family paid the secretaries' salaries, and their employment marked the growth of the first lady's secretarial staff from one to three, a clear measure of

Hoover's expanded public activism in comparison with her predecessors. This increase paralleled similar changes in the president's
support staff and reflected the rise of the bureaucratic White
House, inclusive of the president and the first lady. Finally, it
showed how Lou Henry Hoover's pre–White House management
style carried over into Washington.

The first lady was a demanding boss. Mildred Hall Campbell recalled, "we always worked—the Hoovers never stopped, you know.
Sundays, Mondays through Saturdays we were working there at the
White House." Campbell recounted, "I wrote her letters, I bought
some of her dresses and hats. I even tried to write her speeches! At
least, with my manuscript she knew what she didn't want to say! I
made most of the first of the 1928 campaign trips and all of the 1932
campaign trips with her."[23] Reliance on ghostwritten speeches and
letters provides another indication of Hoover's bureaucratic style
and her hectic schedule. Like her husband, Lou believed in hard work
for its own sake. Her dogged routine revealed the extent to which an
activist, independent woman could remake the role of first lady.

Despite Mary Randolph's talents and her connections with the
capital city's social elite, Washington gossips wondered how long it
would be before Lou Hoover replaced her. Calling her boss "a difficult person to convince," Randolph wrote, "every day I was trying to
persuade Mrs. Hoover to go slowly, for the First Lady should never
rush her jumps. No good comes of that, and every White House
Secretary should try to prevent it. However, insistence on this course
brought Mrs. Hoover face to face with grave difficulties."[24] In her demeanor, Randolph adhered to an old-fashioned understanding of
how elite women should comport themselves, which was both rigid
and unsympathetic to Hoover and her modern agenda.

Hoover used her organizing talents to ensure an efficient flow of
mail in her office. The various categories of mail included personal
correspondence, items requiring immediate attention ("called the
'fire alarms'" by her secretaries), fan mail, and various requests for
assistance. Individually typed form letters were used for the simpler
requests, but Hoover typically returned the urgent matters with
clear directions for handling, recalled one Hoover secretary. Certain
gendered notions of proper decorum hampered the first lady's efforts at modernization. Randolph believed that all correspondence

to the first lady should be handwritten, whereas the outgoing mail from the first lady should be typed. But even Grace Coolidge had cowered at the thought of sending her friend Lou Hoover a typed letter. Coolidge explained, "I shall try to conceal my guilt by addressing the envelope by hand and writing my name in the upper left corner in the hope that I may get by."[25]

Sue Dyer explained that Randolph's traditional, "formal" style conflicted with Hoover's innovative but bureaucratic approach. Additional discord resulted because Randolph could not "manage" Hall and Fesler.[26] She finally resigned as Hoover's social secretary in late May 1930, without public comment, and there was speculation in the press whether she would marry or assume another secretarial post (she found other employment by the end of the year). Hoover had no immediate plans to replace Randolph, preferring instead that Hall and Fesler assume additional duties, at least until the start of the fall and winter social season.

Questions of whether Hoover intended to name a new social secretary or return to past tradition, "when White House hospitality reflected only the spirit of the hostess," became intertwined with skepticism about her overall public demeanor. Pundits attributed her decisions to socialize with her private friends on her own terms, drive her own car (a precedent for first ladies), and shop alone to the lack of guidance from a professional social secretary. These behaviors threatened the provincially minded Washingtonian elite. Hoover viewed the matter differently; she believed that her staff "would be more cohesive if all were on the same status and directly under her own guidance."[27] Thus, Hoover's secretaries—Fesler and Hall—and F. Lammot Belin, the White House director of official entertainment, handled the formal entertaining. Such actions typified Hoover's attempt to balance tradition with her modern, even casual, ways.

The press, though, showed little sympathy for these changes. The Washington social pages, and others throughout the country, depended on the first lady and the White House for news and drama. As one Washington reporter noted, "should Mrs. Hoover have a dispute with her secretary . . . over flowers for the White House table, most of the dinners and tea parties of Washington are buzzing over the incident twenty-four hours later." More tolerant reporters suggested that although previous first ladies had melded into Washington's social machinery, Lou Hoover, as "the most cosmopolitan and widely traveled mistress of the White House," taught her personal staff the methods of her predecessors and "then, firmly but quietly, she threw out the old machinery and substituted her own." Said a *Boston Globe* correspondent, "The traditions that she will uphold are her own."[28]

The less tolerant termed "the first year of the Hoover administration an outstanding social failure" for its willingness to overturn the status quo. Such writers described Randolph's departure as "a serious problem," arguing that Ruth Fesler would face "hard sledding" if she attempted to fill Randolph's shoes. As the depression wore on, political gossip columnists tried to make the Randolph resignation into a controversy about Hoover's indecision and her unrealistic demands for " 'something exquisite—something original—something which none of our predecessors has had.' " One journalist indicated that Hoover never provided specific directions, but in fact, her papers contain lengthy instructions for social affairs. Supposedly the first lady became angry when Randolph's efforts were not "satisfactory," despite doing "the best she could," so Randolph "left."[29]

Ironically, this social criticism came from traditionally minded female journalists, who, by their own employment, had broken that same tradition but nonetheless held it up as sacred to their readers. Thus, Lou Hoover found herself in an impossible situation, akin to what women activists faced in other fields such as politics, education, and social reform movements when they challenged traditional gender mores. The mixed to negative reactions they received illustrate the exceedingly difficult task of Hoover and the first ladies who followed her as they tried to give their White House responsibilities a more modern orientation. Indeed, solidifying first-lady activism as an acceptable, mainstream approach to the unpaid, unelected position of presidential spouses was one of the last traditional gender barriers to crumble in the United States. Put simply, even as the American public slowly accepted new roles for average middle-class women in the 1920s and 1930s, it was not ready for an activist first lady. Hoover's modern, activist take on her post, then, was pathbreaking, even though it contained elements of tradition.

Just as practical elegance had been her forte before entering the White House, Hoover maintained that approach during her husband's presidency. Although concerns about dinner-party decorations seem entirely traditional, Hoover took this feminine preoccupation and modernized it. In the late 1930s, Hoover explained her centerpieces for the White House dinner table: "I endeavored to have table and flowers as nearly as possible in harmony with architecture, decoration and furnishings of the house,—that is, with the very simple dignity that goes with what some call 'the early Federal' period." She typically allowed one of the gardeners to make the flower arrangements, unless the occasion called for additional planning. Apart from the "strongly governing principle . . . of the White House," Lou preferred "to run away from conventionality in table decoration," using centerpieces composed of pine cones of various sizes and shapes, autumnal gourds and corn, and miniature Christmas trees. "I like doing without flowers," she noted. "On suitable occasions I love to pile a big brass tray with vegetables,—purple cabbage and eggplant, a pale green or white squash, green and red peppers, tomatoes,—group themselves gorgeously!"[30]

Because Lou Henry Hoover was a prototype for the bureaucratic, corporate wife, she relished the increased personal responsibilities that the East Wing staff changes required. According to Philippi Harding Butler, "Mrs. Hoover was her own social secretary" after Randolph's departure. The decision, albeit unwise, to micromanage her office in that manner resulted because Hoover could not discern another way to navigate the chasm between traditional entertaining and a more modern approach. When the demands of her work on depression-related relief projects, along with the difficulties of managing the details of social precedents, grew to overwhelming proportions, Hoover finally hired Doris Goss, a social secretary amenable to her modern, activist perspective. The hiring of Goss enabled Hoover to avoid the "professional social secretaries schooled in the intricacies of Washington society."[31]

Although Hoover wanted stately receptions, she disliked the "stiffness" of the Randolph approach, preferring instead for her guests to mingle. As a result, cabinet members and other officials "no longer sat like puppets in a row." The new, democratic mode of entertaining challenged those who had benefited from the exclusive status quo. Hoover made the switch in the hope of mixing the best of a Girl Scout camp meal with a White House state dinner, and she ignored the predictable criticism. A friend said that Lou Henry Hoover transformed the White House into a "cheerful place."[32]

Despite all her preparation and planning, Lou Henry Hoover encountered controversy over the issue of race and White House protocol. On 12 June 1929, Jessie DePriest was a White House guest at a tea party honoring the spouses of members of Congress. As first lady, Hoover hosted the event, which received no publicity beforehand but produced a nationwide controversy afterward. DePriest was the wife of Republican Oscar Stanton DePriest, the first African American member of Congress since 1901. He represented a Chicago district and reflected the expansion of black suffrage in the North. At the same time, Herbert Hoover and the Republicans were courting white southerners away from the Democrats. This social occasion had strong political overtones, and it embodied Lou Hoover's efforts to combine activism with tradition.[33] Never a progressive on civil rights, Hoover nonetheless recognized the most egregious aspects of discrimination within official circles in Washington, D.C.

The enforcement of a rigid color line at the White House had become standard practice with the advent of exclusionary Jim Crow legislation. Many of the laws and customs crafted at the end of the nineteenth century sanctioning a racial caste system actually veiled white southern concerns about women, who were spending more time in the public sphere. Most blatant were the railroad car restrictions, designed to ensure the purity of white women who might otherwise come into contact with African American men while traveling alone on public transportation. Arguments in favor of such measures augmented a nationwide rollback of most, if not all, of the Reconstruction-era advances. Theodore Roosevelt's 1901 White House dinner invitation to conservative African American leader Booker T. Washington angered white southerners and was the last integrated social event in the executive mansion until Lou Henry Hoover became first lady. That DePriest broke the color line at the White House—and in the presence of white women—made the event intolerable for racists in both the North and the South.[34]

Ironically, despite all the controversy it generated, DePriest's visit was not the first instance of an African American guest in the White House during the Hoover years. Robert R. Moton, an African American political leader and the president of Tuskegee Institute, came to the White House on 16 May 1929, fully one month before the DePriest tea, and he returned five more times in 1929 and 1930. The first Moton visit, though, generated no hostile press, despite careful reporting in black media outlets and a press conference with White House reporters. There were three reasons for this lack of public outcry: (1) the Moton visit was business in nature, not social; (2) his visit occurred in May, before a northern member of Congress created controversy in June by pushing for racial equality; and (3) Moton made no issue of his visit. In contrast, Congressman DePriest used the White House tea, along with the negative media reaction to it, to advocate a strengthened civil rights agenda.[35] Although these explanations reveal some of the reasons for the white backlash, they overlook the role of gender in the controversy—specifically, the white South's often fanatic attempts to "protect" white women from any harm that might result from their association with African Americans, both male and female.

Lou Hoover had two options, both of which would have resolved the dilemma of having Jessie DePriest as a guest at the White House, but she considered neither of them. First, not having any tea parties for congressional spouses would have damaged her husband's effectiveness as president because of the ill will created between the White House and Congress. Second, excluding DePriest would have been rude and out of character for Hoover, whose life included numerous small but significant testimonials to her belief in equality. Indeed, notions of fairness loomed large in Hoover's approach to race and White House entertaining.

That sense of justice can be traced back to her childhood in Whittier, where she had African American friends, but it was tempered by the racial mores she had absorbed in Texas. When she and her husband purchased a home in Washington, D.C., they refused to sign a restrictive covenant promising that they would never sell or rent to African Americans or Jews. And Hoover had once paid the college tuition of a black maid because she believed that the young woman had leadership potential. Lou Hoover knew that her personal preference to include Jessie DePriest accorded with her official duty.

The story of how the tea was staged shows Lou Hoover's independent thinking with regard to this social justice issue. In late May 1929, her secretary wrote to Walter Newton, a leading political aide to the president, and inquired, "the question arises as to what can be done about the family of our new colored representative. Mrs. Hoover wishes me to ask for your suggestion, and to remind you that we must think not only of this occasion, but of what is to be done during the entire term of the Representative."[36] Hoover's solution was unique: instead of following standard practice and giving just one tea, at which DePriest would in all likelihood receive discourteous treatment, Hoover divided the guest list and hosted several teas. In no sense, though, was the DePriest tea a "segregated" affair. Segregation, as practiced in the United States in 1929, entailed substandard facilities and discrimination against its African American targets. At the White House, DePriest received hospitality on a par with that accorded all other congressional spouses. More important, the separate tea was planned not to insult her but to protect her from boorish behavior. Both Mary Randolph and Newton advised Hoover regarding the event, indicating the dual social and political purpose of the tea.

To prevent any boycotts of the teas, which would have embarrassed the administration and the DePriests, Hoover arranged for DePriest to attend the last tea party. Racist-minded congressional spouses would have looked silly had they boycotted the earlier teas to protest an event that had not yet occurred, so they had no choice but to attend. On the first lady's orders, Jessie DePriest's invitation was not issued until 5 June, the date of the next to last tea party, and Randolph instructed the messenger to keep its contents "confidential" and "refrain from giving information regarding it."[37]

The first teas were substantially larger, approximately 180 to 220 women, than the one DePriest attended, with 1 male and 14 female guests. Besides DePriest and Hoover, the guests at the 12 June Green Room tea included the first lady's sister, her secretaries, the wives of the attorney general and the secretary of war, and other congressional spouses, all supporters of Hoover's motives. Numerous guest list drafts exist in Hoover's papers and give testimony to the assiduousness with which she planned this sensitive event. A few of the women at the 12 June tea had attended earlier affairs at which their racial attitudes had no doubt been scrutinized.

Because of Lou Hoover's careful planning, the event took place without incident. Some of the women shook hands with Jessie DePriest, and others did not; the first lady shook no hands but greeted all her guests warmly (Hoover sometimes shook hands at receptions and sometimes did not). Congressman DePriest reported in the press that his wife had had a good time and had been treated courteously and with respect. Years later, Ruth Fesler said of the DePriest tea, "It was a very momentous occasion. I remember the butler, Ellis—his eyes just popping as he passed the tea cakes around. You can imagine what this meant to him—to see one of his race being entertained by the wife of the President, and he enjoyed it."[38]

The public reaction, however, indicated opposition to equality for both African Americans and women. Several southern state legislatures passed resolutions of condemnation, a vast amount of mail was sent to the White House, and a significant outpouring of newspaper coverage followed the event. More important, Hoover's dual strategy of including DePriest and avoiding offense to the white South failed. Southern criticism of the first lady ran the gamut from polite racism to snide remarks to bigoted speech. A Texas man cautioned that the DePriest tea "can only bring harm to the negroes of the South. . . . This kind of treatment of the negro, does not set well with those of the southland, who love the negro in his place, but not at our dinner table." A Tennessee woman, who penned the word "white" and underlined it twice beside her signature, agreed, noting that "the innocent, law abiding negro citizen of the South will be the one to suffer."[39] Others complained that the timing of the tea in close proximity to the anniversary of the delivery of the Emancipation Proclamation in many of the southern states insulted white southerners.

Paradoxically, male and female writers outside the South wrote equally biased letters. A Nebraska man informed the first lady: "My WIFE and I are dumb-founded tonight to read in the papers that you have entertained a nigger lady. . . . It places them on an equality with the CAUCASIAN RACE, and assists for the amalgamation of the races. I fear you do not understand the amount of damage you have done to this Country." This critic closed with the observation: "I'll admit however its a nigger vote getter for your distinguished husband, whom we all supported because of the fact we wanted an

AMERICAN on guard at Washington, D.C." A Chicago woman proclaimed: "This nation of white people elected you and your husband to take care of the nation and to live in that great place white house we did not think we would have to be ashamed of our actions later on. . . . You *must* love the dirty smelly niggers no decent white woman would invite a nigger. Shame on you forever." Other letter writers correlated white skin color with the White House: "I had always thought the White House was for white people, and not Negroes, . . . I would have thought you had just a little more *pride* than to put your self on the level with niggers, it is a crime to disgrace the White House."[40]

Only northern and liberal periodicals inveighed against the racism exhibited after the tea. Critics and supporters alike saw Hoover's actions as a first step toward civil rights. A Pennsylvania woman who puzzled over the spread of racist behavior from the South into the District of Columbia called Lou Hoover a "noble, brave lady" and declared, "if we only had more women like yourself who would rise above this unholy prejudice, this false estimate of race differences, it would soon be forever banished from our midst. It would be of the things that have been and are no more. So I believe your heroic deed will help to emancipate human thought from the slavery of intellectual and moral prejudices."[41] Others decried the ridiculousness of requiring someone to apologize for being kind to another person, as much of the South wanted Hoover to do for hosting the DePriest tea. Still others justified Hoover's actions from a Christian perspective.

Although there were some supporters of the event, the volume of complaints forced the White House into a defensive and silent pose about the social affair. One historian suggested that this quiescence contributed to the view that the Hoovers had bungled into the controversy, but such a conclusion would be wrong. Neither the president nor his wife ever sought publicity for the sake of publicity. Instead, they behaved as they thought best, rarely apologizing for their actions or justifying their choices. Not surprisingly, Lou Henry Hoover did not follow through with her stand for social justice by chastising her critics or demanding further reforms; she just moved on to the next task needing her attention. As her husband recalled, Lou was "oversensitive" to the politically and racially inspired invective, which she viewed as "just plain wickedness."[42]

Although the tea and its aftermath might have inspired others to a greater assault on segregation, Lou Henry Hoover's "moral standards" for behavior made it impossible for her to enter the political arena. She recognized but did not address the larger social issues that created the controversy. This omission retarded any gains her courageous invitation had achieved, and it revealed the limits of her activism. Indeed, for all her innovations as first lady, she never fully embraced partisan politics as a venue for her talents, preferring instead to work through voluntary organizations for her public policy goals. The behavior of "evil-minded persons . . . often selected by the electors" inhibited any partisan inclinations she might have had.[43]

The East and West Wings of the White House carefully debated how to respond to the public uproar. The memoranda documenting these conversations reflect Lou Hoover's sense of propriety about what she could and could not say publicly. One aide suggested that the first lady contend "that as the wife of the President of the United States it is not for her to discriminate officially against any individual Senators or Congressmen." Another memorandum, likely from the White House social secretary's office, argued, "we realize that Mrs. Hoover is perhaps not the one to make the statements in the questioned paragraphs. But perhaps it would be wise if those facts should get across by somebody else? Should it be signed by Miss Randolph as Secretary since it was addressed to Mrs. Hoover?"[44] Eventually, the volume of mail became so huge that all the correspondence was routed to Lawrence Richey, a secretary to the president. The administration then tried to bury the matter. Thus, the DePriest controversy revealed the political dynamics of Lou Henry Hoover's White House entertaining, and it was also the first significant warning that she should pay close attention to the demands of tradition.

Hoover's quiet dedication and determination to treat all congressional spouses equally contradicted social conventions regarding how an elite white woman holding the position of first lady should behave. Thus, the DePriest tea controversy exposed numerous conflicting views about racial and gender etiquette in 1929. When Hoover purposefully positioned herself on the "wrong" side of that divide, she accumulated many critics who were only too willing to castigate her for other breaks with tradition. Such negative reactions to her entertaining agenda caused Hoover to balance her activist bent with a respect for tradition, especially with regard to White House social affairs.

The DePriest tea also marred the Hoover administration's "southern strategy"—a complex plan to win the support of voters who preferred the economic and social policies of the Republican party. During the 1928 campaign against Al Smith, the strategy had proved successful. Herbert Hoover had carried Florida, North Carolina, Tennessee, Texas, and Virginia, taking these states for the GOP for the first time since Reconstruction. What he most desired was a reformed southern Republican party that ran more substantive campaigns. Such a political shift, he believed, would force the southern Democrats to abandon the politics of white supremacy in favor of issue-based contests. The DePriest tea, though, confused rather than clarified Herbert Hoover's southern strategy by heightening white racism, not ameliorating it.[45] That neither Herbert nor Lou Hoover crafted a public political or moral rebuttal to their critics suggested much about their lack of political flexibility and the weaknesses of their activism.

Discordantly, neither the media nor the public paid any attention to another White House social affair that included both white and African American guests. This event differed because the principals were male, not female. Just weeks after the DePriest tea, the Hoovers hosted the annual garden party for disabled veterans, attended by both blacks and whites. The fact that the men "mixed indiscriminately" in the receiving line further suggests the potency of the double standard in issues involving race and gender.[46]

During her first year as first lady, Lou Henry Hoover faced challenges other than the politics of race. She tried to balance the traditional social obligations of life in the White House with an effort to modernize and democratize official entertaining. In the spring of 1929, one journalist remarked on the lack of "social leeway" afforded the presidential family. Indeed, if the president had had his way, many of the burdensome White House "social routines" would have been eliminated, because the "rapidly moving assembly line of thousands of handshakes" left him exhausted. The first lady, however, possessed a "rigid sense of duty" to the American people, who enjoyed attending or at least reading about the many formal White

*Lou Henry and Herbert Hoover greet African American and white guests at a
White House garden party for the Disabled American Veterans, 27 June 1929.
(Herbert Hoover Presidential Library-Museum)*

House affairs. Bert overlooked the need for positive public relations,
but Lou recognized the value of a favorable image. "To her it was
part of the job," recalled Herbert Hoover, "and she felt also that we
might be considered snobbish if we limited our contacts to our family and official friends."[47]

Lou Henry Hoover, though, challenged that social latitude on racial grounds as well as status grounds. "Traditions now almost as un-
changeable, if not sacred, as the Constitution itself" governed the nature and number of parties held in the White House. The rules of
White House social etiquette dictated every detail, from the individuals on the guest list to the manner in which they were greeted. Adher-
ence to that etiquette ensured success, while any deviation risked controversy. The first lady "must fit into the pattern of a city of many
rigid social classifications, of aristocratic distinctions such as could
exist only in a nation which has no aristocracy of birth," said one journalist, "and—if the whole truth must be told—possessed of an irre-
sistible tendency to gossip."[48] She chafed at the restrictions resulting

from social conventions because she viewed the artificial distinctions as destructive, discriminating, and constricting. That she adjusted some of these precedents reveals both her vision and the force of her personality.

Dolly Gann, sister of the widowed Vice President Charles Curtis, served as her brother's official companion for Washington social functions, thus presenting another social challenge to the first lady. Gann's demands for the social status usually accorded to the spouse of the vice president made her unpopular with the majority of elite women in the capital city, who were jealous of her position. For example, Alice Roosevelt Longworth, daughter of former president Theodore Roosevelt and wife of Republican Speaker of the House Nicholas Longworth, refused to grant Gann social recognition. The ensuing social precedence "war" kept Washington abuzz. Gann countered that she should be the president of the Senate ladies club, a position typically given to the wife of the vice president but denied to her. The Hoovers refused public comment about these media-driven squabbles. As Gertrude L. Bowman, a Hoover friend and Girl Scout colleague, recalled, "Mrs. Gann got along fine. Nothing happened between Mrs. Gann and Mrs. Hoover, and Mrs. Hoover always accepted her."[49]

Vice President Curtis, Dolly Gann, and her husband Edward Everett Gann dined at the White House on the same day that the State Department "placed Mrs. Gann 'after the wives of chiefs of diplomatic missions,'" in terms of official status. That was an insult, from Gann's perspective, and it led Curtis to come to his sister's defense, a move that emphasized the precedence fight. One journalist, who incorrectly assumed that Gann, like her half brother, was part Kaw Indian, observed that her heritage "makes her a good deal more of a real American than the snobs who have tried to relegate her below the foreign ambassadors' wives." A writer for the *New York Times* declared a "new era in the social history of the capital" when Lou Henry Hoover announced a special political dinner honoring the vice president. That move obviated any embarrassment that might accrue to Gann over the precedence crisis if Curtis were entertained along with the cabinet members.[50]

Lou Hoover's diplomatic handling of the Gann matter baffled journalists, who described the first lady as a "mystery" of little interest to Washington society. During the Gann controversy, termed a "social and political crisis," Hoover made her views clear but "never took sides, never spoke out of turn, while nearly every one else in Cabinet circles was moved to side either one way or the other and many unfortunate words were spoken." Her decision to accord both Jessie DePriest and Dolly Gann the courtesy and respect she believed due them led Washington traditionalists to grow skeptical about her approach to entertaining. According to one source, "the usual whisperings and rustlings and craning of necks" that accompany a first lady "have diminished to a great extent. With all the background of a cultured, traveled woman, a woman capable of great mental activity, a woman who casually served tea to men barricaded in the midst of a Boxer uprising, Mrs. Hoover has not aroused the imagination of her people."[51] Such critical ramblings in the press encapsulate the problems associated with sorting out Hoover's White House activism: because she spent little time explaining herself or her past accomplishments to the American people, few understood or appreciated the nature and extent of her modern agenda.

The Gann controversy continued to incite tempers into the second year of the Hoover presidency. At a Camp Rapidan party celebrating Hoover's birthday, a satiric skit staged by White House physician Joel Boone and several other aides illuminated the controversy and the tension it produced for the first family. Boone absented himself from dinner, reappeared dressed as Gann, and declared, "'Brother Charlie' [Curtis] had suggested my dropping in at the camp." The guests laughed "vociferously," and even the Hoovers joined in the fun, with Lou Hoover referring to Boone/Gann as "'Senora'" and the president asking Boone/Gann about Alice Roosevelt Longworth's whereabouts. The following day, though, staff members received strict orders not to discuss the events, as the rude behavior troubled the Hoovers. No doubt, the perspective of a new day explained the Hoovers' shift from participating in the previous evening's shenanigans to criticizing them. Indeed, Lou Hoover was chagrined that any White House guest might be embarrassed in any way. At the end of her husband's presidency, she told Gann that the "'friction'" between Gann and Longworth "existed only in newspaper and magazine stories."[52] By never publicly contributing to the controversy, Lou Hoover helped ensure that it faded away.

When Lou Henry Hoover carried out her traditional entertaining responsibilities, as in the DePriest and the Gann cases, she incited controversy. And when she redefined entertaining to give it a public, political purpose that satisfied her activist bent, she opened herself up to scrutiny even when the White House guest list included no one named DePriest, Roosevelt, or Gann. The *Washington Star* proclaimed, "As hostess, Mrs. Hoover has almost daily extended in the 'wide-open' West Coast way, with guest lists that mount amazingly at the last minute." Multiple breakfasts, lunches, teas, and dinners were typical. That paper's journalist continued, "The 'extra plate' has been known to become an extra half dozen at Sunday night suppers, to which guests are informally bidden by telephone. Yet the place cards have always been properly arranged, and the supper perfect in its appointments."[53] Journalists typically attended White House dinner parties, and at the start of each social season, Hoover wrote to her close friends asking which White House dinner or musicale they would like to attend.

Initially, the constant parade of guests resulted because of the Hoovers' wide circle of acquaintances and their natural predilection toward numerous social gatherings. After the stock market crash and the pressures of ameliorating the depression sapped Herbert Hoover, the dinner parties gained an additional purpose: they helped calm and distract the president from the tensions of his position. Throughout, Lou Hoover struck a unique balance between formal and casual elegance in her domestic crusade to insulate her husband from criticism. In that way, too, her parties had political meaning.

Because Lou Hoover's public activism intertwined with her social commitments, she faced the challenge of balancing her private entertaining priorities against her husband's need for relaxation. For example, Lou told her sister that although she was welcome to bring a female friend to the White House, "I am rather watching the table now in order that it does not keep up such a preponderance of women, and that Bert may have a few men he happens to want near enough to talk with." When too many female guests "flock down on us," according to the first lady, "Bert goes into himself at the table and keeps on thinking about the problems he has been dealing with during the day instead of being lured out of the thoughts of the daily grind into other fields." Lou placed Bert's social and political needs ahead of her own, but in such a way that she retained her social connections with the women in her informal advisory network. She ceased inviting women to the White House other than those "vitally connected through family, old friendships or some committee interest."[54]

Thus, journalists commonly noted, "entertaining there is continuous, if informal, and it is 'news' when President and Mrs. Hoover do not have a dinner party on hand, rather than when they do." Mildred Hall recalled: "One society reporter called one day and asked what news I had for her. 'None,' I said. 'Who will be there for dinner tonight?' she asked. 'As far as I know, there is no one coming,' said I. 'Well,' said my friend, '*That's* news.'"[55] Nonetheless, the routine pomp and circumstance, staged for Bert's benefit, seemed out of place in a nation of starving people.

Sometimes, White House social affairs were constructed entirely for political effect, specifically so that Herbert Hoover could "pour oil on the troubled waters of public affairs." When Senator Simeon D. Fess attacked Senator William E. Borah over his failure to endorse Hoover's agricultural agenda, the controversy threatened to disrupt the Senate Republicans and the Hoover legislative program. To ameliorate the crisis, the Hoovers invited the Borahs to a White House luncheon on Sunday, 12 May 1929, to "'tell the world' that Mr. Hoover didn't subscribe to the attack." Though the Borah luncheon was meant to appease the insurgent Republican forces, Lou and Bert Hoover knew that Fess, the assistant Republican whip, also deserved White House recognition, "and that very same evening, if you please, Senator Fess was himself a White House dinner guest!" His name was penned on the guest list, which Lou had constructed, after the other names had been typed.[56]

As first lady, Lou Henry Hoover attempted numerous smaller revisions to the White House social scene. Each was intended to benefit her husband politically and her guests socially. The changes included separate receptions for the House and Senate instead of one massive congressional reception, three additional receptions for government departments not previously recognized, and the placement of the diplomatic dinner at the end of the calendar of formal dinners instead of second. Other planned entertainments included a diplomatic reception, the traditional New Year's Day reception, and a judiciary reception. One Washington journalist suggested that the new arrangements would "avoid 'crushes,' and . . . give the hosts greater opportunity for personal contact with their guests."[57]

Most of these events also included what were called musicales. This cultural function had begun during Edith Roosevelt's tenure as first lady and reflected Lou Hoover's lifelong interest in the performing arts. Musical performers of different genres and ethnicities participated, making Lou Hoover the first twentieth-century first lady to bring African American and American Indian entertainers—specifically, the Hampton Choir, the Tuskegee Institute Choir, and a Yakima Indian—to the White House. Their presence resulted in no public controversy. Musicales became such a staple of the Hoover White House that years later a friend sardonically quipped, "You know, of course, nobody ever had any music in the East Room until the FDRs and Kennedys moved in."[58]

Early in her first season as White House hostess, Hoover faced a different kind of challenge and reacted with her usual poise. During a 1929 White House Christmas party for the children of the president's various aides, fire broke out in the recently renovated executive offices. While the guests were eating dessert, the chief usher Ike Hoover whispered news of the fire to one aide, who surveyed the problem and sent for the president and the other male guests. They removed Herbert Hoover's private papers from the Oval Office, and someone even threw a wet rug over Hoover's desk. Household objects and firefighting equipment littered the snowy White House lawn. Lou Hoover, who became aware of the danger, distracted the frightened children with Christmas carols played by the Marine band and the distribution of gifts. After the party ended, according to one published report, "a tall silver-haired woman walk[ed] out on the west terrace to watch the firemen battle the flames."[59]

By the spring of 1930, the deaths of Secretary of War James W. Good and Chief Justice William Howard Taft, as well as a Hoover trip to Florida, had disrupted Lou's plans for additional White House dinners and receptions. To make matters worse, Lou Hoover sprained her back on 17 April 1930 when she lost her footing and fell onto a piece of furniture. Because of the injury, she had to limit her activities until she regained her mobility in late May 1930. Said White House physician Joel Boone, "Mrs. Hoover was not at all well. . . . She

spent a great deal of time in her room or in her bed." After the accident, Grace Coolidge told her, "Wilkins keeps those floors so slick
that there are a few well-known treacherous ones. I used to go skating
around some of the corners on the outer edge of one of my heels."
Lillian Gilbreth, a friend and Girl Scout colleague, remarked, "I know
how inhumane you must find it not to be 100% fit, and to have to
rest. I *know* you are impatient,—I just wish I could help."[60]

News of a new grandchild helped Lou cope with her recuperation. Philippi Harding Butler congratulated Lou on her new grandchild, "a perfectly sweet mite, with enormous blue eyes and very def-
initely ladylike little features," and commented, "I just can't conceive
of you submitting to a wheelchair, so it all sounds rather serious. I
do hope not." Lou responded, "How pleasant to get your letter about
Joan and all the rest of the family! You give me such a good picture
of her that I am more eager than ever to see her! The wheelchair has
really been lots of fun and I do think it is a great invention. However,
after this week, I do not expect to see any more of it."[61]

Because of her injury, Lou Hoover lost important momentum in
establishing her reputation as the nation's hostess. In response, one
journalist contended that D.C. socialites were "puzzled" about "the
lagging social program at the White House." To maintain social functions sufficient for each contingency needing to be entertained,
Hoover adopted a "'two-in-one' plan . . . when both the dinner and
reception were given in one evening." Society writers termed the shift
"one of the most brilliant successes of the administration." Furthermore, Hoover added extra musicales to replace canceled receptions.[62] These changes to the social schedule did not satisfy the Washington elite, who carped about the first lady's break from tradition.

The 1930–1931 social season brought further difficulties. California Senator Hiram Johnson failed to receive an invitation to the
dinner for the Senate Foreign Relations Committee and Ambassador Charles G. Dawes. The Hoovers claimed that the oversight was
a clerical error, but Johnson thought differently. The senator and
the president shared a mutual hostility for each other, and, given
both Hoovers' meticulous attention to detail, the White House explanation stretched credulity. Indeed, Johnson recalled in his published diary that the president had purposefully snubbed him and
had bragged to his secretary about it. One journalist wondered "why

President Hoover does not escape from such errors as his predecessors did. On several occasions there has been an ineptitude in the handling of matters at the White House, which are constantly the subject of discussion." Hoover's political personality was such that he preferred not to tend to "things that appear to be details and which in the end prove to be major political blunders."[63] In this case, Herbert Hoover's critics had a point. Lou Hoover suffered the brunt of this mistake, though, for it reflected poorly on her entertaining skills.

For her second winter season as White House hostess, Hoover again planned an ambitious round of receptions and dinners above and beyond the traditional number held in the capital city. Still, the twelve planned formal parties, four more than dictated by precedent, fell short of the fifteen planned for the 1929–1930 season. By October 1930, though, deteriorating economic conditions caused the White House to place "little emphasis on social affairs this winter. The whirl, as a matter of fact, will revolve slowly." Lou Hoover acknowledged that the "colorful functions" typical of the White House would seem out of sync with the national economic malaise and scaled down the grandeur of official functions.[64]

Her decision left members of the Washington social community nonplussed. Smaller, less ornate, and decidedly informal dinner parties became the norm that winter, leading one journalist to note, "scarcely any of the [White House dinner] guests have worn evening clothes. Business suits for the men and long afternoon gowns, without hats, for the women, have been de rigueur." Such affairs required less planning and less notice, with some functions being arranged on the day they were held. "Society, too, resents her informality," declared one unidentified female politician. "It interferes, they complain with their own engagements to be summoned on brief notice to a White House dinner."[65]

The depression marked the 1931–1932 social season. Perhaps the most noteworthy White House event that year was a children's Christmas party hosted by Lou and her grandchildren, Peter and Peggy Ann Hoover. The 200 guests, all children of capital city officials, brought gifts for impoverished families in Morgantown, West Virginia. As Hoover explained in the party invitations, "Santa Claus has sent word that he is not going to be able, by himself, to take care of all the little boys and girls he wants to this year, and he has asked other people to help him as much as possible."[66]

Lou and her grandchildren received their guests at 3:30 P.M. on 23 December. After touring the Blue, Red, and Green Rooms, the children made their way into the State Dining Room, where they decorated several trees to be shipped along with the collected presents to Morgantown. According to one observer, there "were presents enough so that the Morgantown children would never have need of sadness on Christmas Day." The trees and the gifts were packed and shipped to West Virginia by a group of Quakers, who had "taken this provision as their pleasant burden."[67] In this way, Lou Henry Hoover mixed her social obligations with public activism.

The children sat on the floor and played games, and a White House aide who attended the party compared the underaged guests to "butterflies." White House doormen, members of the Marine band, and naval aides served the children. Later, Mrs. Claus made a visit on behalf of her husband and told the children a story. At that point, the president slipped in after signing legislation that extended the European debt moratorium an additional year. One guest observed, "perhaps it is not possible to guess how pleasant an interlude this scene of childhood made for him, in the first minutes of his relief."[68] If not the most glamorous social event of the 1931–1932 season, this party, more than others, encapsulated what Lou Hoover hoped to achieve for each White House affair she hosted—a relaxing and enjoyable time for all that served a larger social and political purpose.

Lou's activism as White House hostess resulted from her public partnership with her husband as much as from her internal muse. When she modernized the official social functions of her office, she had less time for her independent involvement with the voluntary organizations that had been so important to her career in the 1920s. Her decision to realign her activist priorities suggests the depth of her public and private commitment to Bert's administration. Like "all wives," she "kn[e]w how" to influence her husband's agenda by "slipping a letter on the reading table, dropping a quick word about someone's crucial affairs in, at the right moment." This strategy remained consistent with the nature of their marriage prior to 1929, except that now, "a slip or an omission or the lack of a bit of information at the right time might make a serious difference in the nation's affairs, instead of a friend's." As a result, Hoover "consult[ed] with the most meticulous care on any matter having important consequences, like which two statesmen should be asked to the same dinner."[69]

The seamless merger of the private, entertaining function of their marriage with the public, work aspects of their marriage resulted because "one of the delightful things about those two, to their friends, has always been the exquisite way they do not mind the other one[']s business." Thus, the symbiotic nature of their relationship, which resulted from their "adequately matched minds," caused contemporaries to suggest that "the justly blessed wife in the Bible, whose price was above rubies, and Mrs. Hoover would get along perfectly, but their technique is quite different. Their husbands might both be honored in the gates, but not, in the latter case, because he had rubies at home!"[70]

Additionally, friends of the Hoovers realized the intellectual contributions Lou made to Bert's career, noting that often "his words of wisdom came from" her mind. Lou's habit of providing nightly entertainment had public policy implications. Bert's associates "would all drop into dinner some night unexpectedly, at his invitation, and she would make them so comfortable and so soothed and stimulated by good talk that they would, undoubtedly, hardly be able to describe her when they got back home to their wives," recalled one friend. "But she would have the wives in to tea next day, so it would not really matter." Indeed, Lou Henry Hoover was known throughout the government as "a very charming hostess and . . . a very delightful raconteur in the course of the dinner conversation."[71] She did not succeed nearly so well with the general public because average Americans did not understand her social and public activism, because the depression intervened, and because she never fully used the media to her advantage.

Lou Henry Hoover's social agenda functioned to advance Herbert Hoover's presidency. Unfortunately for the Hoovers, the first lady's skills as a hostess were not uniformly appreciated in Washington, D.C. The attempt to entertain Jessie DePriest caused more political problems than it solved. The capital city, which was segregated not only by race but also by gender and class, did not welcome entertainments imbued with political import. Additionally, aborted and canceled social seasons—including the 1932–1933 season, which fell victim to Calvin Coolidge's death—upset those D.C. residents who depended on national politics for their private entertainment. Put simply, Washington was not ready for a sophisticated, modern woman who pursued an activist agenda via the office of first lady. Lou Hoover, though, remained true to her own principles and modernized the White House social calendar. The criticisms she received should be read not as a mark of her failure but as testament to her success against strong odds. The admixture of previously staid social functions and modern political implications created nothing short of an earthquake within the rigid capital city elite, who were accustomed to informal governance over the transitory national political leadership. Of course, Lou Henry Hoover's reforms met with resistance, but she deserves substantial credit for starting the process of social modernization and democratization in formal White House entertaining.

CHAPTER 3

FROM PRIVATE PHILANTHROPY TO RELIEF POLITICS

Just as the stock market crash and the Great Depression remade Herbert Hoover's presidency, these events transformed Lou Henry Hoover's tenure as first lady. Before economic catastrophe became the focus of public attention, though, Lou Hoover established a model of private philanthropy that previous first ladies had never imagined. Hoover's efforts resulted from her concerns about the crisis of modernity. Specifically, she worried that new technologies and modes of behavior had advanced faster than society's ability to care for its weakest members. In her view, the ultimate result of these forces would be the destruction of the communitarian values that had nurtured America's progress and development from its founding. The aim of both her philanthropic and her relief work was to preserve individual communities so that local residents could care for their own. As she had used the Girl Scouts in the 1920s to combat the ill effects of urbanization and consumerism, in the 1930s, she sought relief for a rural community so impoverished that it enjoyed none of the benefits of a pastoral setting. Indeed, her involvement with the President's Mountain School far surpassed the precedent Grace Coolidge had set when she raised money for the Clarke School for the Deaf.

Hoover personally encountered severe poverty when visiting the presidential retreat she and her husband established above Dark

Hollow in the Blue Ridge Mountains near Criglersville, Virginia. Her experience with and reactions to inherited privation reveal much about her evolving conceptions of philanthropy, relief, and community preservation. Initially, she drew on her commitment to education and self-help, working to establish a school for the under-privileged children. She believed that these efforts would protect a blighted population from even further destruction as modern civilization encroached on the area, but by the fall of 1931, the project also typified her private, individual approach to depression relief.

While fishing at their camp in August 1929, Bert received as a birthday gift a fifteen-pound opossum from a mountain boy. The president struck up a conversation with the lad about his school and discovered that he had none. The poverty and lack of opportunity, especially educational opportunity, that characterized life in the mountain South appalled the Hoovers and motivated their strong philanthropic instincts. The result was the President's Mountain School, constructed for the children who lived near Camp Rapidan. Lou Hoover collaborated with her husband on the creation of the school, more so than on any other issue involving the depression. The Hoovers viewed their work with the school not as an official obligation to the country but as private charity. This philanthropic orientation reflected their implicit criticism of modernity's tendency toward public display. Lou Hoover nurtured the school's development into a community center throughout her years as first lady. She hoped that the school would improve life for the mountain residents, who would soon have to move away because the region was scheduled to become part of Shenandoah National Park.[1] Yet the venture, which unfolded from her concerns about the destruction of rural mores, ultimately strengthened her conservative views about the role of government. Put simply, she believed that private, philanthropic solutions to such problems preserved the dignity of the recipients.

Some days after his visit with the mountain boy, Herbert Hoover, along with his secretary Lawrence Richey, drafted plans for a one-room school. The Hoovers financed construction of the edifice, with the assistance of donations from colleagues, at a cost of approximately $10,000. The privately funded school received the endorsement of state and local education authorities in Virginia. Because of the communitarian focus of the school, local men were employed to work on its construction so that they would become supporters of the project, gain marketable skills, and learn home-improvement techniques. More important, this involvement went beyond the pragmatic need for speedy construction to incorporate the very ethos that drove Lou Hoover to activism—philanthropic facilitation of self-help structures. Philippi Harding Butler declared, "it was so typical of the Hoovers to do something like that—to realize the need for a school and to go ahead and provide a school—very typical."[2]

By the fall of 1929, the Hoovers had surveyed the needs of their Rapidan neighbors, who lived less than 100 miles from the nation's capital. Their discoveries revealed the imperfections of rural life, while also suggesting the failure of modernity, left to its own devices, to address the problem. A Hoover associate explained the dire conditions of the mountain people: "those children had had no schooling at all, and it's amazing that up in those Blue Ridge Mountains there were small communities of big families and they all intermarry and there is no contact with the outside world." According to one of Lou Hoover's secretaries, "the president was very interested in the people and offered to provide a school house and equipment for the neighborhood if the State of Virginia would supply the teacher. . . . The people, of course, could not possibly pay the taxes for the teacher's 'keep,' much less any salary."[3]

The Hoovers hoped that the school would serve more than forty area children. The building, including quarters for the teacher, was to be "modern in every respect." Such an edict reflects the limits of the Hoovers' criticism of modernity. Indeed, they recognized that certain technologies could be used productively to preserve the communitarian values associated with America's rural past. In addition to a furnished apartment, the teacher received a "Ford car" and a horse, the former to "be used as bus for some of the school children." The Hoovers insisted that the school should also function as a regional "'community center.'" Besides educating the mountain children, the teacher would be responsible for doing social work among the adults. "She should be a person who is thoroughly devoted to her work and imbibed with the spirit to serve," explained the Hoovers. "She should be one who has studied the problems of such a community, who has already had experience working with mountain folk and understands their limitations and idiosyncrasies."[4]

When it came time to select a teacher for the Rapidan school, Lou Hoover's secretary wrote to various college presidents and social welfare advocates seeking their input and recommendations. The letters explained the Hoovers' preference for a female teacher, who, they contended, "would be much more useful in developing the community than a man."[5] The Hoovers believed that a woman, more than a man, would know how to help the families pull together into a community, because domestic management skills would be paramount to the success of such work. Furthermore, the Hoovers believed that women, more so than men, possessed the innate strength necessary to live in such a remote location. Such views about the need for a female teacher resulted from another limited infusion of modernity into the Hoovers' thinking about how best to preserve community values, specifically, the expanded public-sphere opportunities available to women. In essence, then, the Hoover plan for the Rapidan school relied on the woman's rights movement of the late nineteenth and early twentieth centuries for implementation.

The county school board superintendent made the final appointment after receiving a recommendation from Herbert and Lou Hoover. The local board retained authority over the teacher and, at the conclusion of the first year, could either renew or terminate her contract. The Hoovers planned such an administrative hierarchy so that the school would be private "only in the sense that the physical equipment is being provided by private funds, and it is a public school in that the State of Virginia supplies the teacher."[6]

When determining how to write the contract for the new teacher, Christine Vest, Hoover's secretary approached the president of Berea College, where Vest had studied, for assistance. Lou Hoover appreciated that the mountain children had been denied a proper education in part because "no one could be found who would undertake the responsibility and the very poor living conditions provided for the *most* inadequate salary," anywhere from $40 to $70 a month. Yet huge variations in the cost of living meant that a salary similar to that paid to urban teachers would be too high. At this crucial juncture, Lou Hoover appreciated the larger implications of the salary question and noted, "we want to set a salary with an appropriate margin beyond comfortable living expenses in order that the authorities in similar localities will realize that they must offer

Lou Henry Hoover surrounded by the children enrolled at the President's
Mountain School. Christine Vest, the teacher, is seated to the far left.
(Herbert Hoover Presidential Library-Museum, © Bettmann/Corbis)

enough to keep the right kind of people in these positions. . . . It
should not go beyond what is reasonable in order not to discourage
the people trying to keep up school conditions in other similar localities."[7] Vest's salary of $125 a month suggested the depth of the
Hoovers' commitment to the school and the community, but not
necessarily the region, for no large-scale proposal for additional
schools throughout Appalachia came from either Hoover.

Because the Rapidan school fit perfectly with Lou Hoover's conception of charity, she worked personally on the selection and purchase of textbooks and furniture for it. This endeavor ultimately involved women's groups, which viewed the school as an ideal charity.
When the leader of a New Jersey girls' club wrote to Hoover inquiring about ways club members could assist the construction and out-
fitting of the school, Fesler compiled a list of "not necessarily essential but very desirable" items, including a subscription to *Child Life*,
classic works of children's literature, and images depicting important people and events in American history: George Washington,
Abraham Lincoln, and the landing of the Pilgrims.[8]

To others who wrote in the summer of 1930 asking how they might help the school get ready for winter, Hoover suggested purchasing shoes: "That certainly is an important item in enabling them to get to school! . . . Perhaps you would prefer to have a share in seeing that the children get a hot lunch after the cold weather sets in? Which would mean milk for soup or cocoa and the other main ingredient. You will be interested in learning that there is even night school up there now, and already one of the men has learned to write his name!"[9] Ironically, although the President's Mountain School encapsulated the Hoover belief in voluntary relief methods, the first lady discouraged the private collection and dissemination of hand-me-downs among the local residents. The juxtaposition of Hoover's statement regarding the man who had written his name— a potentially condescending view that overlooked both the innate intellect of the mountaineers and their educational needs—and her refusal to take donations of secondhand goods suggests a flawed but well-intentioned effort to preserve the dignity of the students and their parents. This contradiction also suggests another way in which the values of modernity permeated Hoover's thoughts.

Hoover's staff coordinated media interest in the opening of the school but arranged for the coverage to be low-key out of respect for the students and their parents. "Please understand that there will be no formal exercises, or dedication," explained Fesler. "It will just be the first day of school. Miss Vest would like to have the President and/or Mrs. Hoover present when the school has its formal opening and they will probably not be able to go up to the mountains until much later in the spring." All interested reporters were requested to make the journey on the same day to assure minimal disruptions.[10] Although the Hoovers wished that others would replicate their experiment throughout the mountain South and in other educationally impoverished areas, the first family brought scant publicity to the cause, which defeated their purpose.

Lou Henry Hoover's hopes for the construction of a community were fulfilled, and she watched closely as the area residents, young and old alike, crowded in on Vest for both practical and academic instruction. One mountain woman noted soon after Vest's arrival, "what a difference it would have made in my life if I ever could have had a home like this [Vest's]." In fact, after the school had been in place for some time, Hoover and her colleagues began noticing substantive efforts at home improvement among the mountain people.[11] These changes resulted because Vest's pragmatic curriculum, with the Sears-Roebuck catalogue for a textbook, encouraged domesticity and self-sufficiency. Vest proved so successful that she was able to enforce Virginia's school attendance laws, which required a good excuse for any absence. In the first year, seventeen students enrolled for classes, and by May 1931, the student body had increased to thirty-two, but average daily attendance was much lower—eighteen.

Lou Hoover maintained a great interest in the children. She supported Vest's plan to take them to the county fair and even paid for their discretionary purchases there. The White House approved the use of a Marine truck to transport the children. The Hoovers funded vaccinations for the children at the school. To demonstrate the children's progress, Vest had them write letters to Hoover: "We thank you for the nice fruit you sent. We thank you and the president for our school. Won't you visit us again. We like to have you to come."[12]

When she visited the school for the first time, Lou Hoover brought a picnic lunch and watched a class. Vest recalled, "she seemed very pleased with what she saw and the children enjoyed displaying the knowledge and skills they had gained." Vest explained years later, "The children had a genuine affection for Mrs. Hoover. They appreciated the school but were genuinely fond of her. They called her 'Miz' Hoover or 'Miss' Hoover. Regardless of how much I tried to emphasize the word Mrs., they always came back to their original way of addressing her," which in the southern vernacular "as applied to an older, married woman is a token of affection, love and respect." Area parents "loved having [Lou Hoover] stop for a visit" when she was out horseback riding in the area. Vest recounted, "I recall once Mrs. Hoover stopped for a visit with Mr. and Mrs. Weakley. Mr. Weakley told of his rheumatism and of some liniment he was unable to get at Syria. I don't know where she procured it, but Mrs. Hoover delivered the liniment in person on her next visit!"[13]

The school operated from February 1930 through May 1933 under Vest's instruction and then for several more years. It ultimately closed when the land was turned over to the federal government for the Shenandoah National Park. Vest explained, "I often wonder what their lot would have been if they had not had all this preparation before leaving their mountain. Because of the school, they were able to take their place in a normal way and many have done very well and have nice homes and fine families of their own today."[14]

Dr. Joel Boone, the White House physician and a close ally of the Hoovers, recalled, "It became a broadly expanded institution of education and community development for mountain children and their elders. It seemed to bring the Blue Ridge Mountains of Virginia from a nebulous, local beginning into a wide spectrum of creative and constructive influence in a wide area of the Virginia mountains, broadening out from a core which was the Hoover camp."[15] Indeed, young and old alike learned how to interact with strangers; how to earn, count, and use money; and how to navigate beyond the confines of their Blue Ridge Mountain homes. Such educational efforts proved beneficial as the students and their parents left the only homes they had known for life elsewhere in the more modernized United States.

The President's Mountain School was much less successful, though, in achieving its larger purpose—namely, to overcome modernity's ill effects. The Hoovers' efforts to model private philanthropy got lost in the larger public concern about the stock market crash and the Great Depression, and few people paid much attention to the Appalachian region in the years that followed. (Eleanor Roosevelt's work with impoverished coal-mining families in Arthurdale, West Virginia, the first New Deal resettlement community, was an economic failure.) Thus, Lou Henry Hoover's work must be judged a limited success. She learned much from her experience with the President's Mountain School that later proved important when handling the many pleas for relief that crossed her desk during the depression.

Between the 4 March 1929 inauguration and the 29 October 1929 stock market crash, few Americans realized the misery that would dominate Herbert Hoover's presidency. By any statistical measure in 1930, the economy had worsened. Increased privations caused people to lash out at the president. Shantytowns of homeless Americans were dubbed "Hoovervilles," and some Democrats sang, "Mellon pulled the whistle / Hoover rang the bell / Wall St. gave the signal / And the country went to Hell."[16] By 1931, with no sign of recovery in sight, average Americans and political leaders alike recognized that the Great Depression was decidedly different from the various nineteenth-century economic panics, which had been characterized by relatively quick onsets and relatively quick recoveries. In contrast, the Great Depression of the 1930s developed over a number of years and, once established, remained for a decade. In the last two years of the Hoover presidency, the country cried out for relief—food, temporary shelter, mortgage forbearance, and employment referral.

The travails of the depression overshadowed Lou Henry Hoover's activities as a White House hostess and posed challenges that no first lady had encountered since the 1890s. Hoover devoted much time to ameliorating the lives of her fellow citizens caught in the economic downturn. A cursory examination of her public speeches, which advocated continued spending, cheerful attitudes, and private charity, suggests that she maintained a cautious and limited approach to the depression. There are two problems with such a conclusion, though. First, it overlooks the question of what responsibilities fall to the first lady, an unelected figurehead with no constitutional power or responsibilities. Second, and more important, it overlooks Hoover's use of women's voluntary organizations as a conduit for local relief efforts, much as her husband sought to do on a national scale. As one journalist said of her situation, "In a peculiar way the problems of the American people are ever poured upon the President's wife, perhaps because she is often pictured in the role of Lady Bountiful."[17]

Hoover argued that self-help, an ideal she had always believed in, should dominate relief efforts. Her views reflected her concern about the dangers of anonymity implicit in the urban environment; localism and a concomitant belief in community shaped her attitudes toward depression relief. The economic crisis, in her mind, was symptomatic of modernity's crisis. The solution, then, involved the reassertion of old values as well as financial assistance. In a national radio address given in late 1932 to a women's group devoted to assisting the needy, she contended, "in our country there is an ample supply of food and clothing for us all. . . . We do know that we must give generously, individually; that generous provision must be made by city and town, by county and State, even as the nation has provided generously for a reserve fund."[18]

Since she had funneled assistance to the needy throughout her life, she believed that other Americans should follow her example in the depression. That outlook dictated her strategy toward the mail that deluged her office with appeals for help. She and her East Wing staff, specifically Philippi Harding Butler, redirected the thousands of requests they received to Hoover's contacts in more than forty federal and state relief agencies, as well as voluntary and philanthropic associations. These groups then took their own action. Hoover's responses thus combined formal and informal action with grassroots and bureaucratic methods and paralleled her understanding of the proper balance between private and public, traditional and modern.[19]

The depression crisis marked a further evolution in the Hoovers' public marriage. Whereas the relief problem of the Great War had induced explicit cooperation between the two, the relative political calm of the 1920s had encouraged a less direct policy partnership and more independent action from Lou, albeit in ways that augmented Bert's career. The White House years generally and the depression specifically saw Lou move even farther into her own separate public sphere. In part, this occurred because the demands of the presidency meant that Bert had less time for shared policy endeavors, but more significant was the fact that Lou was emerging as her own person. Herbert Hoover rarely sought policy suggestions from the first lady or drew on her expertise. Certainly, there was almost no correspondence between them or their offices comparable to that of the Great War era. The White House chief usher, Ike Hoover, contended that she "was anxious, willing and capable to enter into the game. Likewise there was confidence on the part of the president to have her do so, but he never just had time to share his responsibilities with her." Lou Hoover, the usher added, "would have loved to play the part like Mrs. [Helen Heron] Taft attempted to do or that Mrs. [Florence Kling] Harding did but it was just not in the cards."[20]

Edgar Rickard, a close associate of Herbert and Lou Hoover since their days in London, also noted in his diary how the first lady was kept in the dark on depression-fighting measures. According to Ike Hoover, Lou "made herself understand [the necessity of] going her own way and getting some satisfaction out of the little part she could play alone, without authority and without prestige from the master of the official household."[21] That the first lady developed her responses to the depression in almost complete isolation from her husband suggests that she was anticipating what Eleanor Roosevelt would do four years later. The Great Depression had rendered almost irrelevant the Hoovers' previously successful public marriage.

To understand her position, a careful review of how she interacted with the unfolding crisis is needed. Appeals for relief started coming to the White House before the stock market crashed. In March 1929, a Pennsylvania woman told the first lady that her family had campaigned for the president, even though their friends had predicted that "Mr. Hoover would not look at us if we were to go to the White House, or if we were in need." That request for money received an icy response from the first lady's secretary, who responded that millions of Americans had voted for Herbert Hoover "because they thought he would be the best choice for our country's welfare." In fact, the letter never reached Lou Hoover because, as her secretary stated, "we do not trouble her with the ones that could do nothing but distress her." Other rejection letters stressed that the president was not as wealthy as people believed. If he were rich, the secretaries said, "it would be such a pleasure to give financial assistance to those who ask for aid!"[22] The imperious tone probably conveyed a different impression than what the first lady had in mind.

When the economic crisis broke in 1929–1930, unemployment soared to 10.7 percent in the last quarter of 1930, up from 5 percent in November 1929. Bank failures numbered 1,352, compared with 659 in 1929. Investment within the economy dropped 35 percent. President Hoover urged businesses to maintain wages, and he called for tax cuts; both these moves accorded with Keynesian economic theory. A slight recovery early in the year gave Hoover hope. He declared on 1 May, "I am convinced we have passed the worst and with continued effort we shall rapidly recover." For the remainder of the year, however, negative numbers characterized the economy.[23]

Lou Hoover became the public face of sympathy for the first family, much as she had been during the Belgian relief effort. Then, her husband had been unable to look at starvation firsthand, and he responded in a similar fashion after 1929. It thus fell to the first lady to supply the human touch where her husband could not. One of Hoover's secretaries explained to a friend, "the people write to her not knowing to whom else to appeal." Hoover became a "'clearing house'" for relief aid. She routed requests to the proper local agencies, some public and some private. This level and type of activism, unprecedented for first ladies, reflected the subtle manner in which she redrew the boundaries of her position, her philosophical perspective on how the depression should be addressed, and her concern for individuality in the face of depression-induced dehumanization. Of one letter she wrote, "this woman doesn't suggest wanting *any* thing from me although she does imply their poverty. It is only advice she asks for,—and really sympathy that probably she needs." Sending the missive on to a friend, Hoover asked that her name not be used, "as it is simply impossible for me to be of any help myself."[24]

Hoover saw the power of like-minded women with whom she collaborated to facilitate depression relief. Thus, she helped forge a women's network for relief activism that shared several important traits: a commitment to voluntary organizations, the merger of maternal values with social policies, and a belief that relief should be handled on the local level. To help with the mounting demands on her time and energy, Lou Hoover reached out to old friends. In the fall of 1930, she coordinated with Lillian Gilbreth, a longtime engineering colleague and a member of the President's Emergency Committee on Employment (PECE), about relief issues. Gilbreth became an important player during the remainder of Hoover's service as first lady. She had worked professionally and personally as an engineer, applying time and motion studies to the workplace and to the rearing of her twelve children. She even became the inspiration for *Cheaper by the Dozen,* a book written by two of her children. These experiences prepared her well, the first lady believed, for work with depression relief.

Hoover and Gilbreth teamed with Bettie Monroe Sippel, president of the General Federation of Women's Clubs (GFWC), to devise ways that women's club members could combat the problems of the depression. In response to Hoover's pleas, the GFWC surveyed local conditions, and the research indicated that women were family breadwinners more often than not. The GFWC also undertook case-management responsibilities for Lou Hoover and her East Wing relief efforts. Ultimately, Sippel and the GFWC became important for Hoover's informal relief activities, providing the first lady's office with regular reports of the many cases handled by club-women. When Hoover read the draft of a September 1931 article Sippel had penned for the GFWC magazine about clubwomen and local relief, she remarked, "I myself really think something may be accomplished by their plans! . . . And I much hope to be able to cooperate in some of the details of your undertaking."[25]

The first lady merged GFWC work with her ongoing East Wing referral service, which catered to her favored demographics—children, families, and the aged. Hoover's priorities for relief resulted from her worries about modernity. Concerned that a society grappling with economic scarcity would forget its weakest members, Hoover sought local solutions that would preserve individual dignity. She believed that women adept at personalized social service could best fill these needs. Hoover's greatest sympathy was for "these very young people, not yet finding a niche in the world nor knowing how to find one," because she feared that they were "perhaps the greatest sufferers in 'hard times,'—they, or the poor, earnestly striving, old people who are being pushed from *their* niche!" Thus, when supplicants indicated that the depression had adversely affected their children, Hoover often contacted area Girl Scout officials, asking them to "ascertain if the children are sufficiently cared for." She was equally worried about the aged. To an old, infirm man who wrote asking only for a plant to "cheer up his wife," Hoover sent an ivy and a begonia.[26]

Because of the impact of the depression on the nation's children, Hoover asked the national office of the National Congress of Parents and Teachers to undertake relief efforts. Otherwise, Hoover referred cases involving children to local Girl Scout officials or local parent-teacher organizations. She hoped that the National Congress could "encourage in the strongest terms that every Parent-Teacher group in every community do everything in its power to see that every child of its community is enabled to go to school." Hoover wanted local parent-teacher groups to search out those in need of aid instead of waiting for appeals to reach their offices. "It is so essential that we keep the children of this country in school,—not only that they may have the education due them, but that they will be kept from the ranks of the unemployed, or not to be pushed into those of the too-early-employed."[27]

Hoover wrote to the Girl Scouts on behalf of a Kansas City grandmother concerned about the future of her grandchildren. Family Service, an organized charity sponsored by the local Girl Scouts, had already been fulfilling the family's basic needs, but it was requested "that some special Christmas cheer goes to them at this time of year." In her letter back to Hoover, the Girl Scout representative for Iowa, Missouri, Kansas, and Nebraska commented, "the report on this case proves that many of the appeals made to Mrs. Hoover are being taken care of locally, and I feel that if we board members can assist in any way in making her burden a little lighter, it is a privilege."[28] Such reports only reinforced the first lady's belief in localism as a relief strategy, which she and her husband had every reason to believe would assuage the economic slump, much as it had during World War I. Indeed, between the October crash and 1931, the Hoovers could not possibly have known how serious the Great Depression would be, and in fact, it was difficult to get reliable information about economic conditions nationwide.

Even by 1931, when it became apparent that voluntarism alone could not resolve the nation's economic dilemma, Lou Hoover remained committed to the relief processes of the philanthropic culture. As first lady, there was little else she could do. Among her various activities were a number of successes, but no matter how much good she did and how hard she and her staff worked, they were bound to fall short. Rarely did Hoover contemplate moving beyond localism and volunteer efforts, even in the face of mounting obstacles and ballooning relief rolls. In the fourth quarter of 1931, unemployment was 18.4 percent, money wages for those still employed had dropped from precrash levels, and significant deflation had caused prices to fall. The thought of an expanded welfare state was anathema to her, so she labored on in familiar ways with the techniques she had always used.[29]

Within the context of sparse information and optimism for a speedy recovery, localism made sense, and gender-based self-help programs proved very attractive to Lou Hoover. When she learned of a group of widowed women in Iowa who had taken it upon themselves to act as relief agents in their local community, she encouraged her former employee, Dare Stark McMullin, to write a magazine article in the hope of facilitating other such endeavors.

She termed it "a wonderfully practical thing" for older women who no longer had family responsibilities "to give a helping hand to those overburdened and in distress."[30] Furthermore, when women's groups approached the first lady for assistance with their relief-based fund-raising efforts, Hoover willingly cooperated. For example, she provided an embroidered facsimile of her signature for quilters auctioning their projects for charity. She viewed such endeavors not only as ideal for depression relief but also as necessary for the preservation of small-town values under attack by urbanization and modernization.

Hoover received numerous letters from women throughout the country detailing their plans for combating the depression. For example, one letter writer appealed to Hoover as an "American mother and homemaker" to help establish a women's exchange club in each state capital, with the wife of the governor in charge. Such entities, the letter writer argued, could help women sell home-produced food and handcrafts. Hoover's secretary responded that the first lady had studied how to make women's exchanges a feasible component of local relief and advised, "the most important things come often from small beginnings, and everything *must* have a start!"[31] Hoover endorsed the concept of women's exchanges and sought to learn of the existence of all such entities throughout the country. Such local solutions reflected the communitarian approach Hoover championed and addressed the nation's spiritual crisis, which the first lady viewed as a larger concern than the economic one.

By the fall of 1932, existing women's exchanges were too overwhelmed to take on any new clients, thus revealing the failure of strictly local, voluntary relief mechanisms. Three years after the stock market crash, economic investment was nonexistent. Between 1930 and 1931, the decline had been 35 percent; in 1932, the drop was 88 percent, or $800 million, off from $16.2 billion. Deflation spiraled downward from 2.6 percent in 1930 to 18 percent in 1933. With a still soaring jobless rate, hunger, if not starvation, had become a real problem. Weeds served as food for the rural poor, while men in cities dug through the garbage for food. For some, rotten meat, complete with maggots, was the only source of nutrition.[32]

Hoover believed that ending the depression required significant sacrifice and action on the part of those people who had financial means. If someone were contemplating the purchase of a major item or a home renovation, for example, she contended that the individual should follow through, because it would mean work for other people. An April 1932 telegram to her sister revealed more of Lou Hoover's views on how to combat the depression. She hoped that her niece and nephew would "do nothing this summer that would keep a paying job from someone else. No one should take remunerative work now who has other resources." Similarly, Hoover told a Girl Scout colleague that she should return to Stanford for a Ph.D. in order to "leave as much of the national income as possible for the absolutely destitute."[33] Such individualistic methods were problematic for two reasons: first, they required significant community spirit and willingness to sacrifice, and second, they were insufficient for an economic problem on the scale of the Great Depression. That Hoover viewed the community crisis to be on a par with, if not more severe than, the economic crisis suggests much about her mind-set during the latter half of her husband's presidency.

Hoover studied successful relief programs in the communities she knew best as she deliberated the requests for assistance that were forwarded to her office. She suggested that all communities adopt similar strategies, but such an attitude overlooked very real and important regional economic differences that should have been apparent to Hoover from her work as national Girl Scout president. The Organization for Unemployment and Relief in Palo Alto, Hoover's adopted hometown, was a model of local relief. She described it as "most interesting" and "quite a constructive program" and even donated $300 to it.[34] Under the mayor's leadership, the organization operated an employment bureau, a used clothing exchange, a benevolence association that oversaw medical and hospital services, and a shelter for itinerants where food and grooming services were available; it also cooperated with the local Red Cross to provide emergency relief. The Palo Alto effort received a third of its funding from the city budget and two-thirds from private contributions.

Hoover would have preferred all cities and towns to follow the Palo Alto model, and her voluntary relief strategies stemmed from a similar philosophy. She believed that human interaction and fellowship were often the most important aspects of relief work; thus she used her contacts in various voluntary organizations to reach out on an individual level to the people who wrote to the White House with their problems. To ensure that no effort was exerted on behalf of fraudulent appeals, Hoover arranged for several colleagues to research each case before providing assistance—a rather slow process, given the extent of the nation's problems.

Sometimes Hoover and her staff doubted the claims presented to them. In one instance, Hoover instructed her aide, Ruth Fesler, to write to Jane Deeter Rippin, a Girl Scout colleague, about a New York family of five that was suspected of being "entirely a fake case." Rippin, as was typical for Hoover's contacts, reported the details of the situation: "the man is really a worthy citizen, glad to work." Nevertheless, when recruiting one friend to research a "quite unknown" supplicant, Hoover noted, "It is queer how very few of these cases are found utter frauds!"[35] This research strategy meshed well with Hoover's local focus and proved beneficial for shoring up community spirit in the face of economic tragedy. From her perspective, who better to discern the nature of and solution to a problem than another resident of the community in question? The strategy, though, was insufficient when applied on a national scale, because Hoover's case-by-case efforts could never provide relief sufficient to the nation's struggles.

Letter writers appealed to Lou Henry Hoover as a wife and mother but hoped that her informal power as first lady could assuage their difficulties. For example, Ida Animus, the American wife of a Yugoslavian immigrant, asked for assistance reentering the United States: "Mrs. Hoover who is the mother of children the same as I am will realize how it is if you have no money to buy milk or anything to eat."[36] Of course, Hoover had never faced such a situation, and her ability to provide relief, direct or indirect, had little to do with her own experiences of motherhood and everything to do with her connections to Washington bureaucrats and to voluntary and philanthropic organization leaders. Hoover contacted officials with the State Department, reminding them of her own work with stranded Americans in Europe just before and during the Great War. She hoped that the remnants of the American Committee, with which Hoover had been affiliated in London, could provide the funds to ensure return passage for the Animus family.

The various State Department officials who communicated with Hoover and her aides repeatedly contended that the family would be an immediate relief case if brought back to American soil. Furthermore, the State Department had no luck turning up a private source of charity. Thus, this particular problem highlights the incorrect perceptions of volunteerism and the policy process from the Great War era. Put simply, the Hoovers wrongly believed that volunteerism had been responsible for their success in Belgium and with the Food Administration. In reality, although Herbert Hoover had cloaked the Food Administration in the language of volunteerism, his program of price controls had been anything but voluntary. A quick end to the war meant that this contradiction went unnoticed and that the fairy tale of volunteerism survived unscathed. Such realities also reveal why volunteerism was much less successful when applied to the economic malaise of the Great Depression.[37]

Lou Henry Hoover received much correspondence describing family problems. Perceptive letter writers appealed to any common characteristic with Hoover that might encourage the first lady to pay attention to their needs. For example, a Missouri woman, knowing of Herbert Jr.'s bout with tuberculosis, asked for help for her husband, who suffered from the same ailment. Although Hoover provided no medical or employment assistance, her secretary sent information about finding suitable medical care at home. When supplicants reported tuberculosis as one of their problems, Hoover paid special attention to the case, because she contended that the "insidious disease" was "more harmful . . . than any temporary" lack of employment.[38]

Typical letter writers displayed their shame at asking for relief, often describing the appeal as "the most embarrassing thing that I have ever done in all my life." Hoover guarded these feelings of independence and dignity. Because protecting the pride of those who asked for help was as important as actually providing the aid, Hoover shunned news coverage. No doubt, the journalist who compared her to Santa Claus upset her sense of dignity, because the comparison revealed a truth that Hoover preferred not to publicize. Letters from Hoover and her secretaries to agency representatives and individuals who were active in voluntary organizations routinely stressed the importance of "*confidentially*" resolving the cases that came to the White House.[39] This respect for privacy emanated from two sources: Hoover's personal approach to relief, and her pragmatic sensibility. If word spread too widely that she would provide help to those who asked, her limited resources and staff would have been overwhelmed by requests.

Sometimes Hoover took charge of correspondence that had initially been directed to her husband. For example, when the unemployed father of two small children appealed to the president, Lou Hoover sought the appropriate voluntary association colleague to investigate and oversee the case. An impending mortgage foreclosure case, though, revealed the nuanced differences between the two Hoovers. Because her father had been a banker during the panic of 1893, and because he had refinanced many notes to save his customers from foreclosure, Lou Hoover hoped for similar results in the early 1930s. After President Hoover read the appeal, however, the West Wing advised nothing more than a referral to the Farm Loan Board, and the East Wing responded accordingly, providing no introduction to a local female activist who might have personalized the relief process. These isolated examples of interaction between the two Hoovers highlight the failures that both amassed in their respective quests for depression relief. President Hoover never appreciated the importance of humanizing relief efforts, as did his wife, while Lou Henry Hoover, even more than her husband, overlooked the weaknesses of a local, personal relief system.

Occasionally, a plea for assistance so moved Hoover that she contributed her own money to the cause. Typical of such largesse was her funding of the college educations of single young women desiring careers in service to their local communities. Such had been her practice for almost thirty years. According to one close associate, "sometimes she made outright gifts and sometimes she made loans." She believed that the latter would not render psychological damage, whereas a gift might. Hoover, though, rarely deposited the repayment checks. When she died and family members cleaned out her desk, they discovered countless uncashed checks that had been sent to the former first lady as repayment of loans.[40]

Augusta Felsen, a middle-aged woman, wrote to Hoover in March 1931 asking for help in raising the $200 she needed to finish her teacher training program. She planned to use her degree to teach in Appalachia among impoverished "Mountain Whites." Her appeal to the White House reflected every major concern of the first lady: education, self-help, women's and children's issues, and communitarian values. After Felsen's background checked out, Hoover paid the $200 for the continuation of Felsen's education but insisted that act of philanthropy remain "*confidential.*"[41] Hoover and her coterie watched Felsen's progress through school and worked hard to help her secure employment when the same depression that had caused her to ask for assistance in the first place resulted in the elimination of funding for additional mountain teachers.

Not all prospective college students were as fortunate as Felsen when they sought aid from Hoover. In the case of Helga Murray, a young white woman seeking a career in physical education, Hoover introduced her to an official of the National Amateur Athletic Federation, a voluntary organization in which she had played a leadership role since the 1920s. For a young white man in Monterey needing college tuition, Hoover did nothing; she contended that his grades were not sufficient to warrant assistance. Clarence F. Munford, a "fatherless" African American, wanted to become a teacher and explained that he was willing to work his way through school.[42] Hoover's office wrote to a few philanthropic organizations and then informed him which one was most likely to provide scholarship assistance. There was no substantive follow-up correspondence to ensure Munford's success either in college or afterward. Such was the typical Hoover pattern, regardless of race. Rare was the supplicant who either received intensive support on a par with Felsen or was rejected out of hand. Given the volume of mail and Hoover's predilection for initial research, little time remained for follow-up.

The case of Sue Congleton, an Urbana, Illinois, woman facing foreclosure, revealed the flaws of Hoover's private, localized approach to relief. None of Hoover's initial contacts could find an individual or a voluntary association able to deal with the pending loss of a home from failure to pay taxes. As Congleton herself noted, her case was hopeless. She told Hoover, "I showed my husband your other letter, it had it seemed a gleam of hope but I don't believe I'll show him this." This pathos pushed Hoover to seek one final remedy. She arranged for Sue Dyer, another friend with contacts in Illinois, to investigate whether "any of your banking friends would be able and willing to give [Congleton] advice," but requested that "the advice should be given directly to the writer without involving anyone here!"[43] Dyer reported her failure, but such structural problems did not motivate Hoover to advocate a different depression relief method. Instead, she intensified her support for communitarian solutions achieved through voluntary means as the best method to combat both the economic and the spiritual crisis of the Great Depression.

In the fall of 1931, Hoover crafted a new role for the first lady as public policy advocate. When she spoke over the radio to 4-H Club members, she used the media to endorse the White House depression relief philosophy. She asked the club members to join local relief efforts in their towns, avowing that individuals could alter the course of the crisis. Though meant to be empowering for her young audience, the speech also reflected a narrow view of the depression. "Many of you have already seen some ways in which you could help lighten the burdens for others. The problems immediately about you, the ways in which you can help, differ greatly," she contended. "Indeed some of us will find the greatest problem *is* the problem of our own family. Some of us are going to find actual need there." Without considering the psychological trauma of poverty, she then encouraged her listeners to face economic scarcity cheerfully and without complaint because such a demeanor would benefit the family. "There is nothing much more discouraging than a moody, complaining child,—even one eighteen years old!" argued the first lady.[44]

Hoover suggested that practical activities were as important as behavior and attitude. She counseled her audience to turn over the milk from their cows and their stored root vegetables and home-canned produce to local food pantries, because "now we know better than we did years ago, how vital milk and vegetables and fruit are in a limited diet." Finally, she counseled the 4-H members living in prosperous communities to ship their excess goods to struggling towns: "There are areas where the crops failed again this year. There are small industrial communities where mills or mines are *all* closed, where there is absolutely *no* one with an excess of money or produce or materials or food to help out the many hundreds who can not get work and who will not have enough food or fuel or clothes to take them through the winter."[45] Although each of Hoover's points was valid, they reveal the priority she gave to community preservation over economic relief, for she believed the latter was not possible without the former.

There were thousands of appeals for assistance, and the typical response to those deemed worthy was to "help the case temporarily" and refer it to the most logical agency or organization for follow-up. Early in 1931, Philippi Harding Butler began managing the numerous pleas for financial assistance, or the "begging letters," as Mildred Hall Campbell termed them. Because "Mrs. Hoover was very concerned" about the many supplicants, she "didn't want just a form letter to go out—'sorry but we're too busy to do anything.'" According to Butler, Hoover realized, "people often wrote to the wife of the President because they felt that that would solve all their ills."[46] Because of the volume of mail, Hoover employed an assistant for Butler, Mabel Heizer, and even funded the extra salary. Butler's new assistant had worked with PECE, and she maintained an extensive network of contacts.

For each case, Butler crafted the initial response, which informed the letter writer of a White House friend who might be able to lend assistance. After permission was granted to pass the case on to an external contact, letters were exchanged seeking the best result for the petitioner. When requests were received from regions of the country that had not previously sought assistance, Hoover directed her secretaries to investigate with whom they should work locally. Such work assignments reflected an innovative use of the first lady's secretarial staff for policy work, as opposed to concentrating strictly on White House entertaining.

"Very often," according to Butler, "Mrs. Hoover sent money through someone anonymously; she never sent it directly. . . . Her generosity was always practical. She just didn't send five dollars here and ten dollars or more there because you asked for it, which no one should. In the worthy cases she'd send much more than that, but she kept her name out of it." For example, when one particularly "pathetic" woman requested about $50 to prevent losing her furniture to foreclosure, Hoover's secretary responded, "she would not want to send them that money when they perhaps need $500, and this would only be delaying the tragedy a few weeks."[47] No records remain as to the total amount of money Hoover gave from her personal funds.

For those that Lou Henry Hoover could not help through one of her many contacts in women's voluntary culture, the first lady arranged for her secretary to direct the petitioners to PECE, an entity created in the fall of 1930 as a clearinghouse for relief coordination. With one in nine Americans out of work, President Hoover created a temporary committee to deal with what he hoped would be a short-lived crisis. With an eye toward the coming winter, he asked PECE to coordinate and facilitate relief efforts via voluntary organizations throughout the country. To oversee the operation, Hoover tapped Arthur Woods, a former New York City police chief and a key player in the 1921 discussions about postwar unemployment. PECE inspired the creation of more than 3,000 local committees. Reliant on local volunteers and state officials, PECE employed only seven field representatives and a small staff in its national offices. State governors told Woods that they preferred to handle the unemployment problem without federal intervention, and even though Hoover asked for $150 million from Congress for unemployment relief, lawmakers responded with only $117 million.[48]

PECE included a women's division, and its members were close associates of the first lady, specifically, Alice M. Dickson and Lillian Gilbreth. Lou Hoover's secretary billed PECE's female members as "sympathetic and understanding," with a commitment to "avoid unnecessary publicity." In fact, Dickson and Gilbreth had handled "cases" for the first lady on an informal basis even before the creation of PECE. In the summer of 1930, Dickson told Hoover's secretary, "I should—no, I must—make a recommendation for continuance [of the informal casework] after this fiscal year, which ends June 30."[49] Nevertheless, the clearinghouse function of PECE proved frustrating to the activist women, who had been schooled in the Hoover tradition of problem solving and were accustomed to the successes resulting from more direct work with voluntary organizations such as the General Federation of Women's Clubs, the Parent-Teacher Organization, and the Girl Scouts.

Ironically, the Federal Emergency Relief Administration, a more successful New Deal agency with which PECE has been compared, originally contained no women's branch. The immediate provision for such within the Hoover administration was likely the result of the first couple's struggling public partnership and their previous work with women's divisions in past crises, such as World War I relief. Regardless of the inspiration, Dickson, through PECE, helped develop vocational education and mortgage abatement programs for the unemployed. She made sure that Hoover knew of her progress. The first lady, in turn, monitored the work of the committee and its women's division, asking for vocational training and retraining statistics, along with the rates of home mortgage and small loan foreclosures. But because she viewed the agency as a last resort, she never advocated expanding its mandate.[50]

Lou Hoover followed the work of the President's Organization on Unemployment Relief (POUR), which replaced PECE in August 1931, with much interest. The lack of accurate unemployment statistics had complicated PECE's work. Walter S. Gifford, the president of AT&T, was named chair of the new entity, which included no significant shift in policy from the PECE initiatives. The encouragement of community relief efforts and upbeat advertising campaigns remained the predominant strategies. Gifford, however, acknowledged that federal, tax-supported relief was needed, and he explained that the current Hoover structure did not permit a change of course. Still, Gifford worked within the existing context and remained hopeful.[51]

Lou Henry Hoover's secretary advised her of the many difficulties associated with local relief throughout the country. State-level relief efforts varied greatly in terms of organization, responsiveness, and financial resources. In states with efficient relief committees, individuals needing assistance were referred to the "central State man," who directed an investigation of the case and then ensured the provision of whatever relief was appropriate. White House secretary Philippi Harding Butler argued, "this is always effective." The overall philosophy of PECE and POUR meshed well with the Hoovers' faith in voluntary relief, and these approaches met with modest success in 1930 and 1931, suggesting that the Hoover analysis of the Great Depression as an outgrowth of the crisis of modernity still made sense. By the end of 1931, though, unemployment was almost 20 percent.[52] In the face of this heightened misery, uneven voluntary, local, and state relief efforts were stressed further as the flawed Hoover system failed.

In states without a functioning relief structure, private charities or well-organized, wealthier counties helped channel assistance to needy individuals or areas. Such a structure proved imperfect. POUR faced the challenge of devising a system to ensure equitable "'distribution'" of relief from wealthy to impoverished areas.[53] Indeed, Mabel Heizer routinely tackled the problems of uneven local relief structures through her casework clearinghouse. For example, in January 1933— one of the most demanding months of her career with the first lady— she received seventy-five new cases while still handling seventy-nine carryover cases. Of the thirty-one cases resolved that month, slightly more than half received relief money or employment, just under a third had the promise of a job, and five were deemed hopeless. The cases that remained active were referred to state or local welfare agencies or some other miscellaneous entity that was well situated to address the unique needs of the particular case. All told, Heizer generated more than 170 letters and memoranda to achieve those results. The volume of requests, though, did not move the Hoovers to reformulate their approach to depression relief.

In the spring of 1931, Lou Hoover inquired about the cost of handling the various relief cases she had referred to the Red Cross. Fifty of the approximately 150 cases she had passed along were chosen for random sampling. The Red Cross had incurred just over $600 in expenses on those cases. The agency also provided Hoover with some statistics about the cases: the overwhelming majority—thirty-nine, to be exact—came from east of the Mississippi River, and the remaining eleven were spread throughout the rest of the country. Red Cross employees had handled 60 percent of the cases, and volunteers had dealt with the remaining cases. Often, church groups, local clubs, and parent-teacher organizations dispensed with the rural cases Hoover referred to the Red Cross. In only ten cases were the petitioners deemed not to need financial or other aid.

Butler calculated the cost, in terms of secretarial and research support salary, for handling new and closed cases through the first lady's office. Salary expenditures averaged $3 per case for secretarial support and $4 per case for research. Butler argued, and Hoover agreed, that the writing of multiple letters, fifteen or more in some cases, and the placement of numerous phone calls were appropriate expenditures of time. Butler explained to the first lady how she had reassured an assistant "that the rescue of a family was quite worth that much effort—don't you think so?" Likewise, Butler and the first lady agreed that detailed work to ferret out the "'no help needed etc.'" cases was "just as worthwhile since they serve to stop various anglings for help and recenter appeals to the community from which they come."[54]

Besides investigating intransigent cases, Heizer managed a heavy workload of new cases—more than 350 in the fall of 1931 and 1,000 in 1932. This increased workload reflected the magnifying crisis; by 1932, unemployment was almost 24 percent. In these circumstances, Lou Henry Hoover's personalized social services were inadequate. The fault rested with Hoover's failure to adjust to the new realities and to realize that, whatever the merits of her approach, it was no longer enough. Even so, the question remains what Hoover could have done differently. As first lady, she wielded no formal political power. Furthermore, the public distance between her work and that of her husband meant that there was little chance for the two to collaborate, as they had during the Great War. As a result, Lou Hoover was trapped with an increasingly unsatisfactory ideological understanding of the economic crisis as a community crisis. Even if she were right in her analysis of the depression as the product of modernity run amok, her efforts to shore up community support networks contained no national implementation strategy—an alien concept to the locally minded first lady—and thus had no possible relief mechanism for a nation seeking food, shelter, and work.[55]

That Lou Henry Hoover could not discern the need for a more comprehensive relief mechanism was the greatest failing of her public policy efforts for depression relief. Nonetheless, Hoover surpassed the activism of all previous first ladies in dealing with this political and economic crisis. Her depression relief work resulted in significant East Wing innovations—the employment of a policy advisory staff, sustained outreach to the voluntary community, and public appeals for conservation and cooperation. That these expansions to the role of first lady went unnoticed was no surprise, given the economic and political climate of the early 1930s. More significant for both Hoovers' historical reputations, their critique of modernity as the cause of the depression went unheeded. After the 1932 presidential election and implementation of the New Deal, Lou and Bert Hoover's positive contributions to economic and social policy were overlooked, as were Lou's attempts to modernize the work of the first lady.

Despite her shortcomings, Hoover's commitment to the problem of depression relief was genuine. Although she implemented policy, typically in a reactive and voluntary fashion, Hoover also requested that her name not be associated with requests for local relief. As her secretary explained, she feared "the welfare agencies who try to relieve the distress in the particular instances are apt to feel that she has some personal interest in the case in question, and often make more particular contribution in connection with it than they would normally." Such a position suggests that Hoover's relief policies were completely divorced from politics. Additionally, Hoover was much more comfortable, and successful, implementing policies of relief in an informal, voluntary, and local fashion than she was designing new national policy. As a result, according to Ruth Fesler, "the principles and policies of Mrs. Hoover were not fully understood by the public."[56]

Such a perspective necessitates a mixed assessment of Hoover's depression relief policies. She deserves credit for noticing and addressing local poverty-induced problems, but her success with individual cases did little for other equally or more seriously disadvantaged families who did not seek help from the first lady. This paradox, more than anything else, typifies Lou Henry Hoover's involvement with depression relief.

Occasionally, Hoover's secretaries indicated the first lady's oblique support for an expanded welfare state. For example, a secretary told a New Mexico woman, "Mrs. Hoover has often had the feeling that we should make better provision in some of the States to care for those who have worked hard through their lives and through circumstances over which they had no control were without adequate provision for their old age."[57] Never, though, did Hoover push for implementation of this idea. Instead, she made grassroots policy activism her forte. As a result, she humanized depression relief with the help of female leaders and local voluntary organizations, but their work never addressed depression-era poverty in its entirety.

Perhaps the greatest testament to the depth of Hoover's commitment to private philanthropy and depression relief can be found in her continued work with local relief efforts after her husband's administration ended. Indeed, she never retreated from her belief that the forces of modernity—especially urbanization—had destroyed America's traditional values and brought about the depression. She received pleas for assistance into the New Deal era, and she operated much as she had when first lady. Hoover's philosophical disagreement with the New Deal approach to relief, which she believed to be overly partisan in design and deed, became apparent when she sought someone to handle an appeal she received early in 1938: "I fancy that most of them turn out to be poor people, like this Mrs. Farley, who need a friend to talk to more than anything else." In Hoover's mind, the woman in question would have had no problems if only her community had remained vigilant about the need for humanitarian action. Still, Hoover recognized, "others are in real, desperate need of assistance, and need help in finding out how to utilize the various agencies of their neighborhood, some one of which can probably care for their particular need. (Although often it is essential that they be Democrats!)"[58]

Indeed, as Hoover told the Women's National Committee for Welfare and Relief Mobilization, a successor to POUR, in the fall of 1932, "Food and warmth and health are not enough to satisfy the desires of life. Occupation and recreation are more vital to those harassed by trouble than to the carefree." For Hoover, depression relief was not about politics, nor was it about immediate, base needs only. She believed that the nation's problems could not be solved without meaningful attention to "educational and avocational occupation, recreational opportunities, and the activities given by what we call character-building organizations."[59]

In her mind, the depression was more than an economic crisis; it was a crisis of modernity that could be assuaged only with communitarian, voluntary strategies. Because her vision won few converts, few observers noticed the substantial changes to the functioning and expectations of her East Wing staff, which resulted in far-reaching innovations to the office of first lady. Hoover's aides undertook policy work, cooperated with philanthropic organizations engaged in relief, and assumed a professional demeanor unknown to the socially oriented East Wings of administrations past. However, neither these changes nor her efforts to explain the depression as a failure of modernity mattered to the voting public in November 1932, when unemployment surpassed 23 percent.

CHAPTER 4

GIRL SCOUTING
AND
THE DEPRESSION

Becoming first lady and encountering the Great Depression caused Lou Henry Hoover to recast her voluntary activism. Her official duties as the nation's premier hostess impinged on the time available for club work, specifically with the Girl Scouts, which had become her priority in the 1920s. Although she retained an affiliation with the Women's Division of the National Amateur Athletic Federation, she gave that organization less of her time than she had when Bert was still commerce secretary. As first lady, Lou Hoover did not abandon her activism but instead refashioned it to meld better with her new duties. At every available opportunity, she merged Scouting work with her responsibilities as first lady.

Said one student of Girl Scout history: "Mrs. Hoover literally carried the Girl Scouts into the White House when she became first lady."[1] Her involvement with Girl Scouting surpassed the outside interests and causes of any previous first lady. More important, her innovations, specifically with regard to Scouting and depression relief, reflected her commitment to protecting humanity from the excesses of modernity. During her years as first lady, Hoover expanded her Scouting work to balance the dual forces pushing American society— celebration of the individual versus celebration of the machine.

Because Hoover had to balance her Girl Scout activism with her entertaining activism, she stressed to her female colleagues the new constraints on her time. When a few Girl Scout leaders publicly suggested that Hoover had abandoned her national office because of her political activity, the first lady's secretary quashed that notion. Representatives of the East Wing told Girl Scout Executive Director Jane Deeter Rippin, "Mrs. Hoover gave up her *active* National work only last autumn, when it became impossible to get to New York every month or so. 'Politics' had nothing to do with it, as Mrs. Hoover never *did* do *any*thing with politics."[2] This midground mentality, though, had little practical effect on her Girl Scout productivity, and Hoover's commitment to the Girl Scouts remained strong. In fact, the restructuring of Hoover's voluntary agenda did not lessen her involvement with Girl Scouts, which for years had been her most treasured public activity. Although she still worked with other organizations, including the General Federation of Women's Clubs, 4-H, and the Red Cross, the overwhelming majority of her available time and energy went to Scouting.

By 1929, the Girl Scouting hierarchy extended throughout the country. Unfortunately, it retained a contradictory leadership mix of outward democratic structures and inward authoritarianism. Hoover had been tapped for the presidency in the 1920s to counter this problem, and she had been successful in easing some of the personality conflicts. She hoped that as first lady she might have the clout to weed out the remaining vestiges of autocratic behavior within the organization. As a result of her effort, writers of the time termed Hoover "a good scout."[3]

Scouting values—specifically, "citizenship training" and "mutual understanding"—permeated Lou Henry Hoover's approach to being first lady so completely that one cannot understand her public activism during her husband's presidency without appreciating her work with the Girl Scouts. She viewed the Scouting experience for young girls as integral to the healthy functioning of American democracy. The combination of outdoor and domestic training fostered a self-sufficiency that Hoover believed was lacking in modern life. Girl Scout programs highlighted those skills, as well as a respect for modern technology and scientific efficiency. The Girl Scouts were equally pleased that Hoover retained her commitment to the organization while first lady. In the fall of 1929, Harriet C. Barnes, the corresponding secretary for the Girl Scouts' national office, wrote, "if Mrs. Hoover is glad to be 'playing around' with the Girl Scout organization, all parents and others working with girls should be interested."[4]

Hoover's Scouting work was both individual and bureaucratic. The first lady enjoyed personal interaction with the girls, for in her mind, such relationships were at the heart of Scouting. Lenna Yost, a Republican colleague and Girl Scout leader, told Hoover of "a wayward girl" with an unfortunate background who had met the first lady at a Girl Scout camp. "She must have attracted your attention for you put your arm about her and made some kindly expression of interest and regard," Yost recounted. "That girl not only was made radiantly happy, but she says that her whole life is changed; she realizes that the world is really kind. To have had you, the First Lady of the Land, single her out for special attention has made life a new and wonderful thing to her."[5]

Hoover's bureaucratic agenda during the White House years was equally impressive, but on a much larger scale. Hoover worked with her Girl Scout colleagues to increase membership from 200,000 to 500,000 in conjunction with a major fund-raising campaign, helped professionalize Scouting leadership while democratizing the Scouting experience at all levels, and functioned as a resource person when problems arose. Perhaps the most significant Girl Scout crusade—in terms of ambition, if not accomplishment—was in response to the Great Depression. Hoover conceptualized and began implementation of the Rapidan Plan, which argued that Scouts should become agents for relief work in their local communities. Viewed together, these undertakings reveal not only Hoover's continued commitment to Scouting but also her efforts to give the next generation of young women the tools to expand their sphere and balance the tensions between individuals and mass technology.

In the spring of 1929, the editors of *American Girl* magazine asked Hoover to write an article about her childhood. Since Hoover's own life history exemplified what she and the Girl Scout organization hoped all young women could achieve, this request made sense. Who better to model the benefits of the pioneer spirit combined with scientific progress than Lou Henry Hoover? The first lady's secretary replied somewhat sarcastically that the overwhelming number of articles written "*without* permission" caused Hoover to wonder why "it was necessary for the AMERICAN GIRL to *ask* permission to print one!" Additionally, Hoover's secretary noted that there was no available writer with sufficient information to produce an article about the first lady's early years, nor did she have the time for extensive interviews. "The only reason she does not write it herself is because of that factor of time," suggested her secretary. "I will see if I can get something out of her on the subject. But don't be too sure of it!"[6] The following summer, though, Hoover delivered the article. The attitude and the delay reveal Hoover's antipathy toward self-aggrandizing publicity, not toward the larger goal of female empowerment.

Such tensions did not prohibit Hoover from working to better the twelve-year-old magazine in other ways. Hoover told Rippin in late November 1929, "After looking over this month's 'American Girl' and then over the numbers of the last few months, it is really a matter of very grave concern to me that we are constantly losing the Girl Scout impress on the magazine." Although Hoover accepted the counsel of those who hoped to make the magazine more appealing to all girls, she objected that Girl Scout coverage had been reduced to two "badly done" pages. She wanted the magazine to focus on issues of particular importance to Scouts, not just on general matters of interest to girls, whether they were Scouts or not. "I think it would be interesting if in time the Girl Scout magazine made enough money to help support its mother," agreed the first lady. "But that I think is as nothing compared to the power a good magazine would have in carrying the best Girl Scout news, pictures, stories and ideals to the Girl Scouts and their Leaders."[7] For Hoover, the magazine functioned in two ways—as outreach to girls and women not currently involved with Scouting, and as democratic communication with those who were already members.

Likewise, Hoover privately endorsed the children's books her sister, Jean Henry Large, had been writing about Girl Scouting. The Nancy books, featuring a Girl Scout by that name, explored the fundamentals of Scouting. Though concluding that "the Girl Scouts need Nancy even more than Nancy needs the Girl Scouts," Lou Hoover indicated that she would not write an introduction for her sister's second book, *Nancy's Lone Girl Scouts,* even if it was about the program the first lady had nurtured in the 1920s. She wanted the book to succeed or fail on its merits, not through a White House endorsement. "I do not think it would be very wise for me to do that either from your point of view or Girl Scouting," argued Lou Hoover. "I am only an honorary officer of the Girl Scouts now and I *am* your sister so I think it would look much better for Mrs. [Mira] Hoffman, or Mrs. [Genevieve] Brady, or Mrs. Rippin to write your introduction for this next volume establishing thereby the fact that you are approved of by the organization, and that your scouting is correct."[8]

Hoover never retreated from Girl Scout activism. At the 1929 annual convention, Hoover announced a five-year plan to boost the organization's membership from 200,000 to 500,000, make it financially self-supporting, and reconstitute its governance structure. Genevieve Brady, who had replaced Hoover as chair of the Girl Scouts' board of directors, had authored the plan in conjunction with Mark Jones, a paid business consultant. Brady was also an important lay leader in the Catholic Church. Possessing a pleasant disposition, she oversaw Girl Scout financial matters with resolute and unwavering conviction. The ambitious plan directly addressed two of Hoover's three most pressing Girl Scout concerns—girls, money, and leaders. She and other plan advocates agreed that because the Girl Scout movement was so important to the development of young women in American society, efforts should be made to expand the number who could join the organization. The plan also highlighted fund-raising, but it targeted new monies to critical areas to ensure the organization's longevity and stability. Although the plan did not directly address the need for additional leaders, such concerns were treated in conjunction with membership expansion. For the plan to succeed, the organization needed to move away from its cliquish, autocratic governance mechanisms; bring the rhetoric of democratic decision making into accord with reality; and professionalize its operations. Such requirements threatened those who benefited from the status quo, and implementation of the "tremendously ambitious" five-year plan became controversial almost immediately after it was announced.[9]

The plan's most far-reaching goal was the $3 million fund-raising campaign. Major gifts—$250,000 from John D. Rockefeller Jr. and $500,000 from the World War I–era American Relief Administration (which Herbert Hoover still essentially controlled)—along with numerous smaller donations meant that half of the fund-raising goal had been achieved. The timing of the campaign, which coincided with the stock market crash and the initial downturn of the economy, made fund-raising difficult, but Girl Scout leaders remained committed to the original goal. The gift from the American Relief Administration (ARA) reflected Hoover's continued use of her husband's colleagues to the betterment of her voluntary agenda. Tapping that source, though, was very different from reinstituting her public marriage, which had never developed beyond the war years. During the White House years, Herbert Hoover had no time for a public partnership with his wife. Nonplussed, Lou Hoover continued her independent career and focused on the long-term success of the Girl Scouts, which she considered crucial to the preservation of American citizenship and values.

Going solo, Lou Henry Hoover played an important and unique role in the fund-raising drive. She articulated her views of social organization with solid and analytical verbal appeals, and she attended fund-raisers. When asked about the Girl Scouts' greatest need, Hoover told the press, "Girls. We want more and more girls for the joy they get out of the organization, because in scouting they help themselves instead of having things thrust upon them. It is what they put into the organization that makes them happy." The first lady used her public remarks to suggest the applicability of that philosophy to "everything in life, not just of the Girl Scouts." Hoover wanted all those with means and with an interest in youth to understand that "we can't give the Girl Scouts what they need as an organization without money. They cannot pay for everything themselves, because they are not all little rich girls and it would not be right in this democracy for the rich to pay for the poor ones, so the dues must be the same for all, and that does not bring in enough money."[10] Hoover believed that any social class engineering within Girl Scouting would fail. Nonetheless, she also acknowledged that poverty inhibited participation. To solve that problem, she appealed to private rather than public sources.

In response to the first lady's fund-raising efforts, Mira Hoffman, an early volunteer in the Scouting movement, told Lou Hoover, "I do want you to know how much we all appreciated everything you did in your own Girl Scout way. No other organization ever had such marvelous publicity. It was so far-reaching, so dignified and altogether so perfect—thanks to you." Hoffman contended that Hoover had "created a real desire on the part of the Executive Committee to carry out the proposed development plan. I am so glad it was possible for you to set in motion the machinery to carry through the plans you have so long had in mind."[11]

Throughout 1929, Hoover was a key player in the internal negotiations about how best to raise funds and publicize the campaign. Hoover worried that Scout leaders had lost sight of the organization's history and would not take seriously the work needed to implement the plan. Thus, she remained involved with Scout work. Her correspondence with Genevieve Brady reveals her bureaucratic insight into how to ensure organizational success. "I am not at all concerned about who gets *the credit* for past work,—from Mrs. Low's first efforts down to the newest little stenographer. . . . It is the result of the work itself that I fear to have scrapped," Hoover stressed to Brady. She closed her cautionary screed with words of support: "it is you yourself who is going to hold it all together and make the success of the effort."[12]

Even before the plan was solidified, the Girl Scouts faced depression-induced budgetary problems. Some Girl Scout allies of the first lady advocated diverting funds from integral projects such as the *American Girl* and the camping program and using them for general operating expenses. Hoover feared that such a tactic would jeopardize the five-year plan because it would harm the Girl Scouts' credibility with large donors who had earmarked their gifts. She wanted the Scouts to use the money they had raised for the original stated purpose, and she employed the ARA to ensure her continued voice within Scouting. When Rippin first mentioned redirecting part of the ARA donation, Hoover insisted that "the ARA fund should be applied toward completing the program for making *The American Girl* a success, and toward an adequate provision for developing the camping program."[13]

Hoover's ambivalence about a highly organized Girl Scout governance structure resulted from her notions of the role of individuals in a modern, technologically efficient but democratic society. Indeed, her views on the Girl Scout five-year plan and efforts to reorganize the administration of this program flowed from these larger concerns, which had animated much of her activism. The following spring,

Hoover told Brady, "I heard a girl the other day referring to the Girl Scouts as being 'not an organization but a fellowship.' The phrase appealed to me tremendously." The egalitarian nature of fellowship reminded Hoover of small-town mores, and she did not want her favored organization to lose sight of what were, in her opinion, its core values. As such, Hoover balanced her desire to shape the future of the organization with her goal of preserving egalitarian leadership and individual autonomy. She then combined rumination on the intersection of fellowship and democracy with a pitch to ensure the success of the new Girl Scout plan. "I think the vital consideration in making the 'new plan' function is this recognition of fellowship-ness,—and the fact that we must strive to make every *one's* thought and incentive and effort be considered and have effect; that *every*one in the fellowship must feel that what she is giving, or can give, goes into the whole thing and has its due proportion of influence and result."[14]

Hoover cautioned against duplicating the mistakes of the Boy Scouts, which had become so hierarchical that troop leaders had little or no opportunity for input and were expected to merely follow orders from headquarters. "So again I am saying, don't forget that it is the spirit that *you* put into it all and that you inspire *all* the other Girl Scout leaders and Girl Scouts to *give,* that is going to make the coming years a success," argued Hoover. "It is not the *picture of an ideal* that is going to carry through to success,—with no vitally interested personnel at the other end and no vital channels of functioning both ways behind it."[15]

Brady, Hoover, and Harriet Barnes (whose husband had been a colleague of Herbert Hoover's since World War I) had been the leading backers of the five-year plan, but not all Scouting officials were in accord. Rippin, the executive director; Hoffman, the current president; and others questioned the plan. Their expressions of discord disguised the specific reasons for their disagreement, but most likely a combination of forces created the dilemma. Opinions were divided over Mark Jones's role and his motivations regarding the implementation of the plan. Some feared that he would profit personally from the decisions he advocated. Others worried that a worsening economy required a new strategy, specifically regarding the expenditure of funds raised as part of the campaign. As was typical,

Hoover tried to mediate between the differing views, but her strong support for maintaining the $3 million fund-raising target hindered her efforts at practicing the politics of compromise. Although she agreed with the criticisms of Jones, Hoover never questioned the wisdom of the plan.[16]

Hoover told Birdsall Edey, an energetic and popular Girl Scout who served as the organization's president between 1930 and 1935: "I know that Mrs. Brady means very well by the Girl Scouts, and the only reason why she seems to break away from the things we have accomplished in the past is that she was so busy with the finances of the organization that she sometimes did not have time to follow all that we have done in executive work." Hoover then defended Brady from charges that she intended to institute an "autocratic form of government" for the Girl Scouts, as "seems to be the end and aim of Mr. Jones' planning,—either consciously or unconsciously on his part." Hoover and her closest friends in Scouting, Edgar and Abbie Rickard, along with Rippin, had been skeptical about Jones since the winter of 1929.[17] Thus, while publicly disavowing active Scout work, Hoover helped disengage Jones from a position of authority so as to preserve Girl Scouting and the five-year plan.

The conflict over Jones and the five-year plan resulted because Girl Scout leaders had never made the transition from "the casual, personal pre-war basis" in which individual voices could easily be heard to a more modern, efficient structure befitting an organization with several hundred thousand members. Originally the brainchild of Juliette Gordon Low of Savannah, Georgia, the American Girl Scout movement began with a personalized, cliquish approach to administration that continued as Low brought other women she knew into leadership positions. Significant expansion of Girl Scouting during World War I prompted the initial efforts to ensure "a firm, cohesive national structure," but because many Scout leaders were recruited through personal connections, such reforms were slow to materialize. The organization, though, was headquartered in New York City, ironically giving this nature-driven movement an urban tinge regarding governance. In addition to the board of directors, Girl Scout oversight included an executive committee and four departments: education, equipment, field, and publications. Regional committees mediated between local councils and the national headquarters.[18]

Hoover sent a letter for dissemination among Girl Scout leaders to Edey. This document implicitly addressed the relationship between the five-year plan and the extant Field Committee, which was composed of the various commissioners along with individuals close to New York City. Hoover believed that the Field Committee embodied the sort of democratic governance she had advocated since the early 1920s, when she first served as president of the national organization. Hoover sought a Girl Scout governing structure that allowed for "inspiration, initiative and administrative ability flowing from the outside toward the center instead of radiating from the fountain-head out,—which to my way of thinking has been the greatest development we have made over the old ways in those years."[19] She had pursued similar goals in the 1920s, and the introduction of the five-year plan offered an additional mechanism through which she might pursue her crusade against authoritarianism.

Hoover indicated: "I really am shocked at the thought that we would be trying in any way whatsoever to limit the various regions' growing democracy in managing their own affairs." She acknowledged a "perfect obsession" with "good government" for the Girl Scouts, which correlated with "a well working little democracy" in each region and subregion that would oversee "its own, governing its own small affairs and personnel directly, and with other similar regions administering the national affairs." Such a development, Hoover contended, was necessary to prevent the adoption of "second rate" governance structures currently employed in other youth leadership organizations such as the Boy Scouts.[20]

Edey, however, was worried that such regional committees "will consider themselves 'little Nationals' and take on a great deal too much authority." Edey had worked with Jones, despite her "prejudice" against him, to ensure that the regional committees remained busy but not domineering. She told Hoover, "the set of duties that he drew up, have caused a flurry, in the New England Region, and may cause more. Most of the Regions liked them, and have written me so." The draft proposal provided that regional chairs would be nationally appointed, but the New England Committee opposed that notion. Edey reasoned, "But when they understand that we only appoint the person *they* select, I think they will feel better. It is really only a matter of explaining a little more clearly."[21]

Hoover recommended that Edey keep in close touch with the committees when she assumed the Girl Scout presidency, recalling, "I tried to get to as many of your Field Committee meetings as I could when I was President." She also counseled Edey, "you must just all keep a very careful watch that the trend does not run away too far to the extreme in either direction, of either too close control from above or too lax 'independence' below." As was typical for her political sensitivities, Hoover advocated a judicious approach to leadership of the organization. "I think, as you do, that the matter of having the more subordinate divisions make their own elections and decisions," Hoover told Edey, "subject in one form or another to the approval of the next higher group, will do much to balance this." Hoover's constant defense of Scouting democracy and balance reflected an appreciation of the governance challenges unique among nonprofessional leaders and a sophisticated understanding of how best to shepherd Girl Scouting to a more secure financial and organizational condition. Indeed, by 1935, the five-year plan had brought an 85 percent increase in membership, to 382,971, and the Great Depression did not adversely affect the organization's financial condition.[22]

Hoover supported the leadership development aspects of Scouting because she viewed excellent troop leaders as vital to the success of the movement. Hoover told a Girl Scout colleague, "I am still worried over the fact that the Girl Scout leaders of today do not have, as far as I can see, any way to study the history and development as one would get if one could read from year to year transcripts of training camps." The first lady envisioned creating a "record of the progress of Girl Scouting practices in these last few years" so that "the new leaders today" could study for themselves the organization with which they were affiliated.[23] Such work on behalf of Girl Scout leadership reflected Hoover's commitment to the organization, especially the empowerment of young women to guide their own destinies.

She also worked closely with colleges and universities that offered leadership training programs for prospective Girl Scout troop leaders. When the academic jurisdiction for the Stanford University program was being debated, Hoover indicated her preference that it be removed from the education department and shifted to the social science department. As Hoover's secretary explained, "from our point of view, it is even more important to contact girls who do not intend to teach than those who do." Typically, students from a variety of majors took the Girl Scout coursework in the spring quarter, but the smaller summer quarter classes were usually made up of rural teachers hoping to bring Girl Scouting to their schools. Low enrollment caused Lou Hoover to push for elimination of the summer program at Stanford, but she hoped to add the coursework at the teachers colleges in San Jose and San Francisco.[24]

Perhaps the most significant leadership crisis that Hoover and the Girl Scouts faced was Jane Deeter Rippin's 1930 decision to leave her post as executive director. Rippin had been with the organization since 1919, when the paid post had been created for her. Her extensive background as a social worker made her the perfect person to help the fledgling organization expand into a national, professionally run program for girls. But because she was the only executive director in Girl Scout history, her decision to leave, especially in tandem with the difficulty of implementing the five-year plan, caused some controversy reflective of the older, more personal operating style that Juliette Low had employed. Rippin had grown frustrated with the internal conflicts over the five-year plan and debate about the organization's governance structure; additionally, her health had deteriorated. One Girl Scout leader described the executive meeting at which Rippin announced her resignation as "not a pleasant meeting." The problem resulted in part because Brady had "made it a personal matter" when Rippin had tried to discuss her status privately, but the more significant reason for the tension was the conflict over Jones and the five-year plan. Brady and Rippin never completely restored a solid working relationship.[25]

When Rippin formally resigned her post as national director of the Girl Scouts, Hoover explained that although she would no longer be the recognized leader, Rippin "will always be a Girl Scout and we can always feel that we can turn to her in matters of either emergency or joy." Hoover viewed the current leadership crisis as "a test of the strength of the democratic organization which we have all been trying to establish." Indeed, Hoover termed the Rippin resignation "a complete tragedy!" Rippin, who "had given so tremendously to the cause," had ensured Scouting's successful maturation. Hoover wrote to her sister of the annual Girl Scout convention: "no controversial subjects were brought up either at the Board meetings or on the floor. The smoothness of the machinery showed how well trained Mrs. Rippin had made the workers."[26] Hoover hoped that the Girl Scout organization could survive this setback and maintain its course toward greater democratization, which she believed was necessary for the citizenship training of the organization's young charges.

Upon her resignation, Rippin compared her record with that of other "national social-work organizations." The Girl Scouts had amassed a reserve fund of $385,000, with $1.5 million in real estate holdings and pledges of $3 million as part of the five-year plan. Such accomplishments reflected well on Rippin, and Hoover praised the former director in the *American Girl* magazine upon her retirement. Said one student of Scouting about Rippin: "Her dynamic energy, business acumen, personal magnetism, and undisputed leadership had been large and vital factors in the tremendous growth and progress of the organization during her ten-year regime."[27]

Hoover was even more direct in her correspondence with Sarah Louise Arnold. "July first apparently saw Jane Rippin leave the National Director's Chair at 670 Lexington Avenue. I am very, very sad about that but did not do anything to stop it in the last months," Hoover explained. "I felt that if they in New York, who had to work together all the time and so would know just what one another were doing, could not appreciate that she was worth any other three of them rolled together, that they had not better feel that she was being forced upon them by any 'outside' influences." Hoover predicted one of two results from the Rippin departure: "Either they will happen upon such a good substitute that a satisfactory transfer into other hands will be made and the organization will be little the worse for the change,—or else they will happen upon such poor hands and things will begin to go to pot in a few months and they will be forced into insisting that she come back."[28] If the latter transpired, Lou Hoover assured Arnold that Rippin would return out of a sense of duty to Scouting.

When Genevieve Brady asked Hoover who the Girl Scouts might get to replace Rippin, Hoover responded that there was "only [one] woman who could even remotely fill Mrs. Rippin's place,—and she, I do not think would *fill* her place by any means. . . . This is Dr. Lillian Gilbreth." Hoover argued that Gilbreth, her old mining colleague and depression relief liaison, "would be immeasurably better than any of the old welfare workers about New York or than people of our staff, old or new." Hoover encouraged the Girl Scout leadership to "call this first year [Rippin's] long-accrued 'vacation,' or 'leave of absence,'" and much negotiation ensued about how to arrange such a designation for Rippin while simultaneously recruiting Gilbreth for the post. The latter attempt ultimately failed, but Hoover convinced Gilbreth to take a position on the Girl Scout board of directors. More important, Rippin's successor, Josephine Schain, a longtime international peace activist, shared Hoover's views about Girl Scout governance. Put simply, Hoover revealed her bureaucratic talents at backstage politics while helping to navigate the transition in the director's office.[29]

Hoover, though, was not entirely satisfied with the resolution of the leadership crisis, specifically as it regarded Mark Jones's relationship with the organization. During the latter half of 1930, Hoover learned of the many criticisms of Jones that had reached the Girl Scout board of directors. His position with the Girl Scouts had been terminated when he "demand[ed] . . . a perfectly unjustifiable fee for alleged work that he had done," but by the end of January 1931, Hoover told Abbie Rickard of rumors she had heard about possibly reemploying Jones. Initially, Hoover had been skeptical of Jones and had even "express[ed]" her "disapproval of his mode of procedure to a number of the active officers of the Girl Scouts. Later many complaints came to me from numerous members of the Board about his unethical procedure or unsound judgment in numbers of directions."[30]

Hoover fumed that discussions about reinstating Jones had occurred without any mention to her. "This whole matter disturbs me very considerably in regard to my relationship with the Girl Scout organization. I realize fully that when I can take no more active part in their affairs than I do at present, that I am in no position to be emphatic in thrusting my opinions before the Board," Lou complained to Abbie. "On the other hand, I do not feel that I can be in the position of bearing the responsibility that an Honorary President does to an organization, when a factor in which I have no trust is so very active in its affairs, and when I cannot depend upon the assurances made on this subject by the acting officers."[31]

Therefore, she debated whether she should continue her affiliation with the Girl Scouts. In a private letter to Abbie, Lou contemplated walking away from the organization she loved: "It seems to me the simple logical course is for me *very quietly* to resign from my Honorary position. I might simply ask that, at the beginning of this spring season, my name be dropped from the organization's official lists as Honorary President, because my practice is to refrain from holding honorary offices."[32] That Hoover failed to act resulted from her deep personal and professional ties to the organization. She knew that if the first lady, an honorary Scout president, resigned, it would reflect badly on the Girl Scouts. Better to fight Jones and the autocratic tendencies from within the organization, she decided.

The discussions as to whether Jones should be rehired inspired Hoover's rather long meditation about her future with Girl Scouting. She sent her musings to Rickard, along with a handwritten note in which Hoover questioned, "if matters are as I have had them intimated to me, I can see no other action for me" than to resign as honorary president. She asked Rickard to retain her screed "for a few days or weeks, in case it becomes necessary to act upon it suddenly,—or show it to other Board members before my taking more formal action. Naturally, I would not connect his name with my communications to the Board. And you can let me know your opinion of the present phase."[33] Hoover communicated her strategy to Rickard in this politically sophisticated message, which relied on a nuanced threat to leave the organization to achieve her objectives. That Hoover's methods differed little from those she critiqued resulted from the immense challenge of modernizing an organization that too often practiced the politics of personality instead of the politics of substance.

Another significant Girl Scout problem that occurred during Hoover's White House years involved the Little House program, which had been Hoover's brainchild in the 1920s and provided laboratory homes, including kitchens and gardens, for troops to practice their domestic skills. The Little House program required reorganization in the summer of 1929. It had never developed as fully as Hoover had hoped, thus causing the Girl Scout organization to scale back its staff. Martha Noyes, who had worked in Washington, D.C., with the Little House, ensured that Hoover learned of the abrupt manner in which Rippin had removed Noyes from her post. Hoover later apologized to Noyes for failing to inform her of the fate of the Little House. "While it has no definite scheme in mind yet," Hoover explained, the Girl Scout hierarchy "feels that they cannot afford but one good salary down here,—and in all probability that must cover a professional home economics person."[34] The first lady felt sorry for Noyes, but she also worked closely with Gertrude Bowman, the woman who oversaw the Little House for the remainder of Hoover's White House years. Because this personnel change benefited the Girl Scouts, Hoover ultimately approved Rippin's management style.

The Little House remained a continuing concern for Hoover. She received word in the summer of 1929 that Bowman's management had "greatly improved the whole house and grounds." The Little House was an outreach project as well as a destination for visiting troops. "There are many out of town people calling at the Little House, this summer," reported one Scout executive. "All seem to take a great interest in the house. They are told about Girl Scouting and oftimes small sales are made from the little stock of equipment."[35]

By the early 1930s, there were seventy Girl Scout Little Houses located throughout the country, but Hoover had hoped for an even wider dissemination of the program. Hoover "believed that here could be gratified the feminine urge, which begins way back in the mud pie days, for domesticity, cooking, playing with dolls, for having one's own spot where mothers may be imitated in every household pursuit." In Hoover's mind, the Little House program functioned as a living classroom in which Scouts could apply their "instinct" for housekeeping "toward practical application" in a community building "recognized as a home-making center." Scouts decorated the rooms and maintained the exterior landscape. Hoover contributed from her own resources to the gardens for the Washington Little House. She insisted, "Girl Scouts do not ostentatiously entertain. They just cheerfully welcome their friends and quietly try to make them happy." This domestic philosophy was not about restricting women to the home but about using homemaking skills to bring people together in community. Hoover argued, "I never 'entertain' . . . I just ask people to come in to see us, and enjoy each other."[36]

Hoover did not ignore what had originally attracted her to Scouting—imbuing women and girls with an appreciation of the natural world. Indeed, being first lady gave Lou Henry Hoover additional clout to assist individual Girl Scout camps. For example, Hoover and her staff enabled Dr. Mabel M. Aiken's Girl Scout camp near Portland, Oregon, to procure some adjoining government land. A private citizen's homestead claim for the land temporarily complicated the acquisition, but Republican congressman Franklin Korell introduced legislation that allowed the Girl Scouts to obtain the property. Such intervention reflected Hoover's willingness to use her connections as first lady to the betterment of Scouting.

Depending on the issue, Hoover sometimes became quite involved in Girl Scout matters while first lady. She told a Scouting colleague, "I too most heartily agree with you that a camp uniform is very desirable,—and I think it would be an excellent idea to have it ready for discussion, and adoption, at the Convention." She preferred either "an attractive *mottled* green" or a "woodsy gray material," because she knew the uniforms "*will* get spotted and the plain materials show up each innocent little mark so blatantly!"[37] Such positions were entirely within the feminine orbit and thus were nonthreatening to those members of society who opposed new roles for women. More important, they indicate the breadth of issues with which Hoover remained actively engaged while first lady.

Because education and physical fitness also mattered to the first lady, she believed that the introduction of a health program for individual troops was necessary. Hoover cautioned, "I very distinctly laid the emphasis on the word 'Tentative' and do not mean that we want to adopt a health program to stand by in all particulars, as firmly as we do to our nature program. I do think with the emphasis that is being laid on child health programs during the coming year, that it would be very well if we recognized a basis of our present work." Lou Hoover hoped that the new health education curriculum would not be "too 'peppy' with too much of an eye for popularity with the girls," as had been the case with a previously proposed and rejected health program.[38] None of her colleagues noted the contradiction between Hoover's support for a centrally prescribed program and her commitment to decentralized governance.

Hoover encouraged Girl Scout "graduates" to continue their community service as adults. Such a stance reflected Hoover's commitment to local charity work, and it also reinforced her independent activism. Because Hoover hoped that former Girl Scouts would become active with the Red Cross, she made this appeal the theme of her December 1929 address to the Red Cross's National Committee on Voluntary Service. "Life-saving and first aid have a particular appeal to the athletic Girl Scout with her love of the out of doors and her skill in sports. Home Hygiene and Care of the Sick offers an ideal opportunity for the development of her womanly qualities," noted Hoover. She then cited the example of the Santa Barbara Girl Scouts who had come to the rescue of the citizens of that city the morning after an earthquake in 1925. As families gathered on the front lawns trying to make breakfast over campfires, the results proved "more amusing than successful" until "the Girl Scouts appeared, like a flying squadron of kitchen coaches. In almost every yard a uniformed Scout could be seen building the fire in regulation manner, frying the bacon and boiling the coffee."[39]

Finally, Hoover concerned herself with the question of ethnic equality in Scouting, thus reinforcing other public stances for social justice she made while first lady, such as the DePriest tea. Even before 1929, Lou Hoover, albeit haphazardly, supported the expansion of Girl Scouting into the Native American community. In 1927, she told Hubert Work, the secretary of the interior, "Girl Scouting [should] be taken up as a very desirable factor in the Indian girl's education." Such a program, though, would cost about $10,000 per year to serve the estimated 6,000 girls who would become a part of it. Hoover commented, "I haven't the faintest idea who would want to donate that much money for that purpose. Do you? Would it in any way work into the Government budget for Indian girls' education or development? Or do you know some philanthropist especially interested in the Indians who would like to meet it?"[40] Work agreed to pursue the matter but accomplished little.

Four years later, in the midst of her term as first lady, Hoover returned to the issue of Scouting and American Indians. Hoover endorsed the Girl Scouts' efforts to provide scholarship opportunities for young women of either European or Native American heritage who were interested in establishing Girl Scout troops among Native peoples, calling it a "splendid contribution." In 1931, she met with much more success in finding money to support her plan. Hoover told the prospective donor, "I feel that we will be accomplishing something very valuable with the Indians if we can get them interested in the true spirit of Scouting."[41] The first lady also had her secretary forward details of the proposed scholarship to Mary Walcott, a scientist, Indian rights activist, and capital city hostess.

The national director of the Girl Scouts told Mildred Hall of the status of "negotiations to have training courses given to the girls of the Indian Reservations." The effort included discussions with the commissioner of the Bureau of Indian Affairs. Although no plan had been finalized, the national office was pleased that "at least a start had been made to reach the Indian girls." Hoover wondered whether Walcott had discussed the matter with "any G.S. authority."[42]

At the same time that Hoover helped establish the Indian scholarship program, she received a letter from a Michigan Girl Scout: "We are what the *white* people call Indian, but Papa says we are all American as this was Our Country first. . . . I sold cookies for the scouts, I got second prize, I think it must be lovely to be a girl scout in Washington, and visit you as I see bye [*sic*] the Detroit paper some of the Girl Scouts have. We have a new baby boy and we named him after the president (Herbert)."[43] Indeed, although Hoover's support of Native American Scouting surpassed her aborted stance on behalf of African American civil rights, her efforts in this area were de-emphasized when other, more pressing matters such as the depression competed for her attention.

Hoover hoped to forge an inventive response for depression-induced misery. The lessons she learned while functioning as a national sounding board and depression relief referral service inspired her thinking. Because of its focus on both volunteerism and young women's agency in the wider world, Hoover used the Girl Scouts as a national conduit for local relief. No longer would Scouts investigate cases presented to the White House. Instead, Hoover envisioned Scouts as the first line of defense against local misery resulting from unemployment, bank failures, and home foreclosures. When the country's economic and social structure faced the threat of collapse, Hoover intensified her advocacy for Girl Scouting, merging her voluntary activism with her traditional work as first lady. The combination had the potential to revolutionize the responsibilities of first ladies, but because Hoover's efforts for structured depression relief via the Girl Scouts ended with her husband's presidency, the experiment's results did not live up to expectations.

In encouraging Girl Scout philanthropy, Hoover recalled the successful efforts of voluntary organizations. Girl Scout relief work incorporated various strategies. For example, an Oregon Girl Scout told Hoover that despite serious spinal injuries preventing her attendance in school, she had "done much community work, and helping the poor which has made me very happy. All this, scouting has taught me, so you see why I love it so." Other Girl Scouts worked with disabled children, assisted impoverished troop members, and staged circuses to raise money to support the unemployed. Individually, Girl Scout troops throughout the nation bought milk for babies, food for people in breadlines, and supplies for the needy.[44] Finally, several troops donated time and energy to the Needlework Guild of America. Working with the Boy Scouts, the Girl Scouts collected 21,583 garments in 1930, which was 1,878 more garments than had been collected in 1929 but still far short of real help.

Such local endeavors mirrored Hoover's own East Wing depression relief efforts with the President's Emergency Committee for Employment. She hoped to institutionalize the Girl Scouts' relief activities with the Rapidan Plan, an ambitious undertaking that called for 250,000 Scouts to perform local relief work in 4,000 communities throughout America. The plan embodied the communitarian values that had animated Hoover's activism for more than two decades. Scouts operating the Rapidan Plan would survey the needs of their local communities and provide appropriate relief services based on their skills and abilities. For Hoover, then, localizing relief was the best method not only for contending with the miseries of the depression, which manifested in different way in different locales, but also for encouraging the younger generation to retain an ethos of community service. This plan marked another significant departure for Hoover's work as first lady within the government.

In late March 1931, Lou Hoover, as honorary Girl Scout president, spoke about the Girl Scouts' depression relief activities during her fourth national radio address. (One of the previous three had been a substantive appeal to 4-H Club members; the other two, one to the Daughters of the American Revolution and the other in conjunction with the christening of a ship, had reflected her ceremonial duties.) In this address, Hoover suggested that the approximately half a million active and former Girl Scouts represented "a typical cross

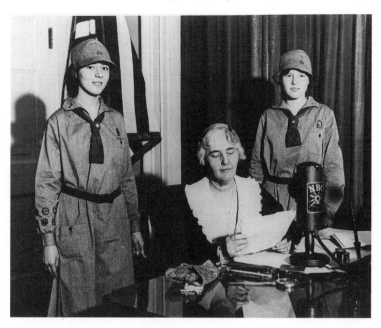

Lou Henry Hoover gives a radio address about Girl Scouting, the Great Depression, and the President's Emergency Committee for Employment, 24 March 1931. Lois Kuhn is on the left, and Peggy Starr is on the right. (Herbert Hoover Presidential Library-Museum, © AP/Wide World Photos)

section of the mass of women and girls of the United States." As such, Hoover believed that members of the organization could "meet" and "overcom[e]" what she termed "the threatening disaster of this national situation." While acknowledging female power to assuage the crisis, she was cautious not to offend male listeners. That posture of compromise flowed from Hoover's own moderate temperament and conciliatory approach to community activism. She contended, "Not for a moment that we are minimizing what the men and boys have done! That we know, and it is marvelous."[45]

Hoover then linked the efforts of the Girl Scouts with those of numerous other clubwomen. These activist women used their various organizations on behalf of the "millions" of "dimly heard" impoverished Americans, who were "often so shy" in their initial requests for help and "even less articulate in thanks. . . . I have heard innumerable talks of gratitude most eloquently expressed. Eloquent I cannot be,—but I do rejoice in passing on to you, girls and women of America, the word that what you have done for those who have suffered innocently this year is borne in their ever affectionate and understanding memory."[46]

Hoover engaged Girl Scouts in systematized relief work. She hoped that this new approach would be an improvement over the haphazard, reactive methods of the early White House years. In developing the new strategy, Hoover learned from Rippin's positive results with other gender-based, volunteerist relief efforts, specifically the Girls Work Committee of the White House Conference on Children. In October 1930, Rippin explained, "what they are really proud of is the fact that you are genuinely interested in work with girls, and this whole group is anxious to get as much of a lift in Girl's Work as is possible. . . . They think the Boys get much more consideration."[47] Additionally, the relief work of local Girl Scout troops impressed the first lady, and she saw the potential for greater results through a coordinated national program focused on the local level—a connection she never made in other aspects of depression relief.

By this time, unemployment had soared to 16 percent, and prospects for Bert's reelection grew dimmer. Talk even circulated of a divided Republican party. Yet there was no direct connection between Lou Hoover's Rapidan Plan for Girl Scout relief work and Herbert Hoover's reelection efforts. The timing of the first lady's programmatic innovation reveals the failure of White House relief efforts and of her moribund public marriage. The pressures of the presidency proved unrelenting for Bert, but he rarely leaned on Lou for policy support. Although their private relationship remained unscathed, neither Lou nor Bert took the necessary steps to reprise the public partnership that had worked so well during the Great War. Greater cooperation between the East Wing and the West Wing could not have hurt and might have helped implement the various voluntary relief strategies the two Hoovers employed against the depression.

In the fall of 1931, the first lady called together her most trusted confidantes to function as a brain trust or think tank. Their task, according to Hoover, was to draft a Girl Scout position paper with significant public policy potential. Lou asked Abbie Rickard's advice about having the Girl Scout executive committee meet at her family's Blue Ridge Mountain retreat, Camp Rapidan. The two women worked closely in devising the agenda for the weekend gathering, where Girl Scout leaders would formalize the strategy for Scouting relief work. For once realizing the importance of publicity, Hoover asked Rickard, "if we have pictures shall we be in uniform?" Hoover knew that "movie people are very anxious to take a picture at camp of the first meeting."[48] Indeed, the various newspaper photographs of Hoover and her Girl Scout colleagues showed the women in their uniforms, indicating that Hoover understood the importance of using an image to push her policy agenda.

Certainly, when news of the meeting reached Hoover's wider circle of confidantes, much praise was sent to the White House. For example, Sue Dyer described the invitation to the Girl Scouts' national board as "a very wise and clever move."[49] Sixteen executive committee members agreed to attend the 23 September 1931 meeting at Camp Rapidan, including Harriet Barnes, Genevieve Brady, Ann Hyde Choate, Birdsall Edey, Lillian Gilbreth, Mira Hoffman, and Abbie Rickard. Six regional representatives confirmed their attendance, along with members of the national headquarters staff.

The rustic camping experience at Rapidan included sufficient household help, revealing much about Hoover's entertaining style and her priorities for the September conference. Hoover made sure that her guests understood that they needed to "tell a Filipino boy before hand, or ask the orderly at the 'office,'" for any individual assistance required in their cabins. Hoover arranged for the Town Hall, located in the center of the camp, to function as "the place of general meeting for anything from Executive Committee Meeting to ping pong and knitting." Guests were advised to "follow your nose's guidance or the movement of the population" to the Mess Hall. To keep warm on cold evenings, guests were instructed to "put on your camelshair dressing gown, wrap your head in a sweater, and throw your fur coat over everything" if blankets and down comforters were not sufficient. Hoover did not want her guests at Rapidan to know that she had planned the arrangements "with great care!" She indicated, "I would much rather it seemed that it was hit and miss."[50] Indeed, Hoover hoped that the natural setting would prove conducive to successful policy deliberation.

One Scout leader told Hoover that the Rapidan meeting "was full of inspiration." Specifically, "Dr. Gilbreth's resume of the unemployment program was so simple and direct I feel convinced we can

all get from it ways to help." No known record exists of Gilbreth's remarks, but her observations obviously impressed the Scouts. Another participant explained: "Then the last evening at the meeting in
the 'Town Hall,' you were wearing a most becoming pink-woolen
ensemble and knitting on a little green sweater, but as Mrs. Gilbreth
told of the unemployment situation and the relief that would be
necessary, you laid aside your knitting and became vitally interested.
I'm sure, right then, we all vowed to ourselves, to work much harder
at helping others and at trying to do good girl scouting." After the
1931 meeting at Camp Rapidan, Flora Whiting told Hoover, "[Abbie
and I] started early Friday morning with a visit to the Scout Headquarters, fired with new enthusiasm. In Westchester County I have
already planned having some of the unemployed women make and
repair clothing for the unemployed. We are going to the department
stores in the County and asking for material that is out of date."[51]
Such reactions reveal the success of Hoover's activist appeals.

If the Rapidan Plan was to transform Scouting, wide dissemination among Scout leaders would be needed. Hoover had purposefully timed the executive meeting that drafted the plan to precede
the annual convention, hoping to build the momentum necessary
for success. In preparation for the Girl Scouts' 1931 national convention, Hoover asked whether there would be time for Lillian Gilbreth
to address the delegates. The first lady hoped that Gilbreth's remarks
could supplement the "excellent report" from Genevieve Brady on
"depression activities for Girl Scouts."[52]

Hoover herself spoke before the national convention in Buffalo
on 14 October 1931 about how the Scouts could use the Rapidan Plan
to transform the world. Attired in a Scout uniform, the first lady
talked for about eleven minutes, and the National Broadcasting
Company transmitted her remarks over the radio. She noted, "I am
here just to listen to you these days," but clearly she intended to
challenge the Girl Scouts to rise to new heights during the economic crisis of the depression. "This is a year for us to take stock of
the serious side of Girl Scouting, of its much encouraged 'service,'"
argued Hoover. She listed the various ways that Scouting, more
than any other entity, prepared its charges for adult responsibilities:
"for years now, we have seen our theories justified as the maturing
Girl Scouts meet their growing responsibilities of citizenship and

of homemaking. This year gives us an excellent opportunity to prove that they will also meet their responsibilities of service." Hoover hoped that "in this year of trial and depression," Girl Scouts would "take, individually and collectively," a significant role in the "alleviation" of the crisis. She continued, "there has, as yet, been no general program for this winter advanced for the organization as a whole. This is the first considerable meeting of the Girl Scout leaders since the days of strenuous need have been upon us."[53]

In the rest of her speech, Hoover celebrated what individual troops were already doing for depression relief. She noted that troops in more affluent areas had already "taken a positive part in the actual supplying of necessities where needed." Similarly, in troops with significant economic stratification, "those with means were helping the less fortunate in a truly sisterly fashion." The first lady reported that the various troops in one particular urban area "had pledged themselves to see that no [local] Girl Scout should be in want of food, warmth, medical care, or the necessities of clothing and books to make school attendance possible." Those Scouts, according to Hoover, hoped to ensure the economic well-being of the impoverished Scouts' families as well. She contended, "This would be no small relief to the community chest of that city!"[54]

Girl Scout troops, according to Hoover, undertook sewing and knitting bees, the canning and drying of fruits and vegetables, and rummage sales to aid the destitute. "Some troops in localities fortunate as to employment were 'adopting' Girl Scout troops from less fortunate areas," she noted. "There was a troop taking care of the children of some mothers who had found work when the other wage earners of their families were temporarily unemployed. Great numbers were helping where and how they could in the efforts of the adult relief measures of their own communities." Troops without the resources to assist others helped "keep up 'the morale' of one another, their families, of the communities" by sponsoring activities such as local talent nights to replace trips to the movies. Hoover argued that such amusements brought "joy into a sad neighborhood," causing her to wonder, "who can say that this is not giving as vitally as is the giving of food and of clothing?"[55]

Scouts working under the aegis of the Rapidan Plan cooperated with the President's Organization on Unemployment Relief but channeled their efforts through the twelve Scout regions. Said one chronicler of Scouting history, they did "work that could not be done so effectively by any other group; that would avoid conflict between the regular and the emergency activities and contribute finally to the character-building which was the primary Girl Scout objective." Following Hoover's lead, Scouts divided their charitable work into four categories: food, clothing, medical care, and Christmas relief. Administrators of the effort ensured that Scout work augmented existing relief operations instead of competing with them. The mixture of priorities—from sustaining the basic necessities of life to providing spiritual and cultural fulfillment—reflects Hoover's commitment not only to relief from suffering but also to the preservation of community values and civic-mindedness, which she feared were endangered by both the depression and the onslaught of modernity.[56]

After the convention was over, Lou Henry Hoover continued to press for increased community service, despite the fact that the media paid scant attention to her Rapidan Plan. She told an Ottawa, Kansas, troop: "the spirit of service in every Girl Scout's heart will lead her to rise to the emergency of our country's present need." A Benton Harbor, Michigan, Girl Scout troop incorporated the Rapidan Plan into its fall and winter 1931 activities. A local newspaper described the troop as "Santa's helpers." According to a member of the troop, "My captain said the last meeting before Christmas that she heard you speak over the radio so I don't know if that is where she got the idea of serving for the Welfare." In addition to making Christmas gifts for the needy, this troop planned "to help the city to make baby clothes for the poor." Other components of the Rapidan Plan included community fruit and vegetable canning projects, school breakfast and lunch programs, lectures on household economy measures, and health care services through hospitals and visiting nurses.[57]

Although troop members responded to Hoover's call, they could never realistically hope to solve the problems of the depression by themselves. Still, Girl Scout officials and students of the organization termed the Rapidan Plan "an immediate success." Membership increased at least in part because the organization communicated a message of relevance in the face of economic crisis, and Scouts thrived in relief work. Between 1931 and 1932, membership rose almost 20,000, from 276,855 to 295,940. Thus, Lou Hoover's plan must be judged a success, for it encouraged thousands of young women to remember the less fortunate in their communities. Hoover's innovative thinking reveals the scant policy options available to her and her creative efforts to transcend these limitations. That her Rapidan Plan did not combat the Great Depression for all its victims matters less than its many local, individual successes and its institution of a community-service ethos among the young women who carried out the plan.[58]

Despite these successes, concern about the depression and how Girl Scouts might help ameliorate the nation's economic woes remained paramount for Hoover. In a speech that was later broadcast over a nationwide radio network, Lou Hoover told the Girl Scout convention on 7 October 1932 that notions of "being friends to all" and "doing a good turn daily" had "become so interwoven in the pattern of our consciousness that they are a real, an almost instinctive, motivation for Girl Scouts." She celebrated the accomplishments of Girl Scouts in the field of depression relief even before the announcement of the Rapidan Plan, noting the extent of their activities. As a result, she explained, "the whole relation of Girl Scouting to national distress,—which really is always local,—was seriously studied." For Hoover, the most rewarding feature of the Rapidan Plan was "the national impetus of the girls themselves" in embracing depression-induced community service.[59]

She reported, "during the last year, Girl Scouts have not only carried out suggestions made, but have themselves made splendid contributions in thinking through many ways of helping. The most interesting thing is that they have found if they could help other groups to help people, it did more for their morale than anything else." Among the work the Scouts undertook as part of the Rapidan Plan was orphanage relief work and assistance to the elderly. Hoover told the convention delegates, though, "that grandmothers were more anxious to give than to receive." She argued that the "effectiveness" of the Rapidan Plan resulted in an increased volume of invitations to Scout troops "to participate in plans for relief and recreation this winter. This means that our work will be much more serviceable because it will be better coordinated with other service work being done in the community." The nationwide radio talk was billed as a "non-partisan address to the young people of the country."[60]

Relief efforts by individual troops continued the following year. In December 1932, Hoover received an invitation to visit the Washington, D.C., Girl Scouts and inspect "their gifts for the less fortunate." In 1931, that troop had made between 1,500 and 2,000 garments to be given away. One of the local leaders observed that the "donations are a very real contribution to Christmas cheer." Hoover's staff marked the invitation as "important."[61]

Although Hoover certainly viewed such activities as vital, her Rapidan Plan probably did more for the young women who participated in it than it did to address the national economic malady. Lou Hoover's plans for voluntary relief, though admirable, were not sufficient by themselves; however, they were never intended to function independent of other relief operations. Even though the New Deal proved to be a much more successful remedy for privation than was Hoover's voluntary activism, it did not bring about full recovery from the Great Depression. Both approaches—the voluntary activism of the Hoover years, as embodied in the Rapidan Plan, and the government activism of the Roosevelt years, as embodied in the New Deal—involved a philosophy of social organization and values that attempted to address economic and social modernity. The former sought to lessen the emphasis on aggressively consumerist approaches to competition and to foster cooperative, communitarian values, whereas the latter sought a government solution to ensure the economic status quo. Society's rejection of the economic, political, and value systems that Lou Henry Hoover favored caused much bitterness in the former first lady.

For Hoover, the end of her husband's presidency also meant a slight shift in her relationship with the Girl Scouts. Hoover told Brady, "Of course I have been joking with different members of the Board about not letting them drop me from the Board. But it was only joking. I had no doubt that they will make me an Honorary Vice President as they did Mrs. Coolidge! I don't remember what the constitution provides, but I hope I may go to Board meetings and do all the talking I want!" In her official letter of resignation as honorary president, written in January 1933, Hoover observed, "during the time I have served in this capacity, the thought of this association has always been a very pleasant one. But the other duties devolving upon me have compelled me to forgo much of the real work with the Girl Scouts. However, now I am looking forward to a more active participation in their affairs in the future."[62]

Girl Scout executives were understandably saddened about the power shift in Washington, D.C. Brady told Hoover, "It is to be my painful duty to go to Mrs. Roosevelt about being the Honorary Chairman. You know our personal feelings do enter into things in spite of our trying to think just of our organization."[63] For Lou Henry Hoover, being a former first lady meant that she would have more time for Girl Scouting and the other voluntary activity to which she was committed. Being in the White House had caused her to redirect many of her energies toward entertaining, but at the same time, she had broadened the scope of her office beyond the narrow ambitions of her predecessors. Her work with Girl Scouts was the best example of that shift.

Hoover took a significant, if unheralded, women's voluntary organization that had mushroomed in the United States since World War I and gave its operations a larger political and social purpose. By using the Girl Scouts to try to combat the ill effects of modernity and the depression, Hoover reminded Americans of the importance of community service in their increasingly anonymous, urban world. Girl Scout officials implicitly recognized Hoover's concerns and accomplishments in the *Girl Scout Annual Report for 1933:* "In these times of social and economic change, the need for a citizenry more conscious of civic responsibility becomes increasingly apparent. It is, therefore, especially significant to note that, as a result of their contact with various organizations, Girl Scouts are becoming more interested in civic affairs; are playing a greater part in community activities, and are influencing their parents to participate also."[64] This glowing evaluation described a reality so idealistic that it never completely materialized. Hoover nonetheless deserves credit for attempting to inspire the better angels among America's younger generation.

CHAPTER 5

LOU HENRY HOOVER IN PUBLIC AND PRIVATE

Midway through the Hoover presidency, Grace Coolidge remarked to Lou Henry Hoover, "I hope we may get together sometime and really tell one another what we think and feel. Perhaps 'twere *better to* wait until we are both private citizens and *feel* that we have jurisdiction over our own tongues."[1] Coolidge's comments emphasized the strains and pressures that Hoover experienced as first lady. From the outbreak of war in 1914, Hoover emerged as an important activist within the voluntary and philanthropic community. Well known in those circles, she nonetheless preferred anonymity in her private life. Becoming first lady meant not only that she had less time for work with the Girl Scouts and other causes but also that the media sought access to more of her private life.

Coolidge's comment accurately reflected the constraints that bound first ladies in the early twentieth century. Although the suffrage movement specifically and the women's movement generally had remade gender roles for average, middle-class women, first ladies were still expected to adhere to traditional feminine behavior; first ladies were to be ornamental, ceremonial counterparts to their political husbands. Lou Henry Hoover never possessed those characteristics. Arbiters of public opinion did not welcome comment from a president's spouse on substantive issues, but Lou Hoover had made numerous public speeches prior to 1929. Previous first ladies had never given formal public talks, especially on the radio, yet Hoover broke that precedent many times while in the White House. These contradictions made the problem of image and identity much more intense for Hoover than it had been for previous first ladies. Put simply, her media strategy was embedded with contradictions: she revolutionized what a first lady could do with mass communication but never fully appreciated how to convert the media into an ally in the administration's fight against the depression.

Lou Henry Hoover modernized the office of the first lady between 1929 and 1933. She advocated public policy, spoke on the radio, and carved out new terrain for presidential spouses, but Hoover did so while respecting the social obligations handed down from an earlier generation. Since she covered her garb of activism with the cloak of traditionalism, and since her husband's presidency failed, the country never had the opportunity to recognize or appreciate the benefits of her public works. Because she despised self-aggrandizement, Hoover avoided discussion of her charitable endeavors or her private life. She nonetheless used the media in innovative ways to advance projects less directly associated with her. Finally, since the depression had almost destroyed her public marriage with Bert, she could no longer retreat to the safety of joint ventures to satisfy her humanitarian ethos. Because the Hoovers had grown accustomed to acting independently, and because she faced the limitations of her position, Lou Hoover crafted a new style of activism different from that which she had employed in the 1910s and 1920s. The irony, then, of her years in the White House was that while she expanded the policy options for first ladies, she also encountered a restricted public agenda compared with her pre-1929 activities.

Despite the ruination of her public marriage, Lou retained a very strong matrimonial bond with Bert. The traditions of family sustained Lou Hoover when an increasingly critical media offered no peace. According to close friends and colleagues, the Hoovers "were a very affectionate couple." When greeting each other, they hugged and kissed without "demonstrating too much." Lou Hoover worried quite a bit about her husband. After each of Herbert Hoover's speeches, Lou telegraphed him laudatory assessments, much like Lady Bird Johnson would do years later for Lyndon Johnson. The first lady, according to Philippi Butler, was "more of an extrovert," whereas the president "was quite reserved, but with a nice sense of humor and real warmth in his relationships with friends and associates."[2]

Lou Hoover emphasized work on behalf of children, especially girls, sometimes to the exclusion of other pertinent issues. One colleague contended that if Lou had not made her life into a public partnership with Bert, she likely would have been the president of a women's college or a progressive school. In fact, the majority of her public speeches were to youthful constituencies. Hoover stayed out of the more political arena. For example, when Lou's good friends from Stanford, Jessie and David Starr Jordan, requested that her office schedule a visit between the first lady and a California representative of the Women's International League for Peace and Freedom and the National Council for the Prevention of War, Hoover's official secretary replied: "in Mrs. Hoover's present position as wife of the President of the United States she can not receive anyone sponsoring causes which are international in scope, all communications concerning such matters being automatically considered by the Department of State."[3]

Because the public spotlight was so intense, there is no one perfect source from which to glean information about Lou Henry Hoover. She garnered a reputation for never giving interviews about herself, and she preferred not to talk to the press unless speaking on behalf of a particular cause. Her reticence stemmed from a number of journalistic miscues in the years before her husband's presidency. She was so guarded in her public and private statements that even her closest associates knew only certain aspects of her personality. A friend of Hoover's, possibly Dare Stark McMullin, wrote a revealing essay about the first lady designed to "tell me what she's really like." In the piece, the author indicated that the best way to learn about Hoover's personality was to visit her, which was, of course, impossible. She noted, "nor can the wife of the President of the United States come forward and explain what she is like, though that is a very pertinent part of her husband's fitness for his job." The writer noted, "that admitted impossibility, by the way, must be a comfort to Mrs. Hoover," who valued her privacy so much that she "has never given an interview in her life except on some impersonal subject she has been very keen on. What she would do if she had, by custom, to talk about herself I just don't know. She and the interviewer would be on some other subject so fast no-one would know how they got there."[4]

Nonetheless, said one journalist after the 1928 election, "Mrs. Hoover is a favorite with newspaper women." These words of praise resulted because the soon-to-be first lady "mingles with woman writers and gives them every opportunity to use their own wits and judgment." A female journalist reported that although Hoover was open with the press, "it greatly displeases her to have her little philanthropies and acts of kindness and charity discussed." Still, "in an almost girlish manner," Hoover invited the Women's National Press Club to a garden tea party in late 1928, where she "answered their dozens of questions, but refused, as she laughingly said, 'to be quoted.'" Always cautious about how her words might be used in print, Hoover understood "that the price of residence in the White House is the loss of liberty and freedom of speech and action, or if not of liberty, at least of privacy."[5]

That point was borne out when reporter Bess Furman disguised herself as a Girl Scout to get a story about the 1930 White House Christmas party for children. To carry out this plot, Furman sought the help of Gertrude Bowman, then an official with the Girl Scout Little House in Washington, D.C. Bowman provided Furman with a uniform because she thought that the planned news story would benefit the Girl Scouts and the Hoovers' public reputation. In furtherance of the charade, Furman removed all her makeup and stuffed her hair under the uniform's cap. Such alterations were necessary because Furman found herself face-to-face with several White House staff members that she knew well. Standing taller than any of the forty authentic Girls Scouts, Furman hid herself in the back row of the chorus. She had difficulty, however, with the hymn "Good King Wenceslas," which was not among the repertoire of Christmas carols she had learned as a child in the Midwest. "I gave up trying to make my jaws move in rhythm, and concentrated on trying to memorize the scene before my eyes," recounted Furman. "And so it was that I was able accurately to record the charming Hoover custom whereby the youngest boy and youngest girl present rank highest on Christmas Eve and, with the President and First Lady, lead the grand march to the dinner table." Lou Hoover, who never learned of the deceit, deemed the news story to be "very nice."[6]

Often when speaking with reporters, Hoover asked that they sit cross-legged on the floor, as would the members of a Girl Scout troop. The request resulted from Hoover's policy never to give formal media interviews but instead to discuss issues related to her favorite organization in the most informal of settings. Only female journalists, though, sat on the floor. Male journalists stood in the rear of the room. From her chair, the first lady used the seating arrangements as a control mechanism to govern access to information. Hoover believed that the ban on formal interviews protected her from unwarranted intrusions into her privacy while allowing her the freedom to discuss subjects of her choosing, but in reality, it only furthered an unflattering public image. Hoover would have been better served had she simply acknowledged such discussions as formal press conferences instead of disguising them as Girl Scout troop meetings.

Newspaper writers were not her only concern. Mary Austin's 1932 book *Earth Horizons* troubled Hoover because it exemplified her lack of control over what was said about her in print. It depicted Lou as a social failure and Bert as incapable of converting an idea into action. As she explained to her son Allan, "The insinuations she tries to make would be amusing but for the fact that some people will magnify them and believe them." The Hoovers had socialized with Mary Austin prior to the Great War, but as Lou explained, Bert became "so completely engrossed in [the war] that he could not squander even a few minutes of time, intellectually, on my" friends and acquaintances. An angry Austin "waged a guerilla warfare whenever opportunity offered against either or both of us."[7]

The realities of the media made contact with friends all the more important to Lou Hoover, but even before her husband was inaugurated, she felt inundated by the mail she received. Because it was nearly impossible for her to read even the correspondence from her close friends, family members, and voluntary association colleagues, she counseled individuals such as Evelyn Wight Allen, with whom she most wanted to have contact, to "slip [their letters] into another envelop saying on the outside 'Personal to Mrs. Hoover from Mrs. Allen,' and put that in an envelop addressed to me. (And don't tell anyone else but your most intimate friends that this is the way to reach me, or I'll be swamped with all sorts of letters from all sorts of people!)"[8]

Hoover, though, was unwilling to let the demands of her social correspondence limit her public activities entirely. To counter the problem, she employed modern technology, specifically the Dictaphone, to increase her efficiency in tackling the mail. Hoover even arranged for a similar machine to be sent to Grace Coolidge so that her last days in the White House might be less hectic. However, Mary Randolph, Coolidge's secretary, responded that Coolidge "feels that just now she has not time to devote to a proper study of its intricacies, and so she will not put you to the trouble of having the dictaphone brought here."[9] This exchange reveals much about the difference between the two women and the changes Hoover would bring to her post as first lady. Hoover was much more experimental and adventurous than her predecessor as she prepared to enter the White House.

After she became first lady, Hoover maintained a close friendship with Grace Coolidge. Coolidge told Hoover, "I follow you in the pictures and in the printed word with keen interest. It is great to be an *Ex*—not the 'X' of the unknown quantity—but the ex of experience."[10] Interestingly, Lou Hoover's correspondence with the former first lady rarely included requests for advice. Instead, Lou used Grace as a safe sounding board to whom she could describe the problems of her position. Rare were the women and men who could relate to Lou's difficult duties, so correspondence with Grace provided that outlet.

By 1929, modern technology set the stage for innovation as broadcasters hoped to get the first lady to make a radio speech. Lou Henry Hoover seemed a likely precedent setter because she had delivered countless public talks in the years before her husband became president. Insecurity about her speaking voice, though, sometimes made her hesitate, and Hoover had once declared the prospect "too appalling to consider." Broadcasters had lobbied Grace Coolidge to give a radio talk, and although she enjoyed the new medium of communication and entertainment, she opted not to break the precedent that a first lady should never "make a set speech." Journalists who were debating whether Hoover would prove more accommodating noted that she had made one broadcast "a year or so ago." The 24 March 1928 remarks had been entitled "Feeding the Children," and they previewed themes she would explore in detail as first lady. Indeed, on 19 April 1929, just a month after her husband's inauguration, Lou Hoover made a "gracious little speech." Her radio address for the Daughters of the American Revolution celebrated the dedication of Constitution Hall.[11] In this way, Lou Hoover entered new territory for first ladies while remaining true to the ceremonial constraints of the post. Yet as her White House tenure unfolded, Hoover would make substantive radio speeches about matters of public policy.

A few weeks after her husband's inauguration, Hoover established another precedent for first ladies. While hosting a group of geologists at the White House, she delivered a professional talk based on her training at Stanford University to a group of 400 to 500 members of the Geological Survey, an organization commemorating its golden jubilee. Although she felt "entirely at home in the company of geologists," the first lady recognized that the theory and procedures of the field had progressed since her training in the 1890s.[12] She acted in an accomplished, professional manner, but when she spoke, she camouflaged her intellectual and scientific abilities.

In May 1929, Hoover agreed to address the 4-H Club members being entertained by the Department of Agriculture in Washington, D.C. These young people were the outstanding 4-H Club members in their states, with each state sending no more than four representatives. Officials at the Department of Agriculture wrote Hoover's speech for her, prompting her secretary to respond, "without doubt she will encompass all the points given in these drafts. I am more than sure that she will put these ideas in her own words as I have never known her to give a speech prepared by anyone else."[13]

The Radio Corporation of America broadcast her talk nationwide, but it almost did not happen. The day before the address was scheduled, Hoover decided to deliver it from a remote connection at Camp Rapidan. The engineers made every effort to string the necessary wires, but thirty minutes before the broadcast, all signals from the camp were lost. Thus, Hoover delivered her address from a tent in the middle of a rainstorm, complete with thunder and lightning. Her second radio speech reached approximately 700,000 4-H Club members in the United States and Hawaii.

This breakthrough speech contained a thoughtful analysis of how social roles for boys and girls should evolve. Officials in the Agriculture Department termed Hoover's rewrite of the speech "very

very fine," saying that it "couldn't be better." She began her remarks by celebrating the spirit and experience of camping: "there is an inimitable deep refreshment in sleeping out of doors. I think the very best sleep of all, snakes and ants and such permitting,—is that which I can have with only a strip of canvas between my blankets and the ground, and nothing between my head and the stars."[14]

Hoover praised the "simplicity" of camp life, complete with "its primitive factors. In its most limited resources we find all the elements of home,—of a satisfactory home or an unsatisfying one. In it we can make a bed comfortable or uncomforting; we can prepare the simplest food in a manner appetizing or repellant. We can arrange it before us in a beauty of symmetry and cleanliness, or in an inchoate mess of unattractiveness."[15] Such views, though perhaps unexpected from an elite women such as Hoover, were entirely in keeping with her rugged individualism and thus were nonthreatening to her audience.

She then compared these realities of the camping experience with those of "home-making" in such a way as to challenge accepted gender roles for men and women. "Girls and boys in home-making and farm accomplishment,—that is what you are, isn't it?" asked Hoover. "I say that very deliberately,—especially the juxtaposition of the 'boys and homemaking' parts." She recounted for her audience the agricultural chores routinely performed by women and then asserted an even more important point—that "every boy and man" had within himself the power to "help or hinder in homemaking." She asked the boys in her audience to reflect on their role in the home. "*Can* or *do you* do anything, in your home today or in one you think possible in the future, to help *make* it a home?" asked the first lady. She defined myriad tasks—painting, carpentry, dishwashing, cleaning, and decorating—as appropriate homemaking tasks in which men should regularly participate. To further challenge male thinking about gender roles, Hoover suggested, "Just as surely . . . it is 'farming' when the girl provides good meals and clean comfortable beds and healthful, well-ventilated, pleasant rooms; for that *is* helping with the farm work, for without these things a lower percentage of farm work would be done."[16]

Still, Hoover wanted the boys in her audience to understand that her message was mainly for them. She hoped young men would realize that the "spirit" with which they approached homemaking was far more important than "those material ways that you do your share in homemaking." Taken together, her remarks advocated an equitable, egalitarian approach to homemaking. "Cheerfulness, consideration of others, appreciativeness, a recognition of the accomplishment of others, an interest in the concerns of others, punctuality, dependableness, helpfulness, and a score of other characteristics *you* can name," argued the first lady, "all these make a home,—otherwise it stops being a 'home' and becomes some kind or another of a 'boarding house.' Boys,—remember, you are just as great factors in the *homemaking* of the family as are the girls. And remember too, that the *spirit* of your contribution is of even greater worth than the material value of it."[17] Her remarks, which were laden with plans for how American gender roles could and should be remade, proved much more substantive than the radio address she had given the previous month on behalf of the Daughters of the American Revolution.

Several days after her talk, the chief of the Extension Service for the Agriculture Department told Hoover, "in almost a single day, your acts have made the 4-H Club movement known throughout the United States and beyond the seas." Hoover received equally positive reviews from the campers themselves. She agreed that the department could use her talk for further publicity purposes, but she wanted it made known that she did not "consider this talk in the nature of a prepared 'address' at all. It was just a hastily constructed little after-dinner talk to the boys and girls, and we would not want anyone to think that it was the result of many hours of labor—or considered an 'address'!"[18]

Jane Deeter Rippin told Hoover, "We all enjoyed so much your radio speech on Saturday night. Everyone was listening in. . . . Your voice was so clear that we had a feeling we were sitting just outside your tent listening to your talk." Later Hoover worked with Rippin on the production of a Girl Scout film. This task was not at all contradictory for the publicity-shy first lady, because the Girl Scouts benefited, not her husband or herself. Rippin told Hoover, "You have been so generous that I hesitate to remind you of our conversation regarding the motion picture the *Girl Scout Trail* and the possibility of its first showing at your home."[19]

After viewing the film, Hoover "hastily asked in the members of the Girl Scout Council" to watch it with her again at the White

House. As she explained to Rippin, "I made no comments on the picture at all, but simply told them that it had been produced by some National Leaders and was up for discussion at present. We made very few remarks about it while it was being shown, but when it was finished, I suggested that they all jot roughly down their impressions before we talked to each other about it." Among the group's objections were "too great self-Scout-consciousness to the child who observes it," combined with concern that "the adult observer" would conclude "we were endeavoring to instill an impossible priggishness or smugness in the children."[20] Such involvement indicates not only Hoover's continued commitment to the Girl Scouts but also her use of her position as first lady to advance those causes vital to the country's well-being. Further, her work with the film reveals an understanding of the media that was not apparent when she herself was the topic of discussion.

Although Hoover's retreat from the public spotlight resulted in a lessening of her public activism, she remained a strong figure within her immediate and her extended family. As she had done for years, Lou kept a watchful eye out for her sister Jean's family. Hoover paid close attention to her niece Janet Large's college application process, inquiring about Swarthmore's admission requirements, evaluating Janet's high school grades, and overseeing her study habits.

More serious problems ensued for Lou's son Herbert Jr., who contracted tuberculosis in 1930. Lou told her sister about the plans for her son's treatment and recovery, which included spending the warmer months at Camp Rapidan and the cooler months in Asheville, North Carolina. The newspapers reported that the first family was "having investigations made all over the country" to discern the best sanatoriums, but Lou told Jean that between the White House physician and the Baltimore specialist, such research was unnecessary. Ultimately, Herbert remained on the East Coast because "we have discovered that Bert is going to be so restless if Herbert is west that as much for his father as for him we want them to be near together."[21]

When queried by the press about Herbert Jr.'s condition, Lou Hoover responded, "My son is getting along nicely. He just needs to rest up for a while and put on a little weight." Said White House physician Joel Boone, Herbert Jr. suffered from "a mild tubercular infection." The Hoovers used their son's malady to educate the public about tuberculosis, and Boone noted, "The modern conception of tuberculosis, when diagnosed early and properly treated, is not viewed with alarm. It is believed that in a case of this sort a complete cure results when such course is pursued." His treatment involved a year's sabbatical from all business activity. For the duration of Herbert Jr.'s confinement, his three children lived in the White House. Lou Hoover became angry when one newspaper ran a story indicating that the White House was "no playhouse" for her grandchildren, noting in pen at the end of the article, "just not one word of 'fact' in it!"[22]

Protecting her family from inappropriate media exposure occupied Lou's days both during and after the 1928 presidential campaign. Although she realized that images of her family must be made available for public dissemination, she ensured that certain "sentimental" photographs were withheld from the press. Such control tactics almost guaranteed that the public would never see the human side of the president. Lou gave meticulous directions to her assistant about the release of family photographs: "We are very sorry that we can't give them permission to release any that have the babies in, or the one of Herbert with his father's portrait." Photographic studios that took pictures of the Hoover family hoped to offer selected images to the press, and although Lou Hoover compromised with the studios that she believed had respected her privacy, she would not release photographs that might exploit private family bonds for the sake of public political acclaim. She explained, "we regret that [we cannot release certain photographs], because they have been so good about doing so many of them, and because they have not violated their trust,—particularly in regard to the babies,—as another firm has."[23]

Lou Hoover failed to understand that modern technology such as the radio and photography for publication had effectively narrowed the scope of privacy accorded not only to elected officials but also to their families. Both Lou and Bert lost valuable political capital at a moment in history when his administration was most in need of favorable public opinion. Isolating their very warm and loving family life from public view intensified Herbert Hoover's dour, uncaring image. Hints from friends that such exposure would be beneficial went unheeded.

Sue Dyer told Hoover, "You have no idea what a joy it is to occasionally hear a Hoover voice over radio. Last night, for example, the

President's broadcast was just perfect and when I heard 'Hail to the Chief,' I could just see the two of you leaving the hall." Positioned near these overlooked lines of advice, though, were other words of commiseration that reflected Hoover's increasing frustration with the media. "Every where I go I am asked how you are both standing it," wrote Dyer. "I wonder myself how you do keep your serenity."[24] Such views only reinforced Lou Hoover's inclination to maintain the sharp delineation between public and private views of her family.

Evelyn Allan told Hoover, "Like so many others of your friends, I watch the papers and marvel at all the President is doing to mitigate suffering in these hard times. I want so much to have his big heart catch the imagination of the people." She also praised a photograph in the 13 October 1930 *Time* magazine that depicted Bert receiving Lou on the back platform of a train. "I wish very much that that attitude of his had been flashed on the screen at the movies instead of the formal picture delivering an address in Boston," Allan stressed. "It is these intimate things that the people need just now, all of which the President would call 'sentimental' if I talked to him in this strain."[25]

Lou Hoover considered coverage of the family's private life exploitation. For example, when a tourist company purported to represent the true nature of the Henry family life in Monterey, the first lady was incensed. She learned of the situation from a friend and asked her sister to investigate and correct the misinformation. Lou Hoover fumed: "the first thing the professional arranger for tourists said to his party was, 'well, the very first thing you want to see is the house the Henrys lived in while Miss Henry taught school here,' — the whole idea being that Miss Henry taught school and the family came there to live on her bounty while she did it!"[26] Indeed, all such false representations of her life heightened Hoover's skepticism toward the media, even though, in this case, the majority of the fault lay with the local opportunists giving the tours.

Ironically, as the depression worsened and the Hoovers needed the press more than ever, Hoover retreated from all but the most specific and controlled media contact. Marie Mattingly Meloney, editor of the Sunday magazine for the *New York Herald Tribune,* sent an anonymous excerpt to Lawrence Richey from a member of the Women's Press Club in Washington and recommended that "it

would be a good idea if it is possible for something to be done officially for the Woman's Press Club by Mrs. Hoover." Apparently,
some female journalists felt snubbed by Hoover, especially when
compared with Grace Coolidge and Florence Harding, who had
hosted elaborate parties for the media. As this journalist explained,
Herbert Hoover, like his predecessors, routinely attended the Gridi-
ron Club dinners and was generally solicitous of male reporters.
Such was not the case, however, for female journalists during the
Hoover years. An anonymous female reporter told Meloney, "it is
difficult to exaggerate the resentment toward the White House felt
by the women who do newspaper work in Washington. I think it
isn't so much personal as professional." These media frustrations resulted because Lou Hoover did not "realize how much these things
mean to these women."[27]

Philippi Harding Butler investigated these charges for the West
Wing. She reported that none of the female officers or friends of the
Women's Press Club had requested an East Wing function. As a result, Lou Hoover and her staff believed that journalists would have
considered an invitation to be "a White House bid for publicity,—in
the interests of politics, if you wish!" According to Butler, Mary
Randolph, who remained as White House social secretary until 1930,
had arranged for Grace Coolidge to invite the club members to a tea
and a garden party. And earlier in the Hoover administration, Lou
Hoover, on Randolph's recommendation, had hosted the club officers at a tea party to balance the Cabaret Grill dinner at which Herbert Hoover had been a guest in February 1930.[28]

According to Butler, this unfounded criticism made Hoover's
social responsibilities all that more difficult to uphold, especially
since she had been contemplating just such a party prior to the re-
ceipt of the anonymous missive. Butler asserted that if the club's
officers agreed with the criticisms, "it would almost necessitate
Mrs. Hoover not giving the garden party invitation she had contemplated. It would quite take away from any spontaneity there
might be in such an invitation from her, if officers or friends of the
Club appeared to be holding her up for it!" Early that summer,
though, Hoover did host a garden party for female journalists, and
the following year, Hoover entertained a contingent of female journalists at Camp Rapidan just months before the 1932 presidential

election. In a two-paragraph story, a writer for the *Christian Science Monitor* contended, "the First Lady gave the news, publicity and fiction writers a glimpse of the personality she has insisted remain unexploited. The rule of confidence prevailing, Mrs. Hoover chatted in a lively manner."[29] Such affairs, though enjoyable for the guests, occurred so late in the administration that they had little impact. Had the Hoovers consistently used the press in this manner throughout the administration, more favorable public opinion could have been generated.

Journalists also criticized Hoover's radio performances in the fall of 1931. The *New York Times* intimated that her recorded remarks from a previous speech were "hardly audible" when "projected on movie screens." Such negative reviews caused Hoover to install a voice studio in the White House to practice her delivery of future radio speeches—another first for first ladies. Not long after she initiated these practice sessions, word leaked to the press. In November 1931, the White House investigated how members of the capital press corps had learned of Lou Hoover's secret "'talkie' voice tests." Revelations about the second-floor studio irritated the first lady and caused her to end the practice sessions. Typical of the reports was one in the *Times*, which suggested, "[Hoover] is seeking a method of speech and intonation that would make her voice record better." The unwanted publicity about her practice sessions caused Hoover to cancel the filming of a November 1931 talk before the 4-H Club. Ironically, just days before this round of stories, another journalist had noted that if Lou Hoover "were not the President's wife, but was merely an American woman looking for a job," she could have had a career in radio broadcasting, given her "'natural'" talent.[30]

Friends such as Lillian Gilbreth remained supportive: "your speech came over beautifully, all our love and thanks." Grace Coolidge told Hoover, "I heard you on the radio and liked everything you said and the way you said it." Small-town and local papers were equally praiseworthy. One newspaper writer commented after a Hoover radio address, "She possesses a highly cultured, well modulated voice. . . . We sincerely hope Lima clubwomen who read papers in sing-song, nasal droning voices, stumbling pronunciation and slurring vowels, heard the finished address of the gracious First Lady of Our Land."[31]

Despite these problems with the press, Lou Hoover took an active role in the 1932 campaign, often traveling with her husband. The contest was difficult because the depression had worsened, with unemployment at 24 percent on the eve of the election. Herbert Hoover's plummeting popularity, though, had no effect on perceptions of Lou Hoover. While traveling through Illinois on a train with her husband, she proved to be a crowd favorite. Her contradictory record of media involvement—conceiving new roles for the first lady while guarding her privacy—worked to her advantage with Republican audiences. The GOP loyalists needed someone to cheer, and Lou easily outstripped Bert in that two-person contest. More important, because she blended sometimes contradictory images of female behavior—independent woman, humanitarian activist, and traditional wife and mother—she appealed to a wide range of Americans without offending ideologues at either end of the spectrum regarding female comportment.

One journalist explained, "Cheers for the President had been none too enthusiastic, but when Mrs. Hoover appeared there was a spontaneous burst of applause." Such was the typical reception for the first family throughout the White House years. Said one journalist covering the contest, "Frequently she has preceded the President to the rear platform, and on every occasion she was clearly seeking to remove from his laden shoulders much of his burden. Mrs. Hoover follows every word of her husband's speeches. . . . Her lips seemed to read his speech with him."[32] A half century later, Nancy Reagan employed a similar technique.

Lou Henry Hoover's partisan activity involved much more than traveling with her husband. She was the first first lady to help plan campaign strategy and voter outreach efforts. Her work occurred behind the scenes with conservative women's organizations, specifically Pro-America, a group that originated in the Pacific Northwest and sought to increase voter participation among women. One year before her husband's reelection battle, Lou Hoover told a colleague, "[Pro-America] can be one of the best recruiting agencies for the regular Republican Clubs." She believed that such an organization would be attractive to "women who have been thus far non-politically minded" because of its focus on "'study'" groups as opposed to "strictly Party institution[s]." Hoover also hoped that careful analysis of public policy concerns would encourage more direct partisan, political action. She argued, "I feel very strongly that the officers and clubs of Pro America should have a very cordial, friendly relation with the regular Party Woman's Republican Clubs."[33] This work competed for Hoover's attention during the 1932 campaign season but became a crusade after her husband's defeat. Being first lady had heightened her interest in partisan politics, but respect for that post caused her to proceed cautiously.

Indeed, the first lady was a willing, if very private, supporter of partisan outreach. During the White House years, Hoover arranged to send Lenna Yost, a friend and GOP activist, a list of names of women that the Republican party could "depend [on] to reach other women." Likewise, Hoover directed her secretaries to pass political intelligence reports to Alice Dickson, a friend who had helped Hoover with her depression-related philanthropies and who followed up on these partisan items. Hoover realized, though, that public knowledge of her partisanship could be problematic. Thus, when individuals with no prior connection to the Hoovers queried the first lady about political matters, she had her secretary disguise her partisan behavior. Said one Hoover secretary, she "does not take an active part in politics at all, and it would, therefore, be impossible for her to advise you."[34]

Likewise, when Republican party officials presented Lou Henry Hoover to the public, the vehicle and the message were typically traditional. For example, when officials with the Republican National Committee wished to secure an article about Lou Hoover as a homemaker, Carol Hyatt suggested focusing on Hoover's management of Camp Rapidan, the Blue Ridge Mountain retreat built by the Hoover family: "since most of the reporters have been guests at the Rapidan Camp they will know at first hand how she puts her guests at ease and what has given her the reputation she has for being a perfect hostess." Hyatt hoped that Hoover would discuss with reporters such topics as the differences between summer and winter housekeeping at the camp, her daily household activities, and the various situations in which she had kept house.[35] Whether Hoover ever assisted with the preparation of such an article is unclear.

In other interactions with the press, Hoover remained traditional, at least outwardly. For example, in conjunction with her speech at the 1931 Girl Scout national convention, Hoover gave a rare formal interview to the press but specified that she would respond only to questions about the Girl Scouts. When a reporter tried to elicit her views on whether Herbert Hoover would seek reelection in 1932, Lou Hoover retorted, "Young man, I rarely give interviews and when I do the limit of time permits me to give them only on stated subjects. The stated subject today is Girl Scouts. I am afraid your question is not pertinent."[36]

Nevertheless, Lou Hoover occasionally discussed the depression with the media. She told a reporter for the *Washington Post* that women should continue to spend money for household items when feasible and cited the example of the White House, which needed new curtains: "I suppose the frayed edges might be cut and made to do. But the man in Washington who would make the new curtains is having a difficult time. An order for curtains for the White House windows—they are so awfully big—would be of considerable help to him." Journalists remained skeptical. An editor at the *San Diego Union* juxtaposed Lou Hoover's call for continued spending against Herbert Hoover's announcement that appropriations for the Navy Department would be cut by $61 million and asked, "if Mr. and Mrs. Hoover do not happen to agree as to the economics of recovery—which of them is right? We have no means of knowing what the women of this republic think about this question, but we have a comprehensive idea what the navy's answer would be." Other editorials disagreed with Hoover's advice to keep spending by posing the question, " 'Yeh, but what with?' "[37]

In her private correspondence, Lou Hoover sometimes showed a lack of sympathy for those affected by the depression. The commotion over the 1932 Bonus March, a political protest in which World War I veterans marched on Washington demanding fair and immediate compensation for their service, troubled her. She believed that veterans who faced "actual distress" should have their problems "met by local or state action . . . except insofar as their trouble is the direct effect of their service." Although she recognized that many local communities had failed to meet their obligations to impoverished veterans, just as they had with the poor generally, Hoover contended, "that, alas, is a matter of human failure,—and it would be no less great,—in fact it would be greater,—if all such relief were to depend on human nature as exerted through Federal Government instead of human nature exerted through local, county and state governments."[38] She blamed much of the recent discontent in Washington on individuals within the bonus movement, some of whom were not even veterans, whose purpose, she wrongly said, was to stir up discontent and to advocate communism.

She also defended her husband's decision to call out the federal troops to deal with the problem: "of course one has to remember that Washington has not the advantage of any other city in our country of being able to call upon a county or state police or militia for protection. There is nothing to back up the District police but the forces of the Federal Government," noted the first lady. "So the President was faced with the alternative of leaving the population of the District under the dictation of a mob of this sort, obeying directly communist and other irresponsible leaders, or of calling troops in for their protection."[39]

Hoover closed her observations by arguing against the bonus on principle: "I do not think that an able bodied man, unharmed by his service, now thirty-five years old, should have in adversity preferential treatment by reason of his enlistment, over a man twenty-eight years old, who was too young to have the opportunity of enlisting."[40] Such views reveal the manner in which the nation's economic crisis remade her attitude toward poverty and deprivation. Ironically, both Hoovers privately provided food, clothing, and bedding for the marchers, even as they publicly denounced their threat to democracy. Lou Henry Hoover's internal conflict between progressive-minded philanthropy and a conservative political ideology imploded after her husband was defeated in 1932, but her rightward-leaning politics was evident in the election contest that year.

In July 1932, after reading the "downright lying" of journalists sympathetic to the Democratic party, Lou Hoover typed an eight-page letter to her sons and her grandchildren countering the partisan argument that Herbert Hoover had spent his presidency trying to save the "bloated plutocrats" from the Great Depression. She contended that during his presidency, as he had during his entire adult life, Herbert Hoover had worked on behalf of the "little" or "common" or "forgotten" man, a class of the population that "had *never* been 'forgotten' *by him*!" Said Lou Hoover, partisan opponents decried the indirect assistance of the Reconstruction Finance Corporation, which provided loans to banks, railroads, and other large businesses to prevent their capitulation to the Great Depression. Lou Hoover defended the soundness of such relief measures: "these *must* in turn distribute it to the 'little man.' (And not only must they distribute it to him in wages and salaries or sales, but the actual ownership of most of them is very largely in the hands of 'little men' now,—in the shape of stocks and bonds. For more little men than big ones go down in these days when a big enterprise fails. And with the banks, the depositors lose as well.)" She contended that her husband had become president because he believed that "he could give more opportunity to the least privileged classes of our communities than he could from any other point." Still, she found much of domestic politics to be "utterly rotten."[41]

As Hoover watched the progress of the campaign nationally, she paid special attention to California. This interest, though, was never sufficient to motivate her to return home. Lou told her sister, "the idea of our going West for a short time for Bert to accept the nomination was just the figment of some newspaper writer's imagination, or the dream of some politician who was thinking more of California than the welfare of the nation." Sue Dyer kept Hoover posted on presidential politics back home: "I can't help but wish that the State Central Committee had more push to it. A friend of mine went over to Oakland one day last week trying to locate the Republican Campaign Headquarters and was told that there was none." Hoover asked Dyer whether the State Central Committee had "greatly augmented" its activities. She was curious whether enough headquarters had been opened in the state and what the focus of each one was. Speaking of concerns in Oakland, Hoover declared, "Perhaps it is a headquarters carrying on for some local officers and paying no attention to the Presidential campaign?" Later, she indicated that "California should take care of itself and let him stay on here to take care of the many enormous problems that he has."[42] Hoover's divided loyalties—desiring GOP success in California, but also concerned about her husband's workload as president and as candidate for reelection—made it difficult for her to discern effective campaign strategy.

Dare McMullin, one of Lou's assistants, told Alice Dickson that the first lady would deliver a national radio address the evening of

Thursday, 13 October, intended for Girl and Boy Scout leaders, "but equally interesting to other adults and young people." In this effort to publicize Hoover's talk so that it would achieve maximum political benefit, McMullin had to be very careful in her promotional efforts. She told Dickson, "I thought you might like to tell some of your groups but of course it is essentially not political material and Girl Scouts must not be embarrassed by having it politically announced. Will you emphasize [the] latter part to anyone at your present headquarters who becomes interested."[43]

Mechanical problems prevented the live transmission of Lou Hoover's speech about women's role in depression relief to the Girl Scout leaders' convention in Virginia Beach, but Hoover repeated her performance for national broadcast purposes. Mildred Hall insisted to Lenna Yost that any mention of the broadcast must avoid talk of the looming political contest to "not embarrass the Girl Scouts." Yost assured Hall, "Happy to know about the broadcast of Our Lady. We are sending out the word to many of our friends, but in no way political. It is splendid that we are to have this speech broadcast, as so many were disappointed in not hearing it before."[44]

Declarations that the speech was not political stemmed from two interconnected beliefs: preference for an elite, male version of formal political debate that excluded the socially focused female style of political intercourse, and a circumscribed, traditional role for first ladies. Nonetheless, when Lou Henry Hoover issued the clarion call to American women to become active in the local politics of relief, she pursued the same course of partial activism that marked her years as first lady. In the midst of the depression and a bitterly partisan campaign, it proved attractive only to those Republicans already devoted to party and president.

Hoover believed that Girl Scouting was one method for combating the depression, and her radio comments urging women of all ages to function as agents of relief in their local communities provided fodder for others. Listener feedback on the speech suggested that the "nonpartisan" talk nonetheless had political impact. A Syracuse, New York, man said of the first lady, "I shall be able to use the material [in her speech] and the prestige of the speaker to great advantage during the Community Chest Campaign." An architect wrote to Hoover because he understood that she was "interested in

public welfare" and declared, "your inspiring speech over the radio
to improve public welfare by enrolling girls in the girl scouts to
teach them better and higher value of life is with out a doubt the
soundest and safest foundation of stronger and healthier womanhood. Truth and nothing but the truth and enacted as such, is the
only everlasting light."[45]

In addition to giving pseudo-campaign speeches, Hoover continued to travel with her husband. That fall, Lou Hoover logged many
miles on the campaign train with her husband, marking another innovation for women in her position. Other presidential wives had
traveled with their husbands, but the Hoovers were inseparable during the campaign season. After Herbert Hoover's speech in Detroit,
Lou Hoover wrote to Alice Roosevelt Longworth, who planned to
join the Hoovers on the campaign train: "That was a good speech if
the President and I do say so who perhaps shouldn't and how perfectly thrilling in its purely physical aspects. It must have felt un-
canny to have heard his actual voice around our globe. Thanks for
your telegram." According to the *New York Times,* the two women
shared a mutual dislike of Franklin D. Roosevelt. That trip marked
Hoover's "fourth October whirl into the mid-West," and on each
stop, she displayed "the cumulative enthusiasm of the seasoned
campaigner." The *Cleveland Plain Dealer* reported, "She sat on the
platform . . . sometimes watching her husband, but more often
watching the crowd and its reception of his speech. . . . When his
barbs at his opponents got over and many in the crowd laughed or
shouted their appreciation she flashed them a broad smile as if she
had been waiting to see if they'd 'get' it."[46]

Said one writer for the *Washington Star,* "Mrs. Hoover, who has
been at the President's side throughout all this electioneering, made
no campaign speeches, but she many times talked from the rear
platform to the station crowds." Lou Hoover's remarks, typically informal and complimentary to the local community, were geared "especially to the mothers and children." The local Republican committee or the local Girl Scouts routinely provided the first lady with a
large bouquet of flowers, which she later gave to women and children at subsequent train stops.[47] The significance of these speeches
rests not with their content but with the fact that Lou Henry Hoover
made them at all. She was the first first lady to address crowds on be-

*Lou Henry Hoover (left) waves to the crowds during a 4 October 1932 campaign
stop in Des Moines, Iowa. With her are Governor and Mrs. Dan W. Turner
and Herbert Hoover. (Herbert Hoover Presidential Library-Museum,
© AP/Wide World Photos)*

half of a presidential candidate, and in so doing, she helped infuse
her post with substantive responsibilities along with the traditional
ceremonial duties.

Lou Hoover earned the nickname "generalissimo of the back
platform" because she greeted local dignitaries when they boarded
the train for a short ride. The first lady proved equally solicitous of
schoolchildren who wished to get a glimpse of her husband. To ensure that result, Hoover moved into the doorway and encouraged
the rest of the platform dignitaries to do likewise. At one stop
where the crowd would not quiet down so that Herbert Hoover
could speak, Lou Hoover accomplished that task when she "held up
two [fingers] and said, 'Sh-h-h,' and got the people quiet enough in
her immediate vicinity that they could hear the President say: 'I
don't think you need any statement from me. The enthusiasm I find
here is a speech in itself. Your enthusiasm is a far better speech than
any I could make.'"48

Those Americans who were enthusiastic about four more years of a Hoover presidency were in the minority. Indeed, more than 57 percent of the vote went to Roosevelt, while Hoover captured just under 40 percent. After the 1932 presidential election was decided, Lou Hoover sent word to longtime family friend Alida Henriques, "the fact, as you say of staggering through the next four years, is not that the same President may be elected again in 1936,—for as he has often said, the personalities count for little,—but it is the accomplishments they leave that matters." Indeed, she did not foresee the possibility of Bert running and winning the presidency in 1936 so much as the need to preserve his work and his political philosophy as favorable public policy, so that other like-minded public servants might build on it. "We don't want the pieces ground into dust and left so that they can never be used again," exclaimed Lou. Her bitterness over the election results was reflected when she quipped that even she might not have voted for her husband if she had believed all that had been written about him in the press.[49]

Although most observers agreed that a huge chasm separated Herbert Hoover and Franklin D. Roosevelt, Lou Henry Hoover and Eleanor Roosevelt shared important similarities. After Hoover made her radio speech to the Girl Scouts about women's role in the Great Depression, at least one journalist drew a favorable comparison between the outgoing and incoming first ladies, both of whom were interested in depression relief and women's issues. "There is striking similarity in the taste of the two women and the effect of their convictions has a far-reaching effect on womankind in general," declared a writer for the *Washington Star*. The negative contrast, according to this journalist, was not between Hoover and Roosevelt but between Eleanor Roosevelt and Edith Kermit Roosevelt, who had had a "merely social reign." Said the journalist, "Nowadays both Mrs. Hoover and Mrs. Franklin Delano Roosevelt give of themselves and frequently lend their presence where it will do most good."[50]

Other writers contended: "Lou Henry Hoover and Anna Eleanor Roosevelt are both remarkable women. There is no question of comparing them—each is a personality distinct. Yet contrasts are few and far to seek, for broadly speaking, their lives run parallel. In greatness of heart, in quality of mind, in education, in spiritual independence, in vivid approach to living and in depth of experience they are sisters." That Lou Hoover was less well known than Eleanor Roosevelt after four years in the White House resulted because "the times have been against that." Before the depression settled in, Hoover's attention had been devoted to her elder son's recuperation from tuberculosis. Once this health problem had been alleviated, most Americans, according to one journalist, were already "looking gloomily at our flat pocketbooks and waiting for Congress to do something about them," and they were not receptive to Lou Hoover's charm, activism, or talent.[51]

Indeed, the depression more than anything else shaped the Hoover presidency and Lou Hoover's public image. Their four years in the White House exhausted the Hoovers, and the events of election night 1932 testify to that fact. Mildred Hall, one of Hoover's secretaries, recalled: "The night he was defeated, you know, in 1932—we knew it very early in the evening and everybody was—well, the people were coming in and going out, but mostly there weren't as many coming as we expected, and Mrs. Hoover was so tired she just put her head on my shoulder and I just knew that she was so unhappy and so hurt with all of it." The March 1933 inauguration was equally traumatic. Philippi Harding Butler described the train that carried the Hoovers out of Washington after Roosevelt's inauguration as "so somber and sad-looking. It was almost as bad as the Harding funeral train." Still, Lou Hoover received favorable reviews for her dignity. At the conclusion of the Hoover presidency, the *Kansas City Star* editorialized, "[Lou Hoover] 'stood by' in splendid fashion through an ordeal that aged and wearied the man at her side."[52]

One writer argued that because Lou Hoover "had affairs of her own, too, to occupy her . . . she wasted as little as possible on formality and useless ceremony." Such a demeanor helped explain some of her precedents, such as driving her own car. Additionally, her bearing as "a direct, unpretentious person" contrasted with the Washington preference for traditional first-lady behavior. "Manicurists, shop girls, civil service employees resent her riding in a car no better than theirs. Taxpayers do not like her buying her own car. They would prefer her to ride in theirs and so be under obligations to them," said one unidentified female politician. Such views reflect the tension between a desire for pomp and circumstance among a ruling elite and an equally strong belief in democracy. Because the two opposing perspectives were merged within the American mind, occupants of the White House navigated challenging and difficult shoals. Indeed, argued the same female politician, "This is, perhaps, where Lou Henry has made a mistake. She has been so busy with her job that she has failed to make the White House appear like a court and herself like a personage."[53] Such frustrations trace back to Hoover's flawed media strategy. Although she used the media in important ways—providing veiled interviews, making serious radio speeches, helping the Girl Scouts make a promotional film, practicing oration, and delivering pseudo-campaign speeches—she never used the press to augment her reputation or to convince the American people that they should embrace a new range of activism for presidential spouses.

Put simply, under the best of circumstances, the American people would have had difficulty with a modern woman like Lou Henry Hoover as first lady, but the crisis of the depression all but assured her lack of success with the general public. Her many media innovations achieved only partial success, and they were not employed to tell her own story. This lapse encapsulates the irony of Lou Henry Hoover's public life. She eschewed all unnecessary attention and devoted her energies to the numerous causes that interested her. Working for public approval via the media would have required that she be a very different person. Nevertheless, her activism, her desire for privacy, and her independent spirit were new to the White House, and this combination of traits made it difficult for Lou Henry Hoover to connect with the American people, proving that first-lady activism without explanation, justification, and communication would never win over the American public.

The disintegration of her husband's presidency shaped Lou Hoover privately as well. Even though she had not been enthusiastic about the prospect of life in the White House in 1928, she had given Bert her full support, as she did in all his ventures. Despite her sadness about her husband's public defeat in 1932, Lou Hoover looked forward to the relative anonymity of private life and the freedom to return to her voluntary career on her own terms. She had approached her work as first lady with an activist agenda—White House entertaining, adoption of a depression relief strategy, work with the Girl Scouts, and maintenance of a public face. That she

achieved mixed results should not detract from the significant progress she made in modernizing the institution of the first lady.

Upon leaving the White House, she expressed her conflicted
views about those four years to one of the few women in America
she trusted. In a poem for Grace Coolidge, Hoover assessed the impact of the White House on her own life: "Up and down and
around about / The house, you have gone with me. / In years gone
by it has often been, / But in these days, constantly. / The house of
beauty, the house of joy, / The house of sadness, of history. / Some
ghosts are stately, and some grotesque / Some tragic, some gay,
some humoresque."[54] In retirement from her White House post,
Lou Hoover focused on the tragic ghosts of her White House years,
as bitterness over the Roosevelt administration dominated her personal and political views.

CHAPTER 6

CONSERVATIVE POLITICS AFTER THE WHITE HOUSE

For Lou Henry Hoover, 4 March 1933 was a bittersweet day. Though never completely comfortable as first lady, Hoover felt her husband's loss to Franklin D. Roosevelt the previous November both deeply and personally. At every turn, she encountered the often vituperative attacks that blamed Herbert Hoover for the Great Depression. Wild rumors that accused the outgoing president of hoarding a supply of gold from the U.S. Treasury followed the Hoover family on their journey out of Washington.

Lou Hoover's most immediate worries were for her family's financial future. She planned numerous economies to balance their losses in the stock market. These public and private defeats changed the former first lady. No longer a benign, above-the-battle figure, she waded into the partisan debates about Roosevelt's New Deal programs. Hoover disguised her efforts on behalf of the Republican party generally and its women's organizations specifically, though, with patriotic rhetoric. Indeed, she believed that her work was not partisan but in the best interest of all Americans. Even as she became avowedly political in her own right, she still participated in old and new voluntary organizations, including the Girl Scouts and the Friends of Music at Stanford University.

Hoover's contributions to Girl Scouting proved satisfying as she recovered from her White House years. Serving again as president of the organization, Hoover approached her duties much as she had in the 1920s, even if there was less for her to do. She mixed immediate crisis management—for example, creating a radio Scouting program for a California community under quarantine because of a polio epidemic—and long-term planning. The result helped her regain her center within the volunteer world, a place where she had made a career for herself. Indeed, in a moment of self-defense, she told a potential biographer in February 1942, "All kinds of projects I should like to have put through. A number of professions or callings I should like to have followed, and was prepared to begin. But always duties, interests, or the movement pushed farther back the moment for taking up any long-to-be continued cause or profession."[1] Such words echoed Hoover's modesty, along with a sense that if she had not made her marriage such a significant component of her career, she could have accomplished even more in the world than she did.

Hoover's other major and more significant frustration after 1933 was Franklin D. Roosevelt and the New Deal, but she ensured that such matters never intruded into Girl Scouting. Despite her bitterness about the 1932 presidential election, Hoover was able to temper her criticism of the Roosevelts, at least when it came to the Girl Scouts. In the spring of 1933, some Hoover partisans involved in Scouting fumed that the Girl Scout Better Homes week included honors for the new first family. Hoover told Abbie Rickard, "We must remember that the President and his wife have always taken part in the first of these occasions after an inauguration and in some of the later ones, and that the wife has *always* (I believe) participated in the later ones if the President himself has been too busy." Therefore, "it would be against all Girl Scout traditions not to have this one built around the President and Mrs. Roosevelt."[2]

Later, Hoover cautioned that Washington-based Scouting events should conform to capital city society etiquette. "For instance, nobody who knows how to do anything ever asks the President or his wife to any function without asking them whom *they* would like for the other guests," Hoover explained to Rickard. "It would be a pity to have the Girl Scouts have breaches of manners! Of course Mrs. Roosevelt would be just like me under the same circumstances and would not take a mistake as a personal affront, but would just say, 'Oh well, poor dears, they haven't had any experience and don't know any better.'"[3]

Lou Hoover had a chance to put her respect for Eleanor Roosevelt to the test at the Girl Scouts' 1933 annual convention. Because Scouting was so important to her, Hoover attended the convention even though Roosevelt was to be installed as honorary president. Before the opening ceremony, Hoover met privately with Roosevelt and a few other Girl Scout officials, and the two first ladies—former and current—spent approximately half an hour talking about the White House and its furniture. When the two women were in public view, however, they did not speak, causing journalists to speculate about tension between them. As one Girl Scout official noted, the two women were "not thinking of themselves as part of the circus and of clasping their hands . . . like prize fighters."[4]

The bulk of Hoover's work with Scouting after 1933 involved image control. She wanted her favorite organization to maintain its preeminence and its public goodwill. As such, Hoover admitted to reporters that the Girl Scouts were following the National Recovery Administration codes regarding their publications and their procurement and sale of Scouting merchandise, even though she personally decried that New Deal program. She also fought to preserve Scouting as a separate organization. When critics suggested that the Girl Scouts should merge with other voluntary groups for young women, such as the Camp Fire Girls, Hoover retorted, "The fathers of these girls have hundreds of organizations. There are Lions and Elks and Rotarians and Eagles and many, many others. Why should there not be as many for their daughters? And they do not overlap, we find."[5]

In October 1935, Lou Henry Hoover was named Girl Scout president, her term to run through 1936. Hoover observed that she felt like she was "going backward through the looking-glass of time" to the "very happy period" of her life in the 1920s when she had previously served as Girl Scout president. Though Marie Mattingly Meloney, a New York City editor, congratulated Hoover on exiting her "quiet corner," such was not entirely true. Hoover employed a more passive leadership style than had been the case in the 1920s, largely because of evolution within the Girl Scout organization; the presidency had become more of an honorary post and less of a job requiring daily attention.[6]

In 1937, after her reelection as national president of the Girl Scouts, Hoover told an interviewer for *Sunset* magazine that the organization had well surpassed Juliette Low's promise that someday there would be more than 5,000 Scouts. "Today there are 400,000. It's growing so fast that we have a hard time training enough new leaders for the girls who clamor to be Scouts," declared Hoover. She explained why the organization was so popular: "It aims to fill a little nook of young democracy between home and school and church. It tries to supplement them, not to overlap. The Girl Scout leaders try not to give orders; not to teach. They try to be just cooperating grown-up friends of the Girl Scouts." Hoover contended, "of all the Girl Scout activities—sports, nature lore, citizenship, and so on—home-making is the most popular."[7]

Hoover's other significant activity within Girl Scouting followed from the limited civil rights precedent she had set by entertaining Jessie DePriest during her first year in the White House. Hoover provided financial support for African American churches and youth camping programs in Palo Alto. She was especially concerned with the segregation that African American Girl Scouts faced on camping trips. Out of deference to white prejudice, though, she did not challenge discrimination directly, instead adopting the more limited solution of funding camp fees for impoverished girls at segregated facilities. Finding locations for black Girl Scout camps proved difficult, however, because park officials often denied permits to African Americans out of concern that "people won't come . . . if they see negroes there—and unfortunately that is perfectly true!"[8]

Hoover told her brother-in-law Theodore Hoover, "Nationally the Girl Scouts have no policy regarding the colored situation. It must be decided in each area by the Council thereof, because Boston and New Orleans, California and Florida, cities and small towns look at all with such different eyes." She explained that in Palo Alto, if white troops wanted "to take in a colored member who is in their class at school . . . there is no question made of it. If they want to take her to camp with them, she goes." However, Lou also noted that not all African Americans were welcome in Palo Alto Scouting. "In the last very few years, I am told, a new group of colored people has come into the southern outskirts of Palo Alto," said Hoover, in a patronizing defense of the situation. "Even our own better colored people exclaim to each other, 'Why did you know there were such colored folks! They's just the kind they sometimes put in stories and movies, and we never believed they were true.'"[9]

Specifically, Lou worked with a Mrs. Moulden, whom she described as "the outstanding woman of her race in Palo Alto." Hoover credited Moulden for recognizing the "difference in their various types." As such, Hoover and the Palo Alto Girl Scout Camp Committee provided Moulden and her Scouts with access to a camp after the local white troops went home. But the experiment failed, according to Hoover, because "they were not good campers; they didn't have well enough trained leaders; and they did not keep nor leave the camp clean nor in good condition." As a result, Hoover's committee accepted prevailing white bias and "decided that under no consideration could they let them use it again until they had some practical demonstration of the colored people's ability to maintain the standards in camping that we had set for ourselves."[10] Still, Hoover sought other camping opportunities for Moulden's girls. Such a turn of events was entirely in keeping with Hoover's views of how to handle race problems in America. Although she sympathized with the plight of middle-class African Americans facing blatant discrimination, Hoover never surpassed the white ethos of her era. She did not possess the capacity to grow intellectually beyond her stance in the DePriest controversy.

In September 1937, Hoover prepared to leave the Girl Scout presidency for the last time, saying, "I think I would like to play with many different things,—none of which are quite so exacting in their demands as being the head of a big, definite organization. Having more time, for instance, to play with things like Stanford music!" Indeed, one of Hoover's most significant causes in the years after her second Girl Scout presidency was her work with the Friends of Music at Stanford University. In the summer of 1937, Hoover hosted several meetings at her home for individuals interested in developing the summer music program at Stanford. Hoover contended that it was "a great pity" that Stanford lacked "a real department of music." The result, she believed, was an alumni population without an "adequate *appreciation* of the music that may come their way in the future." That problem ensued because Palo Alto was "an isolated community" and because Stanford had insufficient funds. The administration and the board of trustees recognized the weakness of the curriculum, but, as Hoover explained, the university faced budgetary constraints that prohibited the development of new programs. Thus, she argued, a school of music at Stanford depended on "the millions of necessary endowment coming from some fairy godmother or godfather,—sometime! Meantime, we must worry along on shoestrings as best we can."[11]

Hoover endorsed a plan by Elizabeth Sprague Coolidge, a music philanthropist, as a potential solution. In the summer of 1937, the Stanford community had benefited from a series of performances of Bach's Brandenburg Concertos. Coolidge contended that a similar series could be arranged for the following year at a cost of $4,000. Coolidge agreed to fund half the cost if Hoover could draw together a group of individuals willing to endow the other half. "To accomplish all this," Hoover proposed the creation of "'Friends of Stanford Music,' with a rather large membership and a rather small annual fee. . . . Then 'Friends' with special interests might give much larger donations."[12] Throughout the summer and fall, Hoover wrote numerous letters soliciting support and money for the new Friends of Stanford Music, and because of her efforts, sufficient funds were raised to match the Coolidge gift.

By the fall of 1939, Hoover was lobbying for a change from a summer music program to one held in the spring, "when our full four thousand students are here, instead of the Summer Quarter, when there are less than one-fourth the number."[13] The next year, Hoover worked with the Friends of Music to help it draft the necessary constitution and bylaws to turn the organizing committee into a permanent association. By the fall of 1941, her efforts had succeeded, and Hoover became inactive with the Friends of Music, reasoning that her frequent absences from Palo Alto rendered her ineffective.

Girl Scouts and the Friends of Music provided Lou Henry Hoover with only partial comfort in the post–White House years. Books critical of her tenure as first lady, such as the one by Irwin H. "Ike" Hoover, and overheated partisanship aggravated her already raw sores over America's rejection of her husband. She did not acknowledge any of the reasons for the discontent, choosing instead to ignore all who rejected Hoover Republicanism.

White House servants expressed contrasting views of the Hoovers and the Roosevelts. In the fall of 1933, one White House employee wrote to Lou Hoover about the difficulty of making the transition to the new administration. The most severe complaints

were reserved for Eleanor Roosevelt, who "certainly enjoys herself."
Hoover partisans on the White House staff "often 'go into a huddle'
and how we do talk at the rate of forty miles a minute and say very
dreadful things about her and that partner of hers who likes himself
also." Eleanor Roosevelt's decorum caused one employee to remark,
"I came near sending for the police for a halter to keep her somewhere. She was dancing all over the place first on one foot and then
on the other and calling 'hoo-hoo' across the room to some one at
the end of the line. Such a queer woman as she is and not one bit like
the lovely lady who came before her, and whom we love so much."[14]
These observations no doubt cheered the former first lady, who otherwise had to endure unfavorable comparisons with Eleanor Roosevelt. The words could not insulate Hoover from a series of critical
publications, however. And ironically, they previewed the manner in
which Hoover partisans downplayed Lou Henry Hoover's public career in an effort to show Eleanor Roosevelt's expanding public political activities in a negative light.

Because of the warm relationship between the former first family
and the White House chief usher, the publication of a series of magazine articles and a book by Ike Hoover caused much concern. In fact,
when the *Saturday Evening Post* released Ike Hoover's reminiscences,
Lou Hoover doubted that the former White House usher had had
anything to do with the project, and she asked her secretaries to provide her with the entirety of Ike Hoover's correspondence. In March
1933, Ike Hoover told Mildred Hall that he had "fond memories" of
Lou Hoover. When Ike Hoover passed away in the fall of 1933, Lou
Hoover told his wife, "we have lost a friend who we have all loved and
whose kindliness and devotion to us will ever be one of our most
cherished memories."[15] Journalist Bess Furman, who happened to
visit Ike on the day he died, confirmed that such feelings were mutual.

These views conflicted sharply with Ike Hoover's public words.
Philippi Harding Butler read the chapter of *Forty-two Years in the
White House* devoted to the Hoovers and made extensive marginal
notations refuting and correcting the many errors of fact and inter-
pretation. That chapter contended that "the Hoovers came in and
upset the whole private part of the house." Butler countered, the
"Hoovers were not [the] only ones to change household arrangements! What did Teddy Roosevelt do?! What did Mrs. F. Roosevelt

do?!!—and fast!" Butler's outrage mirrored Lou Hoover's, but nei- ther woman had the power to win over a public that was ready to be- lieve the worst of Herbert and Lou Hoover. Ironically, though, they were right in their anger and in their defense of the chief usher. In his original notes from which his book was constructed, Ike Hoover described Herbert and Lou Hoover as "liberal" and "generous."[16]

After one of Ike Hoover's articles appeared in the *Saturday Evening Post,* Lou wrote a long letter of complaint to Grace Coolidge in which she asserted that Ike had not willingly written the article in question but might have been motivated by economic privation. She specu- lated that he had constructed his narrative from "that series of little books of his." In reality, though, Ike Hoover's workplace diaries con- tained little more than daily lists of White House guests. Lou Hoover guessed, "Someone else probably took either his own outline, or one made after his death, and fitted into it incidents that this 'collaborator' picked out of the pages of his books and enlivened with stories that must have come from other members of the household."[17]

A later publication, *My Thirty Years Backstairs at the White House,* was also damning and of questionable veracity. The author, Lillian Rogers Parks, had worked as a White House maid. She said of the Hoovers: "Mrs. Hoover appropriated the bedroom that was tradi- tionally the President's bedroom, and called it her dressing room. Only it wasn't used for that at all. It was her *workroom.* She used the bed for her 'desk' and had it completely covered with papers." In her Hoover Library oral history, though, Parks spoke warmly of the Hoovers: "they paid for all the food for the help and everybody out of their pockets." In describing the editing process for her book, she said, "they'd try to take out everything and make it different." Parks said that Hoover's voice was always pleasant, and her manner of managing the domestic staff was "very fair."[18]

Ultimately, Lou Henry Hoover knew that she could not focus too much on these published criticisms. A better way to redirect the national political compass, she believed, was through partisan ac- tivity. She found refuge in an orphaned organization of conserva- tive women, Pro-America, which had first emerged during the 1932 campaign but would not gain recognition from the Republican Na- tional Committee until 1939. Elizabeth Hanley wrote to Hoover in December 1932 about her plans for converting Pro-America into a permanent organization made up of partisan Republican women. Hanley hoped that Pro-America would unite "the great mass of women who will not ally themselves with the machinery of Party politics" and "the loyal intelligent women of the regular party machinery." The organization originated in a Seattle, Washington, garden club and, as Hoover explained some years later, encouraged a conservative political orientation with nonpartisan arguments. "They want to progress into a new future, with new methods," she contended, "but adhering to the old, everlasting principles that have guided America so far."[19] Because each of Hoover's own forays into activism had been so designed, she applauded the strategy.

Hanley hoped that the first California chapter could be formed in Palo Alto, in honor of Lou Hoover. Edith Roosevelt had endorsed the plans and was to be named the group's honorary president. However, Hanley also wanted Lou Hoover's cooperation. She asked the first lady, "as soon as all the duties of the White House are behind you could you take an active part in the organization in California and the nation? All the prominent women's organizations prior to this have originated in the East, let this come from the West." Hoover, however, did not have her secretary respond to this missive until February 1933. Furthermore, despite her 1932 campaign season cooperation with Pro-America, she declined to take an active role in the new women's organization, at least until she could "give the matter the proper consideration."[20]

Indeed, Hoover had little to do with the fledgling organization for the first couple of years after her husband's defeat. Her eventual interest in political organizing among women resulted from her promotion of Herbert Hoover's publications; for Lou, this represented the path to political vindication, if only the public could be made to see the error of its ways in 1932. In May 1934, Hoover told Agnes Morley Cleaveland, a Pro-America activist and former Stanford classmate, "A few weeks ago, we finally succeeded in getting my husband to get to work on *his* view of the present condition of our country." But she complained that Bert, in the interest of brevity, had "taken a little too much for granted in the average citizen's knowledge,—rather than in intelligence."[21] In an effort to perfect the manuscript and ensure its success with the public, Lou Hoover sent out advance drafts to people she trusted, such as Cleaveland, for review. Bert had just published *The Challenge to Liberty* that year, and Lou hoped that his next project, *American Ideals versus the New Deal,* would prove successful.

As Hoover explained, she wanted Cleaveland to discern "what Mrs. Average Citizen would think of it and get from it." Hoover's larger concern, though, was whether "it is a good book to give the American people. And then do you think it is a good book to give the American public *now?*" She explained that the men who had read the manuscript varied in their opinions about its timeliness, specifically, whether it would be beneficial to attack the New Deal. Hoover told Cleaveland, "I would just like your unbiased opinion. For that reason I am not telling you what I think about it. But I am enclosing in another sealed envelope my opinion." In that envelope, Hoover revealed her new conservative political orientation, even as she fumed over the "one critic [who] has said that he feels it reads like a stand-pat reactionary exposition."[22]

In March 1934, Hoover told Cleaveland that she had researched the difficulty of procuring copies of *American Individualism,* a book Herbert Hoover had written in 1922 about the pioneer individualist spirit and American prosperity. San Francisco area bookstore operators believed that it was "an ancient volume now 'out of print.'" Such a reaction caused the former first lady to worry whether her husband's writings were known and available at Stanford. She investigated the university reading lists for citizenship courses and the like, discovering "the lists top-heavy with outright socialistic stuff, nearly all very recent." As a result, she asked Cleaveland to help her construct a college reading list that was "not of a partisan political nature." Lou Hoover took pains to ensure that her citizenship project would not be publicized. However, this familiar pattern of self-circumscription occurred for reasons different from those that had caused her to silence her views during the White House years— namely, her recent desire to gain partisan advantage. She explained, "any subject I discuss or recommend is so frequently pounced upon as containing some hidden dynamite, or as being a pet child of my husband's, that I think it is much better to keep still!"[23]

Hoover told Cleaveland of her conversation with some young men who were about to graduate from Stanford University but possessed only "the haziest ideas of what was going on in our country or of what its foundations are." Though critical of the New Deal, communism, socialism, fascism, and Hitlerism, the young men, Hoover explained, were dumbfounded when asked about the "American system." They responded, "'Why, we haven't got a system, have we?' And the other one rather giggled and said, 'No, haven't we just grown up like Topsy?' They knew their ancestors had fought for freedom, but they really didn't have any idea of what that freedom was, or of how said ancestors thought they had anchored it." Ignorant of the Bill of Rights, the philosophy of the founding generation, or the evolution of American government, these young college-educated men troubled Hoover. "A considerable, but a small percentage of them, have imbibed so much from the teaching of Communism and Socialism that they get here with no antidote that they are going out with our label on them, absolutely Red," argued the former first lady.[24]

Hoover wrote to several influential college presidents about this problem. She had two goals, one long-term and one immediate: the creation of citizenship courses for college curricula, and the development of a lecture series that provided a historical context for the country's current political climate. She lobbied President Ernest J. Jaqua of Scripps College about the curricular "propagation of communistic and socialistic doctrine." Her greatest concern was that "erratic" faculty members would declare their intellectual authority over "very young people not yet skilled in the weighing of argument." Hoover contended that speakers should be invited into the colleges to address "our American system" in comparison with that of other countries. Hoover wanted the project to go forward quickly, given that the midterm congressional elections were just weeks away. She argued that the contests were more important than typical off-year balloting because "the choice between steady progress or social chaos is to be determined," making it "something more than politics."[25] Hoover had no qualms about her request or her behavior, which deviated from her political activity during the White House years. She justified her crusade as transcending partisanship.

For the first four years after she and her husband left the White House, Lou had little contact with Pro-America, but her growing irritation with the New Deal, along with her political evolution rightward, made her ready to take on a behind-the-scenes leadership role with the organization. The timing of her metamorphosis was not accidental. Hoover's public debut with Pro-America coincided with the 1936 election season. That same year, Hoover helped negotiate between dissenting factions of Pro-America over whether the organization should become a permanent entity or whether it should disband and reconstitute itself in accordance with the ebb and flow of partisan political elections. Hoover insisted that it become permanent. In addition, the women's organization quibbled over whether to include Democratic women who otherwise disliked the New Deal. Hoover's activism with Pro-America resulted from her newfound conservatism.

As the Pro-America infighting worsened, Hanley complained that Cleaveland had became the national president only because of her friendship with the Hoovers and had "blunder[ed] . . . a very fine idea," specifically, the promotion of Herbert Hoover's political philosophy in order to control the delegates at the GOP convention. Lou Hoover, however, told Hanley that the situation was not as desperate as she feared. She also took responsibility for some of the misunderstanding about whether there would be Democrats as members of Pro-America. Because she valued both Republicans and disaffected Democrats, Hoover contended, "it would really be quite unwise to alter either one to conform to the other, because it would simply mean the loss of many hundreds of followers on the one side or the other."[26]

In early November 1936, Hoover said of the pending presidential election, "No matter who wins in the election tomorrow, there has to be a very serious and successful attempt at the education of our people in what constitutes true Americanism and how we can save it for America." Roosevelt's reelection would mean that Hoover partisans specifically and Republicans generally "must all be prepared for an even more strenuous fight . . . than has been waged these last months." However, an Alf Landon victory would leave "a real battle to convince Congress . . . that the performances of Mr. Roosevelt and his henchmen were not in any way in line with their constant promises," argued Hoover.[27] The resounding Roosevelt victory only heightened Hoover's partisanship and her fight on behalf of Pro-America and conservative women. Unfortunately for Hoover, she had to devote the majority of her partisan activity not to duels with the Democrats but to feuds within Pro-America.

While she worked to bring harmony to Pro-America, Hoover wrote about her larger mission of Republican activism through study clubs, a device she had endorsed since the 1920s. "Our destiny is in the hands of the vast number between the two [parties],— those voters not permanently aligned with either Party, who have been vacillating within the last few years," argued Hoover. In perhaps an overly optimistic fashion, she believed that "these people who get to studying with real intelligence our national problems today must, at least for the time being, turn into the Republican ranks." Hoover then explained the disagreements between Pro-America and Republican party women, but she contended that Pro-America study clubs could be "recruiting fields for Republican ballots," which were needed in large numbers on both the state and national levels.[28]

Lou Hoover was also active in behind-the-scenes work for Philip Bancroft's 1938 U.S. Senate race in California. She liked Bancroft because he advocated a Hoover version of Republican politics. With Agnes Cleaveland, she constructed a statewide women's committee that would "*work* toward his election." She hoped that this committee would end the hostilities between Pro-America women and regular Republican party women and "get the different groups into the habit of cooperating together." But their efforts were for naught, leaving Hoover defeated in her foray into partisan electoral politics. Nevertheless, after the general election was over—a contest in which Republican strength increased dramatically in both houses of Congress—Lou Hoover became optimistic about the political future: "We really feel here that national hope is beginning to raise its head again from its long sleep."[29]

In 1939, Hoover returned to her typical pattern of behavior with voluntary organizations—that is, public, ceremonial involvement, but this time for a partisan vehicle. She agreed to be listed as an honorary vice president of Pro-America, along with Carolyn Harrison, Helen Herron Taft, and Grace Coolidge, "if the others accept." Edith Roosevelt had been the honorary president since the organization was formed. Hoover worried that "if they do not, I am wondering if it might not be better for you not to have any of us on?"[30] The other three women accepted the invitation, and Hoover hoped that their participation would augment cooperation between Pro-America and the regular party machinery.

Lou Hoover was not through with overtly partisan activity, but at the dawn of both a new decade and a new world war, her efforts followed a bifurcated course: cooperation with Herbert Hoover in another tour of European relief work, and criticism of what she termed the dictatorial nature of American foreign policy. Because Bert believed that their efforts would be more productive if based out of New York City, Lou resigned herself to another move away from her beloved California. Bert was bored with California, where he found life too provincial in comparison with the cosmopolitan New York generally and the Waldorf Astoria, their new home, specifically. Even though she moved with her husband, Lou often traveled back to California.

Indeed, when Herbert Hoover again became involved in fighting wartime starvation, Lou Hoover generated contacts and assisted the effort on the West Coast. In June 1940, Lou assumed an advisory role with the Salvation Army's war work, and that fall, she accepted a temporary assignment with a Salvation Army campaign to gather a shipload of children's clothing for Europe. Hoover solicited other women to oversee the work in their particular communities, and approximately 2 million garments were collected. Hoover said of the work, "It was a great satisfaction for all of us to gather together the many boxes of warm clothing that went to you from our Western Area. The response was so spontaneous and generous that there was no work whatever in the appeal."[31]

Along with her interest in the politics of war, Hoover remained attuned to the looming election of 1940, hoping that her husband's views would dominate the GOP and the nation. Bert unrealistically yearned for the presidential nomination that year, but according to family friend Edgar Rickard, he kept his ambitions away from Lou, who nonetheless knew that there was talk of a Hoover candidacy. Alida Henriques, an old family friend, told Lou that she was "apprehensive lest Mr. Hoover be drawn into considering the Candidacy. He is the only person who can save us, and there is a widespread belief of this. But no human being could stand the stress of cleaning up the mess we are in." Lou no doubt realized that her husband would remain involved in national and international problems, but she saw Bert's role as focused on war relief. She wanted Bert to help shape international politics, but Lou also hoped that the "demands upon him" would not be "too harsh."[32]

After Wendell Willkie gained the nomination, another longtime Hoover friend wrote to Lou, "I was ready to campaign for Herbert Hoover—I am not ready to campaign for Willkie but I will do all I can if the Chief believes in him." Lou Hoover shared Katherine Everts's lack of enthusiasm for Willkie. She argued, "no one could be worse in command of the present situation" than Franklin D. Roosevelt, but she also noted that Willkie "has not seemed to have succeeded in putting his best qualities where they are most evident." She advised Everts to "stress what good things he can give us that very evidently the other one has not. Truth seems the very foundation one to me. . . . How can anyone ever believe anything of a man who tells us one week that he does not want to be drafted and has used no effort toward obtaining the nomination! And the next week, in the same tone, tells us that he wishes to and can keep us out of war!"[33] Indeed, Hoover's hatred of Franklin D. Roosevelt, more than anything else, guided her criticism of the methods if not the motives of American foreign policy. It also shaped her partisan agenda.

As much as she relished Bert's take on the GOP position, she despaired of Willkie's poor political skills. Lou praised at length her husband's Philadelphia speech, in which he contended that even if he were to read the Ten Commandments, Democrats would see it as an attack on the New Deal. She groused in a "very, very very confidential suggestion,—not statement," that the Willkie campaign had ignored Bert's offers of assistance. Lou hypothesized that the slight might not be "intentional . . . but rather that the man [Willkie] simply had not gotten the machinery to working so that it would function well enough early enough." After she finished complaining about Willkie, Hoover returned to the larger purpose of her partisanship. "But do remember that we will be another Germany,—or Belgium or Roumania or something,—if we don't throw out this present incumbent. A campaign of opposition alone is not apt to be effective," contended Hoover. "Therefore, as well as using all the arguments *against him,* we must find as many as possible and stress them *in favor* of the other one."[34]

According to the *Nebraska State Journal,* Lou Henry Hoover declared in November 1940: " 'We must think out our philosophy of government. Will it be democracy or will it be totalitarianism? We must not lose the old principles of democracy in our modern trend. . . . We must not let power rest in the hands of a few. . . . I very much disapprove of a third term. There again we must think of our traditional democratic ideals.'" However, the former first lady penned in the margin: "Never said it to press! Perhaps to two or three of the women officers."[35] Such a notation indicates both the intensity of her partisanship and the extent of her move to the right after 1933. It also suggests her realization that displays of partisan zeal by a former first lady might be considered bad form, so she yet again faced a contradiction between her activist self and her traditional self.

The Roosevelt victory in 1940 caused Hoover and her Pro-America colleagues to consider what they might do differently. The first task, they agreed, was to convert the organization into a national entity. Hoover commiserated with Elva Carpenter, the national president of Pro-America, about the difficulty of organizing Pro-America in New York. Those women with the ability lacked the time, and those women with the time lacked the ability. After talking with her friend and colleague Alice Dickson, Hoover consulted with Ruth Pratt and Edith Roosevelt, all of whom concurred that "this whole war matter will largely determine what people will be free to work in such a cause,—what ones, indeed, will feel that they have time to join it. . . . If war clouds really darken over us, I should think that Pro America might develop a very satisfactory program relating to war work, but emphasizing always *pro* America." Carpenter agreed, contending that women must be the torchbearers to save democracy in America by concentrating on education, not politics. Hoover cautioned that the "lighted torch" should be carried with a "less military method of approach than could be done heretofore" because of the potential for war.[36] But beyond giving Carpenter travel advice for her sojourn in New York, Hoover had little to do with the exportation of Pro-America to the nation. In fact, after the United States became a combatant in World War II, Hoover became much less involved in the partisan organization.

She shifted her partisanship to support for Bert's publications. In January 1942, Lou Henry Hoover played a key role in investigating the availability of and advancing the sales figures for Bert's newest book, *America's First Crusade*. Bert's secretary, Bernice "Bunny"

Miller, reported difficulty finding and buying the book in New York. She advised Lou Hoover "to place an order through somebody else but at our expense" for "twenty books each in twenty different towns along Pacific Coast and Mountain States." Such an innovative tactic suggests how interested parties might inflate the popularity of a book through bulk buying. Miller advised that the purchasing responsibilities should be divided among as many people as possible. Hoover and Miller hoped that this subterfuge would "make an impact on the publishing people and reviewers." The former first lady gladly wired several friends to arrange their participation. As a result of these contacts, Hoover later reported to Miller, "Complete *Crusade* blackout in bay area. Not one store has one. Many never heard of it. Others show *Herald Tribune* review as reason. . . . What step shall we take next? Please send me dozen copies at least."[37]

Eventually, Hoover and Miller concluded that Scribners, the publisher, was not promoting Bert's book. Hoover complained that although Scribners had first indicated that the book would be published in early November 1941, they had not received their copies until 23 December. "That is why the thing came out *after* Pearl Harbor! If published when promised, it would all have been digested before that," Hoover avowed. "Of course all this is not to have a certain author's wares publicized, — but to get these facts over to the American people that they can begin thinking about a sane and practical peace instead of the Utopian one of [Woodrow] Wilson." Hoover advocated using diplomats "with practical common sense and a knowledge of the kind of men they will have to deal with." She criticized, "the present peace talk in this country is just as chimerical, — with the idea of our *imposing* our ideas of a *Christian* peace (which we do not live up to ourselves) upon the rest of the world by a permanent police force of millions of our young men whose lives are otherwise vital to our own race. (And hence, better for the world, too!)"[38]

Hoover spent much of her time in the 1940s corresponding and visiting with old friends and family. Less of her time was given over to active work with the voluntary associations to which she had long been committed, and more of her time was spent watching and commenting on world affairs large and small. As had been the case throughout much of her married life, she devoted a good deal of attention to Bert's agenda, in this case, war relief work. She had watched carefully as European war clouds ultimately produced the storm of World War II, and she supported the Allies while criticizing the U.S. government's decisions. In the fall of 1940, when the administration sought every available measure to aid the British, she criticized Roosevelt's "surprise bargain of destroyers and airplane bases," suggesting that there had been "secret negotiations beforehand." Specifically, Hoover feared the possibility of a dictatorship developing in America, and she doubted the ability of many of Roosevelt's aides to handle the tasks before them. In early January 1942, she asked an assistant to stockpile a variety of nonperishable foods, "not by way of fearing a Jap invasion,—but in view of the crazy administration of transportation and other commissions in Washington."[39]

As the decade progressed, Hoover's health failed, and her doctor limited her activities. In the fall before she died, Lou Hoover spoke with a lawyer about arranging her will. He told her that if she made a holographic will, she would need no witnesses, and she prepared such a document. In a letter to her sons dated 17 November 1943, Hoover constructed a handwritten will while also looking back on her life. Perhaps experiencing symptoms of heart trouble, Lou began putting her life in order. She said, "you have been lucky boys to have had such a father, and I a lucky woman to have my life's trails alongside the paths of three such men and boys." She then provided specific directions for dividing her property among Bert and the boys, with the latter being named as executors. She told Herbert and Allan, "I know I can trust your interest and disinterestedness, and judgment, in seeing this tiresome task through."[40]

Outwardly, Lou's health had been fine earlier in the summer of 1943. Her friend and former secretary, Mildred Hall Campbell, visited Palo Alto and noticed only a slight reduction in the former first lady's energy level. Campbell attributed Hoover's pale complexion to her decision not to "use her [war ration] points for meat!" However, the two women had hiked through the foothills and enjoyed picnic lunches. Campbell then commiserated that the Hoover fortune had deteriorated to the point that the family had vacated Lou's beloved home at 623 Mirada, the structure she had designed after World War I. "The Chief was so ashamed of the house they did

Lou Henry Hoover in a 1943 photograph taken about a year before her death.
(Herbert Hoover Presidential Library-Museum)

have. And it was so unlike them," noted Campbell. "I felt very badly that those two people who had given of themselves so much should now be reduced to such an extent in comforts of life."[41]

On Friday, 7 January 1944, Lou Henry Hoover attended a concert with Bunny Miller in New York City given by Mildred Dilling, a harpist who had entertained at the White House and for the Friends of Music at Stanford University. Earlier that day, Hoover had devoted much energy to a program whereby senior Girl Scouts provided occupational therapy to recuperating soldiers in local hospitals. Said the national Girl Scout president, "Mrs. Hoover was also convinced that girls working under the guidance of trained therapists now would be ready to give valuable service in the post-war era." Following the performance, Hoover said, "let's walk home—the air feels so good," but after a few blocks she said, "well, I guess we'd better take a cab." She did not invite Miller in for dinner but instead she went straight to her bedroom.[42] She had spent what would be the last day of her life with two of her favorite causes—Girl Scouting and the arts. Even at the very end, she showed few outer signs of failing health and maintained a busy calendar.

Edgar Rickard recalled in his diary the circumstances surrounding Lou Henry Hoover's death. He had arrived at the Waldorf at 6:30 P.M. to go out to dinner with Herbert Hoover. The two old friends had been talking and listening to Lowell Thomas on the radio while waiting for a third dinner companion to arrive. Before departing, Bert went into Lou's bedroom and found her on the floor of her dressing room. The Waldorf house physician, along with the Hoover family doctor, were summoned, but before they arrived, Herbert Hoover used his pocket knife to split open her dress and provide first aid for the heart attack she had suffered. Rickard recounted, "House Doctor arrived about 7:05 and in few minutes H.H. came out to say that L.H.H. 'was gone.'" The evening was given over to the many phone calls necessary to arrange a simple funeral, with no long eulogies, at St. Bartholomew Episcopal Church in New York City. Rickard remembered that "H.H. . . . keeps his head and finally goes to his room at 11 P.M."[43]

The funeral, which was attended by more than 1,500 people, contained a mixture of Episcopalian and Quaker doctrine. The choir sang one of Lou Henry Hoover's favorite hymns, "Nearer My God to Thee." In addition to various scripture readings, the chair of the American Friends Service Committee, who co-officiated at the services, read from John Greenleaf Whittier's poem "Eternal Goodness" and from Alfred, Lord Tennyson's "Crossing of the Bar." Mourners came from every organization with which the Hoovers had worked and included a contingent of more than 200 Girl Scouts. The immediate family flew back to California when the services were concluded for her burial in Palo Alto (after her husband's death in 1964, Lou Henry Hoover was reinterred by his grave in West

Branch, Iowa, on the grounds of the Herbert Hoover National Historic Site, which she had helped create). At the Palo Alto memorial
service, Ray Lyman Wilbur, a Hoover friend for more than fifty years
and the chancellor of Stanford University, contended, "she was just as
interested in the smallest Girl Scout as in the biggest economic or political person."[44]

Just after Lou Henry Hoover's death, Mildred Hall Campbell told
Ruth Fesler Lipman, "The Ladye's death was a dreadful shock to me
too. Specially so since she was in such good shape this summer. I
admit she was very restless and jittery, but that I felt was because of
lack of help and the feeling that she had so much to do herself."
Campbell had spent some time with her former boss and friend that
summer. She told Lipman, another former employee and friend of
Hoover, "I just felt she needed someone to ease the pressure of work
(although the mail wasn't great) and to give her a hand with those
old files of hers, and someone to talk about the days when."[45]

After Lou Henry Hoover died, one associate told her husband,
"On our Girl Scout trips to-gether, she wore us all out, by her tireless
energy; she extricated us from many a problem situation, by her
quickness of wit; and she won us and her cause friends, wherever
she went, by the graciousness of her personality. Her love of country, her confidence in youth and in her sex, the high standards she
set for herself as well as others, could not fail to have its effect on
many lives." Said another mourner, "Her brilliance and modesty was
appreciated by all real Americans. She was an outstanding model for
every woman to emulate. A wonderful wife and homemaker and
mother and that seemed first in her life. I hope the next President's
wife will follow her example." The president of the Inter-Racial Press
of America declared, "Her death will be mourned by the nation regardless of political beliefs, for she exemplified in her life and deeds
the true spirit of America." In her "My Day" column, Eleanor
Roosevelt wrote, "Mrs. Hoover must have been a wonderful woman,
and I am sure that her loss will be felt not only by her own family,
but by a wide circle of friends and coworkers."[46] She also sent a
handwritten note of sympathy to Herbert Hoover, and he acknowledged it with another handwritten note.

Countless American newspapers commented on Hoover's death.
The typical theme of these editorials suggested that Hoover's great-

ness resulted from her marriage and the wonderful manner in which she supported her husband's career. The *Christian Science Monitor* argued, "not so many marriages can build themselves in the global proportions, and be consummated in the achievements, which characterize the relationship of Lou Henry and Herbert Hoover. . . . Her own scholarship and individual development was to make Mrs. Hoover one of the most notable of Presidents' wives. . . . It was characteristic of her that her charm and talents did not depend on, but rather enhanced, whatever circumstances she found in which to exercise them." Her adopted hometown newspaper, the *Daily Palo Alto Times,* contended, "as long as Americans cherish honest work, neighborliness, truth, integrity, courage and democracy, Lou Henry Hoover's essential spirit will live. She has not said goodbye."[47]

These varying sentiments speak to the many sides of Lou Henry Hoover—activist, problem solver, Scout, and homemaker. Ironically, few of the cards to President Hoover or the published editorials spoke directly of Hoover's long record of activism, instead focusing on her more traditional qualities. Such was the result of an unfortunate, but officially sanctioned, revision of Hoover's life even before her death. She and her allies downplayed her many innovations in favor of demonstrating her conventional traits in order to draw a sharp contrast between Lou Henry Hoover and her immediate successor as first lady, Eleanor Roosevelt. Indeed, bitterness over the Roosevelt administration remained a constant among Hoover partisans. A sardonic piece originally printed in the *Wallace (Idaho) Miner* in July 1940 contended in part "that 'Hoover was a complete failure'" because he took no salary while president, avoided exacerbating class divisions, and never asked farmers to destroy their produce.[48]

Such rhetoric was commonplace among Republicans, and the presence of a copy of the article among Lou Hoover's papers reveals her own frustrations in the 1930s and 1940s. The last paragraph of the editorial inadvertently suggests why Lou Henry Hoover has been forgotten by Americans: "Mrs. Hoover never made speeches or raced hither and yon on unimportant matters. She never wrote silly drivel on her everyday life and sold it to the newspapers and she never sold soap over the radio. Her only public appearance was as an honorary member of the Girl Scouts of

America. She never invited Communist youth to the White House as guests. The Hoover family seems to have made a failure of about everything that goes nowadays."[49] By rewriting and downplaying Hoover's activities while first lady in such a way as to attack Eleanor Roosevelt, Republican partisans actually harmed Lou Henry Hoover's legacy and relegated her to the back pages of the history books. Although Hoover herself no doubt enjoyed this pseudo-anonymity, the result rendered her a forgotten activist who nonetheless modernized the office of the first lady.

Lou Henry Hoover should be forgotten no more. As a well-known public figure, she entered the White House in March 1929 with as much promise as her husband—or more. Despite the fact that the depression became a steady drain on her time and energy, she was among the most innovative first ladies of the twentieth century. She infused her social responsibilities with political purpose; she pursued depression relief policies from the East Wing; she merged her work as first lady with that of the most important voluntary organization for girls; and she used the media more fully than her predecessors had. Within each of these general areas, Hoover made numerous smaller advances.

Although she never advertised her accomplishments, Hoover represented a transition between nineteenth-century conceptions of demure, receding political wives and the emerging, if incomplete, activism of twentieth-century first ladies. Thus, a line connects Hoover with each of her activist successors: Eleanor Roosevelt, Lady Bird Johnson, Betty Ford, Rosalynn Carter, Nancy Reagan, Barbara Bush, and Hillary Rodham Clinton. Hoover's innovations changed the institution of the first lady by aligning it with the realities of modern women. Just as the depression destroyed Herbert Hoover's presidency, it wreaked havoc on Lou Henry Hoover's tenure as White House mistress.

The public marriage that Lou had built with Bert after they exchanged wedding vows in 1899 suffered between 1929 and 1933. The demands of the presidency meant that Bert had less time to communicate with Lou about their shared concerns. Although Lou had been the primary architect of their public partnership, she had also been dependent on Bert's support for her ambitions. Bert never minded Lou's activism, as long as it did not interfere with her responsibilities as a wife and mother, and wealth ensured that Lou could be a successful wife, mother, and activist. To that end, Bert had encouraged her voluntarism before 1929 because it paralleled his various public policy undertakings.

After 1929, the presidency overtook their public partnership, and because of the depression, Lou had to spend more time protecting Bert from his critics. Thus, the public marriage they had built needed restructuring during their White House years because Lou could no longer pick her work. Instead, being first lady became the most important aspect of her public existence. Although her level of activism never wavered, a weakened public marriage meant that Lou Henry Hoover's accomplishments were comparatively less as first lady than they had been before 1929. Her White House record resulted from her individual efforts rather her partnership with Bert, and she should be remembered as the pathbreaking activist she was.

Lou Henry Hoover's diminished public partnership with Herbert Hoover both liberated and limited her. Her successor, Eleanor Roosevelt, suffered no such contradictions. Because Eleanor's marriage to Franklin had been weak for some time, she was much more accustomed to an independent, public life of activism. Eleanor's accomplishments as first lady, though, came more from an improvisational style than from institutional innovations. She did little to organize or change the operations in the East Wing. Thus, Eleanor Roosevelt's record as first lady resulted from her own ideological beliefs projected outward onto the world. Nonetheless, Lou Hoover foreshadowed much of the work Eleanor Roosevelt undertook and expanded as first lady: radio speeches, Appalachian philanthropy, and depression relief.

Lou Henry Hoover's historical importance stems from the substantive manner in which she remade the institution of first lady. Put simply, Hoover deserves more credit from historians and from the public for modernizing the East Wing of the White House. Indeed, her efforts in that regard have had a more lasting institutional impact than did Roosevelt's unique activism, which actually became a cautionary tale for what future first ladies should avoid. Hoover's expanded use of staff, sustained coordination with volunteer organizations, and development of political programs can be found in the works of subsequent first ladies, specifically Lady Bird Johnson, who converted the East Wing into a professional operation. In making the White House a comfortable place for herself as well as for Bert, Lou put her own mark on the East Wing, outdistancing the efforts of Edith Bolling Galt Wilson, Florence Kling Harding, and Grace Goodhue Coolidge. Yet few people in the early twenty-first century know of Lou Henry Hoover's innovations. Such a historical oversight would please the modest woman who preferred anonymity for her activism, but her White House activism is too important to be overlooked any longer.

NOTES

ABBREVIATIONS

AAS

Articles, Addresses, and Statements

GSOGF

Girl Scouts and Other Groups Files

HHPL

Herbert Hoover Presidential Library

LHH

Lou Henry Hoover

LHHP

Lou Henry Hoover Papers, Herbert Hoover Presidential Library

OH

Oral History

PCF

Personal Correspondence Files

SF

Subject Files

WHGF

White House General Files

WHSF

White House Social Files

FROM TOMBOY TO FIRST LADY

1. "A Foretaste of Camp-Life," in "AAS c. 1886–1898—Early Writings Pre-served by Father," SF, LHHP; Helen Pryor, *Lou Henry Hoover: Gallant First Lady* (New York: Dodd, Mead, 1969), 3–5; Nancy F. Cott, *The Bonds of Womanhood: "Woman's Sphere" in New England, 1780–1835* (New Haven, Conn.: Yale University Press, 1977); Barbara Welter, "The Cult of True Womanhood: 1820–1860," *American Quarterly* 24 (Summer 1966): 151–74; Harvey Green, *The Light of the Home: An Intimate View of the Lives of Women in Victorian America* (New York: Pantheon Books, 1983), 48–51.

2. "LHH, School Girl," typescript manuscript by Emma Naumann Bassett, n.d. [c. 1928–1932], in "Hoover, Lou Henry—Articles and Books About, 1929–1960," SF, LHHP.

3. "Texas," 8 June 1888, in "School Papers—LHH—High School—Reports and Miscellaneous, 1886–1890," SF, LHHP.

4. "Universal Suffrage," 18 November 1889, in "School Papers—LHH—High School—Reports and Miscellaneous, 1886–1890," SF, LHHP. On women's issues, see, for example, Jean H. Baker, ed., *Votes for Women: The Struggle for Suffrage Revisited* (New York: Oxford University Press, 2002), and Barbara Leslie Epstein, *The Politics of Domesticity: Women, Evangelism, and Temperance in Nineteenth-Century America* (Middletown, Conn.: Wesleyan University Press, 1981).

5. "The Independent Girl," 31 January 1890, in "School Papers—LHH—High School—Reports and Miscellaneous, 1886–1890," SF, LHHP.

6. "Resolved;—That the Labor Question is one that must soon demand the consideration of the American public," in "School Papers—San Jose Normal—Essays and Reports," SF, LHHP.

7. George H. Nash, *The Life of Herbert Hoover: The Engineer, 1874–1914* (New York: W. W. Norton, 1983), 598 n.110; Pryor, *Lou Henry Hoover*, 18, 21.

8. Herbert Hoover, *The Memoirs of Herbert Hoover: Years of Adventure, 1874–1920* (New York: Macmillan, 1951), 23.

9. Nash, *The Engineer*, 598 n.110; Lou Henry to My dearest [c. April 1898], in "Hoover, Herbert, 1898," PCF, LHHP.

10. Barbara Miller Solomon, *In the Company of Educated Women: A History of Women and Higher Education in America* (New Haven, Conn.: Yale University Press, 1985), 94–114; Dorothy M. Brown, *Setting a Course: American Women in the 1920s* (Boston: Twayne, 1987), 29–47.

11. Susan L. Dyer OH, 29–30 September 1966, HHPL.

12. Margaret W. Rossiter, *Women Scientists in America: Struggles and Strategies to 1940* (Baltimore: Johns Hopkins University Press, 1982), 60–61 (first two quotes); Lou Henry to Evelyn Wight Allan, n.d. (c. June 1898), in "Allan, Evelyn Wight," PCF, LHHP (last quote); Green, *The Light of the Home*, 10–28; Nancy F. Cott, "Marriage and Women's Citizenship in the United States, 1830–1934," *American Historical Review* 103 (December 1998): 1440–74.

13. Florence L. Henry to Mrs. Mason, [1899], in "Hoover, Lou Henry, Marriage," SF, LHHP.

14. LHH Diary, 7 February 1899 (first quote) and 5 July 1899 (remaining quotes), in "Hoover, Lou Henry Diaries, 1899," SF, LHHP.

15. LHH Diary, 9 March 1899, in "Hoover, Lou Henry Diaries, 1899," SF (first quote); Herbert Hoover to Jean Henry, 12 January 1900, in "Henry Family Correspondence, 1900," PCF (second quote); LHH to Jean Henry, 13 July 1899, in "Henry Family Correspondence, 1899–undated," PCF (last quote), all in LHHP.

16. See Diana Preston, *The Boxer Rebellion: The Dramatic Story of China's Civil War on Foreigners that Shook the World in the Summer of 1900* (New York: Walker, 2000).

17. Nash, *The Engineer,* 118, 121, 624 n.32; LHH Diary, 10 June 1900 (first quote), 16 June 1900 (second quote), 17 June 1900 (third quote), all in "Hoover, Lou Henry Diaries, 1900," SF, LHHP; Hoover, *Years of Adventure,* 50–51 (last quote).

18. LHH to Ida Koverman, 27 February 1928, in "Campaign of 1928, Publicity," SF, LHHP.

19. Hoover, *Years of Adventure,* 55, 64–65.

20. LHH to Papa, n.d. [c. 1901], in "Henry Family Correspondence, 1901," PCF, LHHP.

21. LHH to Charles and Florence Henry, 7 June 1903, in "Henry Family Correspondence, 1903, June–December," PCF, LHHP.

22. Hoover, *Years of Adventure,* 76 (first quote); Herbert to H. C. Hoover, n.d., in "Henry Family Correspondence, 1903, June–December," PCF, LHHP (remaining quotes).

23. Mama to LHH, 13 July 1907, in "Henry Family Correspondence, 1904–1908," PCF, LHHP; Hoover, *Years of Adventure,* 77.

24. Mum to My dearest boys, 20 April 1924, in "Correspondence with LHH, 1924, January–July," Allan Hoover Papers, HHPL.

25. Hoover, *Years of Adventure,* 117–19; Pryor, *Lou Henry Hoover,* 69.

26. Hoover, *Years of Adventure,* 117–19.

27. Steven Mintz and Susan Kellogg, *Domestic Revolutions: A Social History of American Family Life* (New York: Free Press, 1988), 107–31.

28. Hoover, *Years of Adventure,* 144.

29. See, for example, Karen J. Blair, *The Clubwoman as Feminist: True Womanhood Redefined, 1868–1914* (New York: Holmes and Meier, 1980); Allen F. Davis, *Spearheads for Reform: The Social Settlements and the Progressive Movement, 1890–1914* (New York: Oxford University Press, 1967); Ellen Carol DuBois, *Harriot Stanton Blatch and the Winning of Woman Suffrage* (New Haven, Conn.: Yale University Press, 1997); Sara Hunter Graham, *Woman Suffrage and the New Democracy* (New Haven, Conn.: Yale University Press, 1996); Anne Firor Scott, *Natural Allies: Women's Associations in American History* (Urbana:

University of Illinois Press, 1991); Rosalyn Terborg-Penn, *African American Women in the Struggle for the Vote, 1850–1920* (Bloomington: Indiana University Press, 1998).

30. LHH to Charles and Florence Henry, 22 August 1914, in Pryor, *Lou Henry Hoover,* 91; "Report of the Chairman of the Resident American Women's Relief Committee of London (Up to 1 October 1914)," in "American Women's War Relief Fund—Reports of Activities and Finances, 1914," SF, LHHP (quote).

31. Herbert Hoover to LHH, 5 November 1914 (first two quotes), 6 November 1914 (next four quotes), LHH to Herbert Hoover, 7 November 1914 (remaining quotes), all in "Hoover, Herbert, 1912–1914," PCF, LHHP.

32. Mummy to Herbert, 25 November 1914, in "Reynolds, Jackson," PCF, LHHP (first two quotes); Mummy to Allan Hoover, 24 November 1914 (third quote), and Mummy to Allan, n.d. [c. fall 1914] (last quote), both in "Correspondence with LHH, 1914," Allan Hoover Papers, HHPL.

33. Hoover, *Years of Adventure,* 211 (first two quotes); telegram from LHH, 12 July 1915, in "Hoover, Herbert, 1915," PCF, LHHP (last quote).

34. Herbert Hoover to Josephine Bates, 18 December 1914, in "Belgian Relief—Correspondence, 1914" (first quote); LHH to Mr. Shaler, 31 October 1916, in "Belgian Lace—Correspondence, 1915–1918" (second quote), both in SF, LHHP.

35. "Belgium's Need: Notes of a talk given by LHH in October, 1915," in "Belgian Relief—Articles about Commission for Relief in Belgium, etc., 1914–1919 and undated," SF, LHHP.

36. LHH to Charlotte Kellogg, 3 April 1915, in "Belgian Relief—Correspondence, 1915," SF, LHHP.

37. Maurine Weiner Greenwald, *Women, War, and Work: The Impact of World War I on Women Workers in the United States* (Westport, Conn.: Greenwood Press, 1980).

38. Dudley Harmon, "Dining with the Hoovers: What a Guest Eats at the Table of the Food Administrator," *Ladies' Home Journal,* March 1918, in "Clippings, 1917–1919," SF, LHHP.

39. LHH speech, 23 July 1918, in "AAS, 23 July 1918, Women's Council of Defense, Rockville, Maryland" (first quote); "Mrs. Hoover Sets Pace in Aiding Saving of Food," n.p., 27 October 1917, in "AAS, 27 October 1917, Opening Food Conservation Week, Baltimore, Maryland" (second quote), both in SF, LHHP; George H. Nash, *The Life of Herbert Hoover: Master of Emergencies, 1917–1918* (New York: W. W. Norton, 1996), 155.

40. LHH to Colonel Winford H. Smith, 5 November 1918, in "American Red

Cross, Canteen Escort Service, Correspondence and Memoranda, 1918–1919 and undated," GSOGF, LHHP.

41. A. J. Pizzini to LHH, 30 December 1918, in "American Red Cross, Canteen Escort Service, Correspondence and Memoranda, 1918–1919 and undated," GSOGF, LHHP.

42. Mum to Allan, n.d. [c. 1918], in "Correspondence with LHH, 1918," Allan Hoover Papers, HHPL.

43. Brown, *Setting a Course,* 49–74; Nancy F. Cott, *The Grounding of Modern Feminism* (New Haven, Conn.: Yale University Press, 1987), especially 11–142; J. Stanley Lemons, *The Woman Citizen: Social Feminism in the 1920s* (Urbana: University of Illinois Press, 1973).

44. Gerald Egan, "Efficient Mrs. Hoover Heads Girl Scouts," *New York Herald,* 25 March 1923, in "Clippings, Girl Scouts, 1923," SF, LHHP.

45. Mayme Ober Peak, "The Woman Power in the Cabinet: Wives of Members Wield a Big Influence," *Buffalo Express,* 15 March 1925, in "Clippings, General, 1925," SF, LHHP.

46. Paula Baker, "The Domestication of Politics: Women and American Political Society, 1780–1920," *American Historical Review* 89 (June 1984): 620–47.

47. Mum to Allan, [c. 29 April 1920], in "Correspondence with LHH, 1920," Allan Hoover Papers, HHPL.

48. LHH to Philippi Harding, n.d., in "Philippi Harding Butler, 1921 March–May" (first quote); LHH to Alida Henriques, 30 June 1927, in "Henriques, Alida, 1926–1928 and undated" (second quote), both in PCF, LHHP.

49. "Wife of Secretary Hoover in Cincinnati," *Cincinnati Times Star,* 29 August 1923, in "Clippings, Girl Scouts, 1923," SF (first two quotes); Andrew R. Boone, "At Home with Mrs. Herbert Hoover," *Stanford Illustrated Review,* in "Clippings, January–April 1922," GSOGF (remaining quotes), both in LHHP.

50. Anonymous, *Boudoir Mirrors of Washington* (Philadelphia: John C. Winston, 1923), 244 (first quote); LHH to Dare Stark McMullin, 15 August 1933, in "White House Furnishings, McMullin Book, Hoover Administration," SF, LHHP (second quote).

51. Arthur T. Dailey to LHH, 23 January 1924, in "ARA European Children's Fund, 1920–1929," GSOGF, LHHP.

52. LHH to Vaal Stark, 4 March 1940, in "Administrative Correspondence, Stark, Vaal (Wally Anne)," GSOGF, LHHP.

53. Ethel Mockler, *Citizens in Action: The Girl Scout Record, 1912–1947* (New York: Girl Scouts National Organization, 1947), 12; Kendrick A. Clements, *Hoover, Conservation, and Consumerism: Engineering the Good Life* (Lawrence:

University Press of Kansas, 2000); John William Ward, *Red, White, and Blue: Men, Books, and Ideas in American Culture* (New York: Oxford University Press, 1969), 21–37.

54. LHH to Marie H. Richards, 2 March 1927, in "Administrative Correspondence, Richards, Marie H.," GSOGF, LHHP; Anne Beiser Allen, *An Independent Woman: The Life of Lou Henry Hoover* (Westport, Conn.: Greenwood Press, 2000), 93.

55. Helen Storrow to LHH, [c. summer 1921], in "Administrative Correspondence, Storrow, Helen," GSOGF, LHHP.

56. "A Manual for National Officers (especially new President!)," in "AAS, February 1922, A Manual for National Officers," SF, LHHP.

57. Untitled document by LHH, 22 April 1922, in "AAS, 22 April 1922, Dissertation of Girl Scout Policies, Washington, D.C.," SF, LHHP.

58. Suggestion for DPA Article, 8 October 1923, in "AAS, 8 October 1923, Stanford Girl Scout Course, Stanford, California," SF, LHHP (first two quotes); Rebecca Christian, "'Don't Forget Joy!': Lou Henry Hoover and the Girl Scouts," in *Lou Henry Hoover: Essays on a Busy Life,* ed. Dale C. Mayer (Worland, Wyo.: High Plains Publishing Company, 1994), 44; The President's Message, Mrs. Herbert Hoover, National President of the Girl Scouts, Eleventh Annual Convention, Boston, Massachusetts, 20 May 1925, in "AAS, 20 May 1925, Eleventh Annual Girl Scout Convention, Boston, Massachusetts," SF, LHHP (last quote).

59. Allen, *An Independent Woman,* 93–94; untitled, undated history of the National Little House, in "Little House History, 1942" (first quote); "Girl Scout Home-Making Activities Stimulated by Aid of Mrs. Hoover," n.p., n.d., in "Little House Clippings and Printed Matter," (second quote), both in GSOGF, LHHP.

60. Text of LHH's speech, [c. 26 October 1923], attached to LHH to Marion Delany, 24 October 1923, in "California Civic League of Women Voters, Correspondence, 1921–1928," GSOGF, LHHP.

61. See Zelma Boeshar to LHH, 12 May 1921, and Hoover's typed replies to Boeshar's questions about women engineers, in "Professions for Women: Views on, 1921–42," SF, LHHP.

62. Letter from LHH, [c. 1924], in "Correspondence with LHH, 1924, January–July," Allan Hoover Papers, HHPL.

63. Ibid.

64. Pryor, *Lou Henry Hoover,* 136–38.

65. Alice Allene Sefton, *The Women's Division National Amateur Athletic Federation: Sixteen Years of Progress in Athletics for Girls and Women, 1923–1939* (Stanford, Calif.: Stanford University Press, 1941), 1.

66. Announcement for the Associated Press, in "Clubs and Organizations, National Amateur Athletic Federation Women's Division, Annual Meeting, 1923, Publicity" (first quote); LHH to Susan Bristol, 29 February 1924, in "Clubs and Organizations, National Amateur Athletic Federation—Women's Division, Bristol, Susan, 1924" (second quote), both in GSOGF, LHHP; Sefton, *The Women's Division*, 6, 8, 37.

67. Mum to Both the Boys, [16 April 1927], in "Correspondence with LHH, 1927, March–September," Allan Hoover Papers, HHPL.

68. Richard Norton Smith, *An Uncommon Man: The Triumph of Herbert Hoover* (Worland, Wyo.: High Plains Publishing Company, 1984), 53.

69. Mum to Both the Boys, [16 April 1927], in "Correspondence with LHH, 1927, March–September," Allan Hoover Papers, HHPL.

70. Ibid.

71. Robert H. Ferrell, *The Presidency of Calvin Coolidge* (Lawrence: University Press of Kansas, 1998), 192–94 (first quote); Sarah Louise Arnold to LHH, 8 February 1928, in "Arnold, Sarah Louise, 1927–1928," PCF (second quote), and W. F. Snow to LHH, [c. spring 1928], in "Campaign of 1928, Publicity," SF (last quote), both in LHHP.

72. LHH to George Akerson, 15 February 1928, in "Hoover, Lou Henry, 1928–1931," George Akerson Papers, HHPL.

73. "Electing a President's Wife: Mrs. Al Smith in the White House," *Women's Home Companion* (April 1928): 10, 63.

74. Advertisement, *Delineator* (October 1928): 3.

75. LHH to Edgar Rickard, 18 February 1928, in "Rickard, Edgar, 1928," PCF (first quote); Ruth Fesler to LHH, 11 July 1928, in "American Institute of Mining and Metallurgical Engineers—Women's Auxiliary Correspondence, 1928, April–July," GSOGF (second quote), both in LHHP.

76. LHH to Caroline Slade, 27 August 1928, in "Campaign of 1928, Women's National Committee for Hoover," SF, LHHP.

77. Fesler to Helen Sutherland, 18 September 1928, in "Campaign of 1928, American Association of University Women," SF, LHHP.

78. Bess Furman, *Washington By-Line: The Personal History of a Newspaperwoman* (New York: Alfred A. Knopf, 1949), 8–9.

79. "Mrs. Hoover Escapes Death in Auto Crash," *Washington Post*, 18 March 1928 (first two quotes); LHH to Lucy Booth Cumming, [March 1928], in "Hoover, Lou Henry Driving Accident, 1928," SF, LHHP (last quote).

80. Ibid.

81. LHH to Doctor H. R. Fairclough, 20 March 1928 (first quote); LHH to

President Glass, [March 1928] (second quote), both in "Hoover, Lou Henry Driving Accident, 1928," SF, LHHP.

82. Dyer OH.

83. LHH to Grace Brosseau, 10 April 1928, in "Daughters of the American Revolution, Correspondence, 1928," GSOGF, LHHP.

84. LHH to Flora Hartley Greene, 17 May 1928, in "Campaign of 1928, General, January–September," SF, LHHP.

85. Penelope Sumerwell, "Campaigning Doesn't Fatigue Mrs. Hoover," n.p., n.d., in "Clippings, Campaign Trip, Newark, New Jersey, 1928" (first quote); LHH to Mary A. Roberts, 15 September 1928, in "Campaign of 1928, Prohibition Issue" (second and third quotes); LHH to Estelle Northam, 28 January 1929, in "Campaign of 1928, Republican National Committee, Women's Activities" (last quote), all in SF, LHHP.

86. LHH to Edgar Rickard, 4 October 1928, in "Campaign of 1928, General, October–November" (first two quotes); LHH to Ludmilla Sayre, 11 October 1928, in "Campaign of 1928, Publicity" (last quote), both in SF, LHHP.

87. Ruth Fesler to Mrs. Phillips, 16 October 1929, "South America Trip Correspondence, 1929," SF, LHHP; Herbert Hoover, *The Memoirs of Herbert Hoover: The Cabinet and the Presidency, 1920–1933* (New York: Macmillan, 1952), 210, 211; David Burner, *Herbert Hoover: A Public Life* (New York: Alfred A. Knopf, 1979), 208, 285; Pryor, *Lou Henry Hoover,* 157–58.

88. David Starr Jordan to LHH, 7 November 1928, in "Jordan, David Starr," PCF, LHHP.

AN ACTIVIST FIRST LADY IN TRADITIONAL WASHINGTON

1. Emma Bugbee, "New First Lady Gay and Grave on Eventful Day," *New York Herald,* 5 March 1929, in "Clippings, Inauguration, 1929," SF, LHHP; Mary Randolph, *Presidents and First Ladies* (New York: D. Appleton-Century, 1936), 118–20; Ishbel Ross, *Grace Coolidge and Her Era: The Story of a President's Wife* (New York: Dodd, Mead, 1962), 255; Anne Beiser Allen, *An Independent Woman: The Life of Lou Henry Hoover* (Westport, Conn.: Greenwood Press, 2000), 120.

2. Randolph, *Presidents and First Ladies,* 121–22.

3. David Starr Jordan to LHH, 19 March 1929, in "Jordan, David Starr and Jessie" (first quote); Philippi Harding Butler to LHH, 16 February 1929, in "Butler, Philippi Harding" (second quote), both in PCF, LHHP.

4. Ruth Fesler to Elsie C. Mead, 22 October 1930, in "Girl Scouts: Administrative Correspondence, Mead, Elsie C.," GSOGF, LHHP.

5. "The Lady of the White House," *The Key of Kappa Kappa Gamma,* n.d., in

"Clippings, LHH, Featured Articles, Magazines, 1929," SF, LHHP (first quote); Mary Roberts Rinehart, "A New First Lady Becomes Hostess for the Nation," *Worlds Work* 58 (March 1929): 34 (second and third quotes); "Mrs. Hoover as First Lady," *Review of Reviews* (April 1929): 121 (last quote).

6. For more background on first ladies, see Betty Boyd Caroli, *First Ladies,* expanded ed. (New York: Oxford University Press, 1995).

7. "Intricate Social Regime Claims First Lady," *Des Moines Register,* 12 May 1929, in "Clippings, Clubs and Organizations, 1929" (first two quotes); Jean Jarvis, "First Lady Keeps up Timed Schedule," *Washington Star,* 28 February 1932, in "Clippings, Miscellaneous (1) 1932" (last two quotes), both in SF, LHHP.

8. Irwin H. Hoover manuscript notes for *Forty-two Years in the White House,* Roll 9, Irwin H. Hoover Papers on Microfilm, Library of Congress.

9. Corinne Rich, "Plans Are Laid by Mrs. Hoover for New Home," *Washington Herald,* 14 February 1929, in "Clippings, White House Furnishings and Grounds, 1929" (first three quotes); "First Lady Sets Precedence in Methods of Entertaining," *Washington Star,* 21 August 1930, in "Clippings, Social, 1930" (remaining quotes), both in SF, LHHP.

10. Rich, "Plans Are Laid by Mrs. Hoover."

11. William Seale, "Lou Henry Hoover and the White House," in *Lou Henry Hoover: Essays on a Busy Life,* ed. Dale C. Mayer (Worland, Wyo.: High Plains Publishing Company, 1994), 86–87; LHH to Jean Henry Large, 5 June 1930, in "Large, Jean, 1930 January–July," PCF, LHHP (quote).

12. Lillian Rogers Parks, *My Thirty Years Backstairs at the White House* (New York: Fleet Publishing Corporation, 1961), 80.

13. Herbert Hoover, *The Memoirs of Herbert Hoover: The Cabinet and the Presidency, 1920–1933* (New York: Macmillan, 1952), 321 (first quote); Secretary to Mrs. James C. Rogerson, 23 May 1929, in "White House Furnishings, Arden House, 1929 April–July," SF, LHHP (second quote).

14. LHH to Anne Hyde Choate, 20 January 1930, in "White House Furnishings, Committee on, Choate, Anne and Mabel, 1930" (first quote); Dare Stark McMullin, "Herbert Hoover, Lou Henry Hoover 1929–1933," in "White House Furnishings, McMullin Book, Hoover Administration" (second and third quotes); "Hoovers Prepare for Moving Day," *Washington Star,* 30 January 1933, in "Clippings, General 1933" (last quote), all in SF, LHHP.

15. Dare Stark, "Heirlooms in the White House," *Woman's Home Companion* (March 1932): 17–18, 104, in "White House Furnishings, Article by Dare Stark McMullin," SF, LHHP.

16. McMullin, "Herbert Hoover, Lou Henry Hoover 1929–1933."

17. Joel Boone Autobiography—Hoover Administration, p. 64C, Joel Boone Collection, HHPL (first quote); LHH to McMullin, 15 August 1929, in "Rapidan Camp, General, 1928–1938 and undated" (second quote), and LHH to James Y. and Jane Deeter Rippin, 27 January 1929, in "Rapidan Camp, Correspondence, Rippin, James Y., 1929–1932" (last two quotes), both in SF, LHHP.

18. LHH to James Y. and Jane Deeter Rippin, 27 January 1929, in "Rapidan Camp, Correspondence, Rippin, James Y., 1929–1932," SF, LHHP.

19. "Mrs. Hoover's Plans for Planting at Camp," c.1929, in "Rapidan Camp, Plans for Camp," SF, LHHP.

20. Choate to LHH, 24 September 1931, in "Girl Scouts: Administrative Correspondence, Choate, Anne Hyde (Mrs. Arthur O.), 1920–1936," GSOGF, LHHP.

21. Martha Strayer, "Once Jobless Washington Stenographer Now Is Secretary to First Lady of Land," *Washington Daily News,* 9 March 1929, in "Clippings White House Secretaries and Aides, 1929," SF, LHHP.

22. "White House Social Secretary Awaited," *Washington Post,* 3 March 1929, in "Clippings White House Secretaries and Aides, 1929," SF, LHHP.

23. Mildred Hall Campbell OH, 24 September 1966, HHPL.

24. Randolph, *Presidents and First Ladies,* 124.

25. Helen Hartley [Greene] White OH, 27 October 1966, HHPL (first quote); Grace Coolidge to LHH, 23 October 1929, in "White House Furnishings, Committee on, Coolidge, Grace, 1929–1932," SF, LHHP (second quote).

26. Susan L. Dyer OH, 29–30 September 1966, HHPL.

27. "Mrs. Hoover May Choose to Have no Social Secretary," *New York Herald,* 2 October 1930, in "Clippings, White House Personal, 1930, SF, LHHP.

28. Robert Allen, *Washington Merry-Go-Round* (New York: Horace Liveright, 1931), 9 (first quote); "Three Secretaries for White House Gaiety," *Boston Globe,* 13 July 1930, in "Hoover, Lou Henry—Memorabilia," Ruth Fesler Lipman Papers, HHPL (remaining quotes).

29. Unidentified clipping, "October Tatler 1930," *Washington,* in "Clippings, White House Personal, 1930" (first three quotes); George Abell, "Capital Capers," *Washington Daily News,* 25 February 1931, in "Clippings, White House General, 1931" (remaining quotes), both in SF, LHHP.

30. LHH to Ethel Obetz Fullenwider, 17 March 1938, in "White House Furnishings, General Correspondence, 1930–1938 and undated" SF, LHHP.

31. Philippi Harding Butler OH, 12 September 1967, HHPL (first quote); "First Lady Gets Third Secretary," *Washington Star,* 22 October 1931, in "Clippings, White House General, 1931" (second quote).

32. "First Lady Gets Third Secretary" (first two quotes); "Tell me what she's

really like, A discussion of Mrs. Hoover, by a friend," typescript manuscript, n.d. [c. 1929–1933; possibly written by Dare Stark McMullin, as per pencil marks on the document], in "Hoover, Lou Henry—Biographical Data" (last quote), both in SF, LHHP.

33. For background on the DePriest controversy, see David S. Day, "Herbert Hoover and Racial Politics: The DePriest Incident," *Journal of Negro History* 65 (Winter 1980): 6–17; David S. Day, "A New Perspective on the 'DePriest Tea' Historiographic Controversy," *Journal of Negro History* 75 (Summer/Fall 1990): 120–24; Donald J. Lisio, *Hoover, Blacks, and Lily-Whites: A Study of Southern Strategies* (Chapel Hill: University of North Carolina Press, 1985), 134–40, 173.

34. See, for example, Barbara Young Welke, *Recasting American Liberty: Gender, Race, Law, and the Railroad Revolution, 1865–1920* (New York: Cambridge University Press, 2001).

35. Day, "Herbert Hoover and Racial Politics," 8, 14.

36. Secretary to Walter P. Newton, 21 May 1929, in "Social Events at the White House, 1929 January–October and undated," WHGF, LHHP.

37. M. Randolph to Mr. Rockwell, [5 June 1929], in "1929, June 12 Tea," WHSF, LHHP.

38. Ruth Fesler Lipman Diary, 12 June 1929, Ruth Fesler Lipman Papers; Ruth Fesler Lipman OH, 26 September 1967 (quotes), both in HHPL.

39. W. C. Jennings to LHH, 15 June 1929 (first quote); Mary J. Reeves to Herbert and LHH, 19 June 1929 (remaining quotes), both in "DePriest Incident, Critical of Mrs. Hoover," SF, LHHP.

40. C. L. and Eunice E. Nethaway to LHH, 19 June 1929 (first two quotes); One of the Club to LHH, 23 June 1929 (third quote); unsigned letter to Herbert and Lou Hoover, n.d. (last quote), all in "DePriest Incident, Critical of Mrs. Hoover," SF, LHHP.

41. Mary Andrews to LHH, 19 June 1929, in "DePriest Incident, Approving Mrs. Hoover's Actions (1)," SF, LHHP.

42. David Burner, *Herbert Hoover: A Public Life* (New York: Alfred A. Knopf, 1979), 215; Hoover, *The Cabinet and the Presidency,* 324–25 (quotes).

43. Ibid.

44. Undated, untitled draft reply (first quote); memorandum to Mr. Akerson, 14 June 1929 (second quote), both in "DePriest Incident, Miscellany," SF, LHHP.

45. Lisio, *Hoover, Blacks, and Lily-Whites,* 72–92, 115–40, 159–85, 244–45, 275–80.

46. Notes re Garden Party for Veterans, 4:00 P.M., 27 June 1929, in "Social Events at the White House, 1930 May–October," WHGF, LHHP.

47. "The Lady of the White House," *The Key of Kappa Kappa Gamma,* n.d., in "Clippings, LHH, Featured Articles, Magazines, 1929," SF, LHHP (first four quotes); Hoover, *The Cabinet and the Presidency,* 323 (remaining quotes).

48. "The Lady of the White House."

49. "Mrs. Herbert Hoover Has Upset Capital Tradition by Her Actions," *Mt. Carroll Daily Mirror-Democrat,* 5 April 1929, in "Clippings, Automobile Driving, 1929," SF, LHHP (first quote); Marvin Ewy, *Charles Curtis of Kansas: Vice President of the United States, 1929–1933* (Emporia, Kans.: Emporia State Research Studies, 1961), 47; Gertrude L. Bowman OH, 6 and 12 November 1966, HHPL (last quote).

50. "White House Friendliness," *Le Grand Monde,* 1929, p. 24, in "Clippings, Social January–March, 1929" (first quote); "Mrs. Herbert Hoover Has Upset Capital Tradition by Her Actions," *Mt. Carroll Daily Mirror-Democrat,* 5 April 1929, in "Clippings, Automobile Driving, 1929" (second quote); "Hoover Doubles White House Social Program; Dinner to Curtis Solves Precedence Problem," *New York Times,* 10 November 1929, in "Clippings, Social October–December, 1929" (last quote), all in SF, LHHP.

51. "Capital Baffled by the Riddle of Mrs. Hoover," *New York World,* 22 September 1929, in "Clippings, LHH, Featured Articles—Newspapers," SF, LHHP.

52. Joel Boone Autobiography—Hoover Administration, p. 430, Joel Boone Collection, HHPL (first three quotes); LHH to Dolly Gann, 26 April 1933, in "Gann, Dolly," PCF, LHHP (remaining quotes).

53. "Mrs. Hoover Gives White House Atmosphere of West Coast," *Washington Star,* 21 September 1929, in "Clippings, General News Items, 1929," SF, LHHP.

54. LHH to Large, 30 April 1930, in "Large, Jean Henry, 1930 January–July," PCF, LHHP.

55. "White House Friendliness" (first quote); Mildred Hall Campbell, "Mrs. Hoover's Secretary," Memoirs of Allen Campbell and Mildred Hall Campbell, 30 November 1971, HHPL (second quote).

56. "White House Friendliness" (quotes). For the dates and LHH's role, see Irwin H. Hoover's calendar for 12 May 1929, Roll 6, Irwin H. Hoover Papers on Microfilm, Library of Congress.

57. "Precedent Set for Functions in White House," n.p., 10 November 1929, in "Clippings, Social October–December, 1929," SF, LHHP.

58. Elise Kirk, "First Lady in the Arts," in Mayer, *Lou Henry Hoover,* 100, 107–8; Dyer OH (quotes).

59. "Fire Fails to Halt White House Party," *Washington Post,* 25 December 1929 (quote); Seale, "Lou Henry Hoover and the White House," 86.

60. Joel Boone Autobiography—Hoover Administration, p. 976, Joel Boone

Collection, HHPL (first quote); Coolidge to LHH, 27 June 1930, in "Coolidge, Grace" (second quote); Lillian Gilbreth to LHH, 29 April [1930], in "Gilbreth, Lillian" (last quote), both in PCF, LHHP.

61. Butler to LHH, 12 May 1930 (first two quotes); LHH to Butler, 27 May 1930 (last quote), both in "Butler, Philippi Harding," PCF, LHHP.

62. Sallie V. H. Pickett, "Mrs. Hoover Given Praise for Her Skillful Solution of Recent Society Problem," *Washington Star,* 23 February 1930, in "Clippings, Social, 1930," SF, LHHP (quotes); Dyer OH.

63. David Lawrence, "White House Dinner Error Stirs Gossip," n.p., 8 November 1930, in "Clippings, Social, 1930," SF, LHHP.

64. Cornelius Vanderbilt Jr., "Hoover Vetoes Lavish Society Life This Year," n.p., 27 October 1930, in "Clippings, Social, 1930," SF, LHHP.

65. Ibid. (first quote); "The Other Presidents: A Well Known Woman Politician Sizes Up the Last Five Mistresses of the White House," n.p., n.d., in "Clippings, Magazine Articles, 1932," SF, LHHP (remaining quotes).

66. Copy of invitation, [c. December 1931], in "White House Christmas, 1931," SF, LHHP.

67. Peter and Peggy and Grandma Give Party in Grandpa's House, in "White House Christmas, 1931," SF, LHHP.

68. Ibid.

69. "Tell me what she's really like, A discussion of Mrs. Hoover, by a friend."

70. Ibid.

71. Ibid. (first three quotes); Butler OH (last quote).

FROM PRIVATE PHILANTHROPY TO RELIEF POLITICS

1. For further background on mountain schools, see, for example, David E. Whisnant, *All That Is Native and Fine: The Politics of Culture in an American Region* (Chapel Hill: University of North Carolina Press, 1983).

2. Darwin Lambert, *Herbert Hoover's Hideaway* (Luray, Va.: Shenandoah Natural History Association, 1971), 90; Philippi Harding Butler OH, 12 September 1967, HHPL.

3. Butler OH (first quote); Ruth Fesler to Idabel M. Porter, 23 October 1929, in "Rapidan Camp, President School, Socio-Psychological Profile of Children," SF, LHHP (second quote).

4. Untitled, undated memorandum, in "Rapidan Camp, President School, Teacher Candidate, 1929–1932," SF, LHHP.

5. Secretary to William J. Hutchins, 4 November 1929, in "Rapidan Camp, President School, Teacher Candidate, 1929–1932," SF, LHHP.

6. Untitled, undated memorandum, in "Rapidan Camp, President School, Teacher Candidate, 1929–1932," SF, LHHP.

7. Fesler to Hutchins, 22 November 1929, in "Rapidan Camp, President School, Teacher Candidate, 1929–1932," SF, LHHP.

8. Fesler to Mrs. William Talbot, 18 January 1930, in "Rapidan Camp, President School, Donations, 1929–1931 and undated," SF, LHHP.

9. LHH to Alma Lorimer, 17 November 1930, in "Rapidan Camp, President School, Donations, 1929–1931 and undated," SF, LHHP.

10. Fesler to Mary G. Armstrong, 17 February 1930, in "Rapidan Camp, President School, Correspondence, General, 1929–1932," SF, LHHP.

11. Susan L. Dyer OH, 29–30 September 1966, HHPL.

12. Della Meadows to LHH, n.d., in "Rapidan Camp, President School, Children's Letters," SF, LHHP.

13. Christine Vest Witofski, untitled manuscript, June–July 1960, in "Clippings, General News Items, 1929" (first quote); "The President's Mountain School, Reminiscences of Christine Vest, teacher Feb. 1930–May 1933" [August 1960], in "Rapidan Camp, President School, History" (remaining quotes), both in SF, LHHP.

14. "The President's Mountain School, Reminiscences of Christine Vest, teacher Feb. 1930–May 1933."

15. Joel Boone, "Preface," in Lambert, *Herbert Hoover's Hideaway,* x.

16. Paul F. Boller Jr., *Presidential Campaigns* (New York: Oxford University Press, 1984), 239.

17. "First Lady Gives Views on Relief," *Star,* 31 August 1931, in "Clippings, Clubs and Organizations, 1931, Miscellaneous," SF, LHHP.

18. LHH speech, 27 November 1932, in "AAS, 27 November 1932, 'The Woman's Place in the Present Emergency,'" SF, LHHP.

19. For an institutional history of women and depression relief during the Hoover administration, see Martha H. Swain, "Prelude to the New Deal: Lou Henry Hoover and Women's Relief Work," in *Uncommon Americans: The Lives and Legacies of Herbert and Lou Henry Hoover,* ed. Timothy Walch (Westport, Conn.: Praeger, 2003), 151–66.

20. Irwin H. Hoover manuscript notes for *Forty-two Years in the White House,* Roll 9, Irwin H. Hoover Papers on Microfilm, Library of Congress.

21. Ibid.

22. Mrs. Joseph Beers to LHH, 11 March 1929 (first quote); Secretary to Beers, 4 April 1929 (second and third quotes), both in "Requests for Assistance: Advice, Clothing, Money, 1929, Bar–Bry"; Secretary to Mrs. T. H. Flack, 18 April

1929, in "Requests for Assistance: Advice, Clothing, Money, 1929, F" (last quote), all in WHGF, LHHP.

23. Richard Vedder and Lowell Gallaway, *Out of Work: Unemployment and Government in Twentieth Century America* (New York: Holmes and Meier, 1993), 77, 84; Robert S. McElvaine, *The Great Depression: America, 1929–1941* (New York: Times Books, 1984), 72–75 (quote).

24. [Secretary] to Louis Losh, 13 November 1931, in "Requests for Assistance: Advice, Clothing, Money, 1931, L" (first quote); Secretary to Edgar Rickard, 22 August 1931, in "Requests for Assistance: Advice, Clothing, Money, 1931, G" (second quote); LHH to Lucy D. Good, 15 September 1931, in "Requests for Assistance: Advice, Clothing, Money, 1931, Coc–Cur" (remaining quotes), all in WHGF, LHHP.

25. Untitled, undated note, in "General Federation of Women's Clubs, 1929–1933," GSOGF, LHHP. The placement of this note in the larger file indicates that it likely refers to the September 1931 article in the *Clubwoman GFWC.*

26. LHH to Carrie R. Johnson, 14 May 1931, in "Requests for Assistance: Advice, Clothing, Money, 1931, K" (first two quotes); Secretary to Sibyl Gordon Newell, 4 November 1931, in "Requests for Assistance: Advice, Clothing, Money, 1931, Mia–Mott" (third quote); Secretary to Mrs. Odell, 6 April 1931, in "Requests for Assistance: Advice, Clothing, Money, 1931, T" (last quote), all in WHGF, LHHP.

27. LHH to Mrs. Hugh Bradford, 25 August 1931, in "Requests for Assistance, Field Investigators, Parent Teacher Association: National Congress of, 1931," SF, LHHP.

28. Margaret A. Field to Daisy F. Hindman, 22 December 1931 (first quote); Hindman to Margaret Hall, 23 December 1931 (second quote), both in "Requests for Assistance: Advice, Clothing, Money, 1931, N," WHGF, LHHP.

29. Vedder and Gallaway, *Out of Work,* 84.

30. LHH to Dare Stark McMullin, 20 June 1931, in "Requests for Assistance: Miscellaneous, 1931, A–M," WHGF, LHHP.

31. Mrs. Llewellyn A. Turnock to LHH, 1 December 1931 (first quote); Secretary to Turnock, 14 December 1931 (second quote), both in "Depression Relief Measures, 1930–1931," SF, LHHP.

32. McElvaine, *The Great Depression,* 73, 80.

33. LHH to Jean Henry Large, 14 April 1932, in "Depression Relief Measures, 1932–1939 and undated," SF (first quote); LHH to Louise Price, 5 July 1932, in "Girl Scouts: Administrative Correspondence, Price, Louise," GSOGF (second quote), both in LHHP.

34. Secretary to W. F. Hyde, 5 January 1932, in "Depression Relief Measures, 1930–1931," SF, LHHP.

35. Secretary to Jane Deeter Rippin, 2 March 1931 (first quote); Rippin to Ruth Fesler, 10 March 1931 (second quote), both in "Requests for Assistance: Advice, Clothing, Money, 1931, B"; LHH to Nelle Evans Johnson, 17 August 1931, in "Requests for Assistance: Advice, Clothing, Money, 1931, Cam–Clo" (last quote), all in WHGF, LHHP.

36. Mrs. Conrad Animus to LHH, 7 August 1931, in "Requests for Assistance: Advice, Clothing, Money, 1931, A," WHGF, LHHP.

37. George H. Nash, *The Life of Herbert Hoover: Master of Emergencies, 1917–1918* (New York: W. W. Norton, 1996); Kendrick A. Clements, "Agent of Change: Herbert Hoover as Secretary of Commerce," in Walch, *Uncommon Americans,* 93–105.

38. Mildred Hall to Maud van Woy, 25 March 1931, in "Requests for Assistance: Advice, Clothing, Money, 1931, Hea–Hyr," WHGF, LHHP.

39. Rose Miller to LHH, [c. September 1929], in "Requests for Assistance: Advice, Clothing, Money, 1929, Mil–Nye" (first quote); Secretary to Mrs. Elbert Johnson, 31 August 1931, in "Requests for Assistance: Advice, Clothing, Money, 1931, N" (second quote), both in WHGF, LHHP.

40. Butler OH.

41. Augusta Felsen to LHH, [c. March 1931] (first quote); Alice M. Dickson to Butler, 13 October 1931 (second quote), both in "Requests for Assistance: Advice, Clothing, Money, 1931, F," WHGF, LHHP.

42. Clarence F. Munford to LHH, 18 April 1931, in "Requests for Assistance: Advice, Clothing, Money, 1931, Mue–Mur," WHGF, LHHP.

43. Sue Congleton to [Dickson], n.d. (first quote); Secretary to Sue Dyer, 12 September 1931 (second quote), both in "Requests for Assistance: Advice, Clothing, Money, 1931, Coc–Cur," WHGF, LHHP.

44. Copy of speech read to the 4-H Clubs' National Achievement Day program, 7 November 1931, in "Four H Clubs, 1929–1931," GSOGF, LHHP.

45. Ibid.

46. Secretary to Mrs. Patrick Hurley, 3 March 1931, in "Requests for Assistance: Advice, Clothing, Money, 1931, B," WHGF, LHHP (first quote); Mildred Hall Campbell, "Mrs. Hoover's Secretary," Memoirs of Allen Campbell and Mildred Hall Campbell, 30 November 1971 (second quote); Butler OH (remaining quotes), both in HHPL.

47. Butler OH (first two quotes); Secretary to Margaret Dreier Robins, 24 February 1930, in "Requests for Assistance: Advice, Clothing, Money, 1930, Wal–Wes," WHGF, LHHP (remaining quotes).

48. David Burner, *Herbert Hoover: A Public Life* (New York: Alfred A. Knopf, 1979), 265–66.

49. Secretary to Clara Beasley, 23 May 1931, in "Depression Relief Measures, 1930–1931," SF (first two quotes); Dickson to Butler, 2 June 1930, in "Dickson, Alice M., 1930–1931," PCF (remaining quotes), both in LHHP.

50. Swain, "Prelude to the New Deal," 151–66.

51. McElvaine, *The Great Depression,* 78–79; Burner, *Herbert Hoover,* 266–67.

52. Re [Mr.] Bane and poor communities, 28 October 1931, by Philippi Harding Butler, in "Depression Relief Measures, 1930–1931," SF, LHHP; Vedder and Gallaway, *Out of Work,* 77.

53. Re [Mr.] Bane and poor communities.

54. Re Heizer Cases, by Philippi Harding Butler, [c. March–April 1932], in "Requests for Assistance, Field Investigators, Heizer, Mabel, 1931–1939," SF, LHHP.

55. Vedder and Gallaway, *Out of Work,* 84.

56. Secretary to Florence B. Litchfield, 12 September 1931, in "Requests for Assistance: Advice, Clothing, Money, 1931, F," WHGF, LHHP (first quote); Ruth Fesler Lipman OH, 26 September 1967, HHPL (second quote).

57. Secretary to Mrs. R. L. Rhodes, 2 April 1930, in "Requests for Assistance: Advice, Clothing, Money, 1930, Ran–Rit," WHGF, LHHP.

58. LHH to Charlotte MacLafferty, 27 January 1938, in "Requests for Assistance, Clothing, Money, 1938–1940," SF, LHHP.

59. LHH speech written for Women's National Committee for Welfare and Relief Mobilization, October 1932, in "AAS, October 1932, Women's Welfare and Relief Article," SF, LHHP.

GIRL SCOUTING AND THE DEPRESSION

1. Ethel Mockler, *Citizens in Action: The Girl Scout Record, 1912–1947* (New York: Girl Scouts National Organization, 1947), 50.

2. Secretary to Jane Deeter Rippin, n.d., in "Girl Scouts: Administrative Correspondence, Rippin, Jane Deeter, 1929 January–May," GSOGF, LHHP.

3. Draft manuscript by Elsie Scott, n.d., in "Girl Scouts: Administrative Correspondence, Rippin, Jane Deeter, 1929 January–May," GSOGF, LHHP.

4. Mockler, *Citizens in Action,* 6 (first two quotes); Harriet C. Barnes to LHH, 28 October 1929, in "Girl Scouts: Administrative Correspondence, Barnes, Harriet C. and Julius H., 1926–1931," GSOGF, LHHP (last quote).

5. Lenna Yost to LHH, 13 December 1930, in "Republican Organizations— National Committee, 1930–1934," GSOGF, LHHP.

6. Secretary to Margaret Mochrie, [May 1929], in "American Girl Magazine, 1926–1933 and undated," GSOGF, LHHP.

7. LHH to Rippin, 29 November 1929, in "American Girl Magazine, 1926–1933 and undated," GSOGF, LHHP.

8. LHH to Jean Henry Large, 20 August 1929, in "Large, Jean Henry, 1929–1933," PCF, LHHP.

9. "Scout Leaders Move to Extend Work for Girls," *Christian Science Monitor*, 8 November 1929; "Mrs. Hoover Here for Girl Scout Fund," *New York Times*, 26 September 1929; Mockler, *Citizens in Action*, 51, 55 (quote).

10. "Mrs. Hoover, Here for Day, Tells Girl Scouts of $500,000 Gift," *New York Herald Tribune*, 26 September 1929, in "AAS, 25 September 1929 Girl Scout Fund Drive Address New York, New York," SF, LHHP.

11. Mira H. Hoffman to LHH, 3 October 1929, in "Administrative Correspondence, Hoffman, Mira H., 1926–1933," GSOGF, LHHP; Mockler, *Citizens in Action*, 51.

12. LHH to Genevieve Brady, 5 October 1929, in "Girl Scouts: Administrative Correspondence, Brady, Genevieve Garvin, 1928–1930," GSOGF, LHHP.

13. LHH to Edgar Rickard, 19 December 1929, in "Administrative Correspondence, Rickard, Edgar, 1922–1941," GSOGF, LHHP.

14. LHH to Brady, 2 May 1930, in "Girl Scouts: Administrative Correspondence, Brady, Genevieve Garvin, 1928–1930," GSOGF, LHHP.

15. Ibid.

16. Ibid.; Anne Beiser Allen, *An Independent Woman: The Life of Lou Henry Hoover* (Westport, Conn.: Greenwood Press, 2000), 139.

17. LHH to Birdsall Edey, 30 April 1930, in "Girl Scouts: Administrative Correspondence, Edey, Birdsall Otis (Mrs. Frederick), 1922–1934," GSOGF, LHHP (quotes); Edgar Rickard Diary, 16 December 1929, HHPL; Mockler, *Citizens in Action*, 51.

18. Mockler, *Citizens in Action*, 28, 39–42.

19. LHH to Edey, 30 April 1930, in "Girl Scouts: Administrative Correspondence, Edey, Birdsall Otis (Mrs. Frederick), 1922–1934," GSOGF, LHHP.

20. Ibid.

21. Edey to LHH, 14 June 1930, in "Girl Scouts: Administrative Correspondence, Edey, Birdsall Otis (Mrs. Frederick), 1922–1934," GSOGF, LHHP.

22. LHH to Edey, 17 June 1930, in "Girl Scouts: Administrative Correspondence, Edey, Birdsall Otis (Mrs. Frederick), 1922–1934," GSOGF, LHHP (quotes); Allen, *An Independent Woman*, 140.

23. LHH to Martha Noyes, 12 September 1932, in "Noyes, Martha," PCF, LHHP.

24. Secretary to Agnes B. Leehy, 24 February 1931, in "Girl Scouts: General Correspondence, 1930 February," GSOGF, LHHP.

25. Hoffman to LHH, 13 April 1930, in "Girl Scouts: Administrative Correspondence, Hoffman, Mira H., 1926–1933," GSOGF, LHHP (quotes); Allen, *An Independent Woman*, 139; Mockler, *Citizens in Action*, 40.

26. LHH to Dolly Lindsay, 24 July 1930, in "Girl Scouts: General Correspondence, 1930 June–July" (first two quotes); LHH to Hoffman, 10 June 1930, in "Girl Scouts: Administrative Correspondence, Hoffman, Mira H., 1926–1933" (third and fourth quotes), both in GSOGF; LHH to Large, 13 October 1930, in "Large, Jean, 1930 August–December," PCF (last quote), all in LHHP.

27. Rippin to Honorary President, 4 April 1930, in "Girl Scouts: Administrative Correspondence, Rippin, Jane Deeter, 1930–1932," GSOGF, LHHP (first quote); Mockler, *Citizens in Action*, 56 (second quote).

28. LHH to Sarah Louise Arnold, 5 July 1930, in "Girl Scouts: Administrative Correspondence, Arnold, Sarah Louise, 1925–1931," GSOGF, LHHP.

29. LHH to Brady, 14 April 1930, in "Girl Scouts: Administrative Correspondence, Brady, Genevieve Garvin, 1928–1930" (first quote); LHH to Abbie Rickard, 7 April 1930, in "Girl Scouts: Administrative Correspondence, Rickard, Abbie, 1927–1930" (second quote); LHH to Brady, 16 April 1930, in "Girl Scouts: Administrative Correspondence, Brady, Genevieve Garvin, 1928–1930" (last quote), all in GSOGF, LHHP; Mockler, *Citizens in Action*, 56.

30. LHH to Abbie Rickard, 30 January 1931, in "Girl Scouts: Administrative Correspondence, Rickard, Abbie, 1931–1935 and undated," GSOGF, LHHP.

31. Ibid.

32. Ibid.

33. LHH to Abbie Rickard, 31 January 1931, in "Girl Scouts: Administrative Correspondence, Rickard, Abbie, 1931–1935 and undated," GSOGF, LHHP.

34. LHH to Noyes, [c. June 1929], in "Girl Scouts: General Correspondence, June 1929," GSOGF, LHHP.

35. Marion Early Sears to Rippin, n.d., in "Girl Scouts: Administrative Correspondence, Rippin, Jane Deeter, 1929 June–December," GSOGF, LHHP.

36. Undated, untitled typescript, in "Girl Scouts: General Correspondence, 1930 June–July," GSOGF, LHHP.

37. LHH to Flora Whiting, 23 August 1929, in "Girl Scouts: Administrative Correspondence, Flora Whiting," GSOGF, LHHP.

38. LHH to Rippin, 16 October 1929, in "Girl Scouts: Administrative Correspondence, Rippin, Jane Deeter, 1929 June–December," GSOGF, LHHP.

39. "The National Committee on Volunteer Service, Annual Meeting Addressed by Mrs. Herbert Hoover," *Red Cross Courier* (1 January 1930): 20, in "AAS, 12 December 1929 Annual Meeting of the Red Cross, Washington, D.C.," SF, LHHP.

40. LHH to Mr. Secretary, 13 March 1927, in "Administrative Correspondence, Work, Dr. Hubert," GSOGF, LHHP.

41. LHH to Barnes, 20 May 1931, in "Girl Scouts: Administrative Correspondence, Barnes, Harriet C. and Julius H., 1926–1931" (first quote); LHH to Helen Storrow, 20 May 1931, in "Girl Scouts: Administrative Correspondence, Storrow, Helen" (second quote), both in GSOGF, LHHP.

42. Josephine Schain to Mildred Hall, 18 February 1931, in "Girl Scouts: Administrative Correspondence, Schain, Josephine," GSOGF, LHHP.

43. Helen C. Jacobs to LHH, 10 June 1930, in "Girl Scouts: General Correspondence, 1930 June–July," GSOGF, LHHP.

44. Henrietta Autenrieth to LHH, 26 January 1932, in "Girl Scouts: General Correspondence, January–March 1932," GSOGF, LHHP (quote); Lewis L. Gould, "A Neglected First Lady," in *Lou Henry Hoover: Essays on a Busy Life,* ed. Dale C. Mayer (Worland, Wyo.: High Plains Publishing Company, 1994), 72.

45. LHH nationwide radio speech, 23 March 1931, in "AAS, President's Emergency Committee for Employment, Washington, D.C.," SF, LHHP.

46. Ibid.

47. Rippin to LHH, 28 October 1930, in "Girl Scouts: Administrative Correspondence, Rippin, Jane Deeter, 1930–1932," GSOGF, LHHP.

48. Ibid.

49. Dyer to LHH, 19 September 1931, in "Servants and Aides, Dyer, Sue, 1931–1932," SF, LHHP.

50. Cabin Allocation, n.d., in "Girl Scouts: Administrative Correspondence, Brady, Genevieve (Mrs. Nicholas), 1931–1935" (first four quotes); LHH to Abbie Rickard, 18 September 1931, in "Girl Scouts: Administrative Correspondence, Rickard, Abbie, 1931–1935 and undated" (remaining quotes), both in GSOGF, LHHP.

51. Mollie H. Page to LHH, 28 September 1931 (first two quotes); Daisy Seiler Hindman to LHH, 28 September 1931 (third quote), both in "Girl Scouts: General Correspondence, September–October 1931"; Whiting to LHH, 1 October 1931, in "Girl Scouts: Administrative Correspondence, Flora Whiting" (last quote), all in GSOGF, LHHP.

52. LHH to Edey, 16 October 1931, in "Conventions: National 1931 Buffalo, Correspondence," GSOGF, LHHP.

53. LHH speech, 14 October 1931, in "AAS, 14 October 1931, Girl Scout Convention Address, Buffalo, New York," SF, LHHP.

54. Ibid.

55. Ibid.

56. Mockler, *Citizens in Action,* 57.

57. "Mrs. Hoover Advises Girl Scout Troop," *Girl Scout Bulletin,* 16 November 1931, in "AAS, 16 November 1931, Letter to White Swan Girl Scout Troop, Ottawa, Kansas," SF (first quote); "Girl Scouts Prove Santa's Helpers; Make Yule Gifts for Stockings of Needy Boys and Girls," n.p., n.d. (second quote); June Schindler to LHH, 12 January 1932 (remaining quotes), both in "Girl Scouts: General Correspondence, January–March 1932," GSOGF, all in LHHP; Mockler, *Citizens in Action,* 57–58.

58. Mockler, *Citizens in Action,* 58–59.

59. LHH speech, 7 October 1932, in "AAS, 7 October 1932, Girl Scout Convention Speech, Virginia Beach, Virginia," SF, LHHP.

60. Ibid. (first four quotes); typed note, in "AAS, 7 October 1932, Girl Scout Convention Speech, Virginia Beach, Virginia," SF, LHHP (last quote).

61. Mary Denman Cheatham to LHH, 14 December 1932, in "Units—Washington, D.C.—Council and Camp, 1931–1933," GSOGF, LHHP.

62. LHH to Brady, 24 January 1933, in "Girl Scouts: Administrative Correspondence, Brady, Genevieve (Mrs. Nicholas), 1931–1935," GSOGF, LHHP.

63. Brady to LHH, [January 1933], in "Girl Scouts: Administrative Correspondence, Brady, Genevieve (Mrs. Nicholas), 1931–1935," GSOGF, LHHP.

64. Quoted in Mockler, *Citizens in Action,* 64.

LOU HENRY HOOVER IN PUBLIC AND PRIVATE

1. Grace Coolidge to LHH, 8 July 1931, in "Coolidge, Grace," PCF, LHHP.

2. Gertrude L. Bowman OH, 6 and 12 November 1966 (first two quotes); Philippi Harding Butler OH, 12 September 1967 (remaining quotes), both in HHPL.

3. [Mary Randolph], Official Secretary to Jessie Jordan, 6 November 1929, in "Jordan, David Starr and Jessie," PCF, LHHP.

4. "Tell me what she's really like, A discussion of Mrs. Hoover, by a friend," typescript manuscript, n.d. [c. 1929–1933; possibly written by Dare Stark McMullin, as per pencil marks on the document], in "Hoover, Lou Henry—Biographical Data," SF, LHHP.

5. Sallie V. H. Pickett, "Mrs. Hoover Fits into Her New Role," *Washington Star,* 9 November 1928, in "Clippings, LHH, Background for Position as First Lady, 1928," SF, LHHP.

6. Bess Furman, *Washington By-Line: The Personal History of a Newspaperwoman* (New York: Alfred A. Knopf, 1949), 58–61.

7. [LHH to Allan Hoover, c.1932], in "Mary Austin, 1932," Allan Hoover Papers, HHPL.

8. LHH to Evelyn Wight Allan, 11 January 1929, in "Allan, Evelyn Wight," PCF, LHHP.

9. Randolph to Ruth Fesler, 24 January 1929, in "Coolidge, Grace," PCF, LHHP.

10. Coolidge to LHH, 3 June 1929, in "Coolidge, Grace," PCF, LHHP.

11. LHH Script as Moderator, 29 September 1927, in "AAS, 29 September 1927, Presiding Officer Speeches, New York City" (first quote); Florence V. Kaiser, "The First Lady Eludes Radio," n.p., [c. March 1929], in "Clippings, Biographical, 1928" (second and third quotes), both in SF, LHHP; "Mrs. Herbert Hoover Talks over Wide Hook-Up, She Is First President's Wife to Make Radio Address—Speaks at D.A.R. Dedication," *New York Times,* 20 April 1929 (last quote).

12. Frederic William Wile, "Precedent Set by 'First Lady,'" *Washington Star,* 24 March 1929, in "Clippings, Clubs and Organizations, 1929," SF, LHHP.

13. Secretary to [Arthur M. Hyde] Secretary of Agriculture, 15 June 1929, in "Four H Clubs, 1929–1931," GSOGF, LHHP.

14. Phone message from Mr. Macburton, [21 June 1929] (first two quotes); typescript of LHH's remarks, 21 June 1929 (last quote), both in "Four H Clubs, 1929–1931," GSOGF, LHHP.

15. Typescript of LHH's remarks, 21 June 1929, in "Four H Clubs, 1929–1931," GSOGF, LHHP.

16. Ibid.

17. Ibid.

18. C. B. Smith to LHH, 26 June 1929 (first quote); Secretary to F. H. Spencer, 2 July 1929 (second quote), both in "Four H Clubs, 1929–1931," GSOGF, LHHP.

19. Jane Deeter Rippin to LHH, 25 June 1929 (first quote); Rippin to LHH, 2 October 1929 (second quote), both in "Girl Scouts: Administrative Correspondence, Rippin, Jane Deeter, 1929 June–December," GSOGF, LHHP.

20. LHH to Rippin, 11 October 1929, in "Girl Scouts: Administrative Correspondence, Rippin, Jane Deeter, 1929 June–December," GSOGF, LHHP.

21. LHH to Jean Henry Large, 13 October 1930, in "Hoover, Herbert Jr. Illness, 1930–1937 and undated," SF, LHHP.

22. "Mrs. Hoover Holds Dish-Washing Housewife Has More Courage than the Big Game Hunter," *New York Times,* 2 October 1930, in "AAS, 1 October 1930, Girl Scout Convention Address, Indianapolis, Indiana" (first quote); "President's Son Has Mild Case of Lung Lesion," *New York Herald Tribune,* 23 September 1930, in "Clippings, Articles about Hoover family, Herbert Hoover,

Jr., Allan, etc., 1930" (second and third quotes); "White House No Playhouse, Hoover Grandchildren Learn," n.p., n.d., in "Clippings, Misrepresentations, 1929" (remaining quotes), all in SF, LHHP.

23. LHH to Gertrude L. Bowman, 19 July 1928, in "Servants and Aides, Bowman, Gertrude L., 1926–1929," SF, LHHP.

24. Sue Dyer to LHH, 3 December 1931, in "Servants and Aides, Dyer, Sue, 1931–1932," SF, LHHP.

25. Allan to LHH, 24 October 1930, in "Allan, Evelyn Wight," PCF, LHHP.

26. LHH to Large, 19 May 1931, in "Large, Jean Henry, 1931," PCF, LHHP.

27. Marie Mattingly Meloney to Lawrence Richey, 18 February 1931 (first quote); anonymous excerpt from a letter to Meloney, n.d., attached to Meloney to Richey (remaining quotes), both in "Hoover, Lou Henry, Relations with the Press, 1931," SF, LHHP.

28. Memorandum to Mr. Richey, 14 March 1931, in "Hoover, Lou Henry, Relations with the Press, 1931," SF, LHHP.

29. Ibid. (first quote); "Mrs. Hoover Greets Women's Press Club," *Christian Science Monitor,* 4 June 1931 (second quote).

30. "Mrs. Hoover Takes Voice Tests to Improve Talkie Technique," *New York Times,* 6 November 1931 (first, second, and fourth quotes); " 'Leak' on Voice Test Annoys Mrs. Hoover; White House Seeks Source of News Story," *New York Times,* 7 November 1931 (third quote); "Mrs. Hoover Fine Radio Talker," *New York American,* 2 November 1931 (remaining quotes), all in "Clippings, Radio Addresses and Voice Tests," SF, LHHP.

31. Lillian Gilbreth to LHH, 23 March 1931, in "Gilbreth, Lillian" (first quote); Coolidge to LHH, Easter 1931, in "Coolidge, Grace" (second quote), both in PCF; " 'Round Lima Hour by Hour," n.p., October 1932, in "AAS, 7 October 1932 Girl Scout Convention Speech, Virginia Beach, Virginia," SF (last quote), all in LHHP.

32. "President and Mrs. Hoover Wave Friendly Greeting to Early Morning Crowd Here," *Decatur Evening Herald,* 17 June 1931, in "Clippings, Clubs and Organizations, Lincoln Tomb—Springfield, Illinois, 1931" (first quote); Erwin D. Canham, "Hoover Ends Campaign in Home State," *Christian Science Monitor,* 9 November 1932, in "Clippings, Miscellaneous (1) 1932" (second quote), both in SF, LHHP.

33. LHH to Bowman, 3 April 1931, in "Campaign of 1932, Bag-Boy," SF, LHHP.

34. Mildred Hall to Lenna Yost, 26 August 1931 (first quote); Secretary to Mrs. Hoover to Mrs. Samuel Ratliff, 2 July 1932 (second quote), both in "Republican Organizations—National Committee, 1930–1934," GSOGF, LHHP.

35. Carol Hyatt to Yost, n.d. [c. 1932], in "Republican Organizations—National Committee, 1930–1934," GSOGF, LHHP.

36. "Keep Spending, Women Urged by First Lady," *Washington, D.C. Herald,* 15 October 1931, in "AAS, 14 October 1931, Girl Scout Convention Address, Buffalo, New York," SF, LHHP.

37. "Mrs. Hoover Urges Living Normal Life," *Washington Post,* 15 October 1931 (first quote); "Which Is Right?" *San Diego Union,* 16 October 1931 (second quote); "Yes, Yes, But with What?" *Coeur D'Alene Press,* 26 October 1931 (last quote), all in "AAS, 14 October 1931, Girl Scout Convention Address, Buffalo, New York," SF, LHHP.

38. LHH to Mary Walcott, 16 August 1932, in "Bonus March, 1932," SF, LHHP.

39. Ibid.

40. Ibid.

41. LHH to Herbert and Allan and their children, July 1932, in "Hoover, Allan 1932," PCF, LHHP.

42. LHH to Large, 7 June 1932, in "Large, Jean Henry, 1932–1933 and undated," PCF (first quote); Dyer to LHH, 28 September 1932 (second quote); LHH to Dyer, 6 October 1932 (third and fourth quotes), both in "Servants and Aides, Dyer, Sue, 1931–1932"; letter from LHH's secretary to Mr. McDowell, 19 October 1932, in "Hoover, Lou Henry—Voter Registration, 1932–1940" (last quote), all in SF, LHHP.

43. Dare Stark McMullin to Alice Dickson, 10 October 1932, in "Campaign of 1932, Dickson, Alice M.," SF, LHHP.

44. Hall to Yost, 10 October 1932 (first quote); Yost to Hall, 10 October 1932 (second quote), both in "Republican Organizations—National Committee, 1930–1934," GSOGF, LHHP.

45. J. P. Behm to Hall, 16 October 1932, in "Requests for Assistance: Miscellaneous, 1932, A–D," WHGF (first quote); Charles H. Bohm to LHH, 14 February 1933, in "Girl Scouts: General Correspondence, January–February 1933," GSOGF (remaining quotes), both in LHHP.

46. LHH to Alice Roosevelt Longworth, 27 October 1932, in "Longworth, Alice Roosevelt, 1931–1933 and undated," PCF (first quote); "Mrs. Hoover Hailed by Mid-West Crowds," *New York Times,* 29 October 1932 (second and third quotes); Norma Hendricks, "First Lady Intent as Husband Talks," *Cleveland Plain Dealer,* n.d. (last quote), both in "Clippings, Campaign Trip, 1932," SF, all in LHHP.

47. J. Russell Young, "Campaign Leaves President Weary," *Washington Star,* 8 November 1932, in "Clippings, Campaign Trip, 1932," SF, LHHP.

48. Norma Hendricks, "Mrs. Hoover Is Heroine of Trip," *Cleveland Plain Dealer,* 16 October 1932 (first quote); "Mrs. Hoover Aids Husband Greet Crowds at Stations," *Pittsburgh Post Gazette,* 6 October 1932 (second quote), both in "Clippings, Campaign Trip, 1932," SF, LHHP.

49. Letter to Alida Henriques, 10 November 1932, in "Servants and Aides, Henriques, Alida, 1929–1932," SF, LHHP; Richard Norton Smith, *An Uncommon Man: The Triumph of Herbert Hoover* (Worland, Wyo.: High Plains Publishing Company, 1984), 28.

50. Sallie V. H. Pickett, "President and First Lady Kept Too Busy during Past Week for Social Activities," *Washington Star,* 27 November 1932, in "Clippings, Society, November–December 1932," SF, LHHP.

51. Alice Rogers Hager, "Candidates for the Post of First Lady," *New York Times Magazine,* 2 October 1932, in "Clippings, Featured Articles, Newspapers, 1932," SF, LHHP.

52. Mildred Hall Campbell OH, 24 September 1966, HHPL (first quote); Butler OH (second quote); "Mrs. Hoover," *Kansas City Star,* 6 March 1933, in "Clippings, General 1933," SF, LHHP (last quote).

53. "The Other Presidents: A Well Known Woman Politician Sizes up the Last Five Mistresses of the White House," n.p., n.d., in "Clippings, Magazine Articles, 1932," SF, LHHP.

54. Untitled poem by LHH, 23 January 1933, in "Coolidge, Grace," PCF, LHHP.

CONSERVATIVE POLITICS AFTER THE WHITE HOUSE

1. Quoted in Richard Norton Smith, "Carrying On: Lou Henry Hoover as a Former First Lady," in *Lou Henry Hoover: Essays on a Busy Life,* ed. Dale C. Mayer (Worland, Wyo.: High Plains Publishing Company, 1994), 124.

2. LHH to Abbie Rickard, 28 April 1933, in "Administrative Correspondence, Rickard, Abbie, 1931–1935 and undated," GSOGF, LHHP.

3. LHH to Abbie Rickard, 25 May 1935, in "Administrative Correspondence, Rickard, Abbie, 1931–1935 and undated," GSOGF, LHHP.

4. Marie McSpadden Sands OH, 30 September 1981, HHPL.

5. Katherine Anderson, "Ex–First Lady Predicts Return to Hearth, Home," in "General Correspondence, November–December 1933," GSOGF, LHHP.

6. LHH remarks, 4 October 1935, in "AAS, 4 October 1935, Girl Scout Presidential Response San Francisco, California," SF (first two quotes); Marie Mattingly Meloney to LHH, 10 October 1935, in "Administrative Correspondence, Meloney, Marie M.," GSOGF (last quote), both in LHHP; Anne Beiser Allen, *An*

Independent Woman: The Life of Lou Henry Hoover (Westport, Conn.: Greenwood Press, 2000), 159.

7. "Mrs. Hoover Talks about Youth," attached to Lee Larsh to Edith Harcourt, 22 January 1937 (first and last quote); Edith Harcourt to Lee Larsh, 25 January 1937 (second quote), both in "Articles re: LHH and Girl Scouts, 1936–1937," GSOGF, LHHP.

8. See, for example, Oscar F. Green to Harcourt, 26 June 1939; typed note, n.d. (quote); and Harcourt to Pearl Moulden, 19 June 1940, all in "Palo Alto Negro Activities, 1939–1942 and undated," GSOGF, LHHP.

9. LHH to Theodore Hoover, 1 April 1942, in "Administrative Correspondence, Hoover, Theodore, 1942," GSOGF, LHHP.

10. Ibid.

11. LHH to Adaline, 16 September 1937 (first quote); LHH to Mrs. Baldwin, 14 August 1937 (remaining quotes), both in "Friends of Music Correspondence, 1937," GSOGF, LHHP.

12. LHH to Baldwin, 14 August 1937, in "Friends of Music Correspondence, 1937," GSOGF, LHHP.

13. LHH to Alfred R. Frankenstein, 25 September 1939, in "Friends of Music Correspondence, 1939 January–September," GSOGF, LHHP.

14. Augusta M. Dale to LHH, 20 September 1933, in "Servants and Aides, White House, 1933," SF, LHHP.

15. Ike Hoover to Mildred Hall, 20 March 1933 (first quote); LHH to Mrs. Irwin Hoover, 14 September 1933 (second quote), both in "Servants and Aides, Hoover, 'Ike,' 1930–1934 and undated," SF, LHHP.

16. Irwin H. "Ike" Hoover, *Forty-two Years in the White House* (Boston: Houghton Mifflin, 1934), 181 (first quote); marginalia in "'Forty Two Years in the White House,' by Ike Hoover," Philippi Harding Butler Papers, HHPL (second quote); Irwin H. Hoover manuscript notes for *Forty-two Years in the White House,* Roll 9, Irwin H. Hoover Papers on Microfilm, Library of Congress (remaining quotes).

17. LHH to Grace Coolidge, 8 February 1934, in "White House History, Ike Hoover Books," SF, LHHP.

18. Lillian Rogers Parks, *My Thirty Years Backstairs at the White House* (New York: Fleet Publishing Corporation, 1961), 216 (first quote); Lillian Rogers Parks OH, 12 February 1971, HHPL (remaining quotes).

19. Elizabeth Hanley to LHH, 12 December 1932, in "Pro-America, 1932–1938," GSOGF (first two quotes); LHH to Alice Dickson, 28 December 1935, in "Dickson, Alice M., 1934–1935," PCF (remaining quotes), both in LHHP.

20. Hanley to LHH, 12 December 1932 (first quote); Secretary to Hanley, 19 February 1933 (second quote), both in "Pro-America, 1932–1938," GSOGF, LHHP.

21. LHH to Agnes Morley Cleaveland, 18 May 1934, in "Cleaveland, Agnes Morley, 1934–1935," PCF, LHHP.

22. Ibid. (first three quotes); LHH's reaction to Herbert Hoover's manuscript, n.d., in "Cleaveland, Agnes Morley, 1934–1935," PCF, LHHP (last quote).

23. LHH to Cleaveland, 20 March 1934, in "Cleaveland, Agnes Morley, 1934–1935," PCF, LHHP.

24. LHH to Cleaveland, 13 June 1934, in "Cleaveland, Agnes Morley, 1934–1935," PCF, LHHP.

25. LHH to President Jaqua, 25 September 1934, in "Educational Ideals," SF, LHHP.

26. Hanley to LHH, 10 March 1936 (first quote); LHH to Hanley, 2 April 1936 (second quote), both in "Pro-America, 1932–1938," GSOGF, LHHP.

27. LHH to Mrs. Hudgins, 2 November 1936, in "Campaign of 1936," SF, LHHP.

28. LHH to Annie F. Brown, 26 May 1938, in "Pro-America, 1933–1938," SF, LHHP.

29. LHH to Ruth Comfort Mitchell Young, 1 July 1938, in "Campaign of 1938," SF (first two quotes); LHH to Caroline Honnold, 9 November 1938, in "Honnold, Caroline, 1938–1939," PCF (last quote), both in LHHP.

30. LHH to Fern Mattei, 18 December 1939, in "Pro-America, 1939–1940," GSOGF, LHHP.

31. LHH to Mrs. Carpenter, 31 January 1941, in "Salvation Army, General, 1940–1943," GSOGF, LHHP.

32. Alida Henriques to LHH, 16 June 1940 (first quote); LHH to Henriques, 29 June 1940 (remaining quotes), both in "Campaign of 1940," SF, LHHP.

33. Katherine Everts to LHH, 28 September 1940 (first quote); LHH to Everts, 30 September 1940 (remaining quotes), both in "Campaign of 1940," SF, LHHP.

34. LHH to Everts, 30 September 1940, in "Campaign of 1940," SF, LHHP.

35. "Friendly Mrs. Hoover Firm in Opposition to Third Term," *Nebraska State Journal,* 1 November 1940, in "Clippings, 1940, Social," SF, LHHP.

36. LHH to Elva Carpenter, 10 March 1941 (first quote), and 22 March 1941 (remaining quotes), both in "Pro-America, 1941," GSOGF, LHHP.

37. Bunny to LHH, 25 January 1942 (first three quotes); LHH to Bernice Miller, 26 January 1942 (last quote), both in "Promotion of Herbert Hoover's Books, America's First Crusade, 1942," SF, LHHP.

38. LHH to Mildred Hall Campbell, 28 January 1942, in "Promotion of Herbert Hoover's Books, America's First Crusade, 1942," SF, LHHP.

39. LHH to Herbert Hoover, October 1940, in "Hoover, Herbert, 1940," PCF (first two quotes); LHH to [Harcourt], [2 January 1942], in "Servants and Aides, Harcourt, Edith, 1942 and undated," SF (last quote), both in LHHP.

40. Mildred Hall Campbell OH, 24 September 1966, HHPL.

41. Campbell to Ruth Fesler Lipman, 22 February 1944, in "Hoover, Lou Henry—Memorabilia," Ruth Fesler Lipman Papers, HHPL.

42. "Mrs. Herbert Hoover's Funeral Will Be at St. Bartholomew's," *New York Herald Tribune,* 9 January 1944, in "Clippings, 1944, Death of Mrs. Hoover, General (2)," SF, LHHP (first quote); Gertrude Bowman OH, 6 and 12 November 1966, HHPL (remaining quotes).

43. Edgar Rickard Diary, 7 January 1944, HHPL.

44. "There Is No Finer Example of How to Live," *Palo Alto Times,* 15 January 1944, in "Clippings, 1944, Death of Mrs. Hoover, General (2)," SF, LHHP.

45. Campbell to Lipman, 22 February 1944, in "Hoover, Lou Henry—Memorabilia," Ruth Fesler Lipman Papers, HHPL.

46. Alice M. Chester to Herbert Hoover, 8 January 1944, in "LHH, Death and Funeral, Clippings, Condolences, Letters Received, C" (first quote); Mildred Burr Schluter to Herbert Hoover, 8 January 1944 (second quote), and Nathan H. Seidman to Herbert Hoover, 10 January 1944 (third quote), both in "LHH, Death and Funeral, Clippings, Condolences, Letters Received, Sa–Se"; Eleanor Roosevelt, "My Day," *New York World Telegram,* 10 January 1944, in "LHH, Death and Funeral, Clippings, Editorials and Comments (2)" (last quote), all in SF, LHHP.

47. "Mrs. Herbert Hoover," *Christian Science Monitor,* 11 January 1944, in "Clippings, 1944, Death of Mrs. Hoover General (2)" (first quote); "We Don't Say Goodbye," *Daily Palo Alto Times,* 10 January 1944, in "Clippings, 1944, Death of Mrs. Hoover General (3)" (second quote), both in SF, LHHP.

48. "Hoover's Mistakes," in "Hoover's Mistakes," Box 59, SF, LHHP.

49. Ibid.

BIBLIOGRAPHIC ESSAY

This book draws primarily from Lou Henry Hoover's papers, which total 182 linear feet and cover her entire life. The papers are subdivided as follows: Personal Correspondence Files in four chronological parts (67 boxes), Subject Files (121 boxes), Girl Scouts and Other Groups Files (60 boxes), White House General Files (79 boxes), and White House Social Files (38 boxes). Cumulatively, 59 feet of these papers document day-to-day White House activities.

The Subject Files illuminate Hoover's multifaceted interests, ranging from the Boxer Rebellion in China to World War I relief efforts and depression relief. This series is arranged topically and spans the entirety of Hoover's life, meaning that it was useful for each of the six chapters in this book. There are two important subsections of this series to which researchers should pay special attention: the Articles, Addresses, and Statements and the Clippings boxes. The former fills part of ten boxes and contains everything from a young Lou Henry's school assignments to the many speeches she gave as an adult, along with speech fragments and notes. The twenty boxes of clippings from 1910 through 1963 are quite thorough. Researchers should be careful in their use of the clippings, however, because journalists often relied on previous articles for background details, meaning that numerous errors of fact were replicated countless times. The Subject Files were helpful in constructing the sections of the book pertaining to politics, the DePriest controversy, the President's Mountain School, Camp Rapidan, Hoover's many servants and aides, and White House redecoration. Lou Henry Hoover kept a diary from early childhood into the first years of her marriage, and although the entries are not extensive, they were invaluable at key junctures. Finally, the Subject Files should be consulted for what little documentary evidence there is about the manner in which Herbert and Lou Henry Hoover communicated and worked with each other.

The Personal Correspondence Files function as a barometer of Hoover's activity level throughout her life. They are subdivided as follows: 1874–1920, 1921–1928, 1929–1933, and 1934–1944. In her busiest years, letters from Hoover's friends were routed through secretaries, while in quieter times, she often wrote detailed and thoughtful replies. Researchers should go to these files for additional insight into the Hoover marriage. Some knowledge of how Lou Henry Hoover worked and who her most valued friends and colleagues were is needed to maximize the usefulness of this series. Although I found valuable material for each of the chapters here, these files should be consulted only after a careful survey of the Subject Files and perhaps the Girl Scouts and Other Groups Files. The correspondents that I found most helpful were Evelyn Wight Allan, Sarah Louise Arnold, Philippi Harding Butler, Agnes Morley Cleaveland, Grace Coolidge, Alice M. Dickson, Lillian Gilbreth, Edith Harcourt, Alida Henriques, various members of the Henry family, Caroline Honnold, Allan Hoover, Herbert Hoover, Jean Henry Large, and Edgar and Abbie Rickard.

The Girl Scouts and Other Groups Files supplement the Subject Files' coverage of Lou Henry Hoover's involvement in the Girl Scouts, as well as documenting her wide-ranging charitable commitments. They also contain evidence of the important role that organizational culture played in Hoover's life and her contributions to it. Besides the Girl Scouts, this series should be consulted for details about the following organizations: 4-H Club, American Red Cross, American Relief Administration, Friends of Music, League of Women Voters, Pro-America, Republican party and related organizations, Salvation Army, and Women's Division of the National Amateur Athletic Federation.

The White House General Files and the White House Social Files tell the story of Lou Henry Hoover's years as first lady. Both series have significant information about entertaining at the White House. The White House General Files also contain approximately ten boxes of material about Hoover's involvement in depression relief that should be used in conjunction with the parallel Subject Files. The White House Social Files provide a thorough history of the various official social events at the White House and reveal the Hoover approach to entertaining.

Several collateral collections at the Hoover Library added nuance to the book. Most important are the Allan Hoover Papers, as Lou Henry Hoover maintained an extensive and often revealing correspondence with her younger son. The Joel Boone Collection contains the former White House physician's unpublished autobiography for the Hoover years. The original and longer manuscript is available at the Library of Congress. In it are numerous references to Lou Henry Hoover, specifically her work with Camp Rapidan, entertaining there, the President's Mountain School, Ike Hoover's dislike of the Roosevelts, and Herbert Jr.'s bout with tuberculosis. The Ruth Fesler Lipman Papers contain a diary describing some of her work as the first lady's secretary, as well as correspondence. The Edgar Rickard Diary suggests much about Lou Henry Hoover's work in the voluntary association world, as well as the nature of her partnership with Herbert Hoover. The Philippi Harding Butler Papers contain a copy of Ike Hoover's memoirs, replete with Butler's marginalia showing where that book deviated from her view of the truth.

Other important collections at the Hoover Library include those of Gertrude L. Bowman, a friend who shared Hoover's interests in scouting and Republican politics; Mildred Hall Campbell, another secretary to Lou Henry Hoover; and Katherine Milbank, a friend. In addition to these miscellaneous collections, the papers of Herbert Hoover flesh out the details of her life. Although there is little explicit or revealing correspondence between the two, any Lou Henry Hoover biographer will need to read her husband's papers judiciously to gauge the high and low points of public cooperation between the two Hoovers. Finally, see the George Akerson Papers for information on the 1928 campaign.

The Hoover Library Oral History Collection contains numerous valuable records, including those of Gertrude L. Bowman, Philippi Harding Butler, Mildred Hall Campbell, memoirs of Allen and Mildred Hall Campbell, Elmore R. Dutro, Susan L. Dyer, Allan and Margaret C. Hoover, Marguerite Rickard Hoyt, Harry Jepson, Ruth Fesler Lipman, Mr. and Mrs. Frederick Loomis, Carrie B. Massenburg, Dare Stark McMullin, Jeremiah Milbank, Jeremiah Milbank Jr., Katherine Milbank, Sydney Sullivan Parker, Lillian Rogers Parks, Helen B. Pryor, Marie McSpaden Sands, Mark Sullivan Jr., Agnes Thompson, and Helen H. Green White.

The popular press printed many articles about Lou Henry Hoover during her adult life, making both magazine and newspaper sources extremely useful. Researchers interested in Hoover's public voice should see Lou Henry Hoover, "The Late Dowager Empress of China," *Contemporary Review* 95 (January 1909): 84–97; and Hoover's "Foreword to 'Play Day—The Spirit of Sport,'" in *Women and Athletics*, ed. Women's

Division, National Amateur Athletic Federation (New York: A. S. Barnes, 1930). An important glimpse into her approach to motherhood can be found in Augusta Hinshaw, "How the Hoovers Brought up Their Boys," *Parents Magazine* 4 (December 1929): 24–25, 66–67. Charlotte Kellogg's "What Is Mrs. Hoover Like?" *Woman's Home Companion* 47 (June 1920): 13, 66, reveals Hoover's background in California, and her September 1930 article in *Ladies' Home Journal* ("Mrs. Hoover," 24–25, 182, 185–86) carries the story forward to the White House years. For Hoover's life through the mid-1920s, see, for example, Anne Hard, "Friendly Impressions," *Woman Citizen* (October 1926): 14–15, 41. Upon Herbert Hoover's inauguration as president, *World's Work* described Lou Hoover as "a strong woman" with "unusual poise and great naturalness," making her uniquely suited for the "First Lady's 'job.'" For the entire article, which also details the expectations that first ladies were supposed to live up to, see Mary Roberts Rinehart, "A New First Lady Becomes Hostess for the Nation," *World's Work* 58 (March 1929): 34–39, 170. Particularly revealing is "The Other Presidents: A Well-Known Woman Politician Sizes up the Last Five Mistresses of the White House," *Good Housekeeping* 94 (February 1932): 18–21, 135, 138, 141–42, 144, 146, 148. See the editorial in the *Journal of Home Economics* 21 (September 1929): 663–64, for excerpts from Hoover's 1929 radio address to 4-H Club members.

There are numerous memoirs from the era of Lou Henry Hoover's public involvement. Hoover did not like the accounts of her activities contained in the anonymous *Boudoir Mirrors of Washington* (Philadelphia: John C. Winston, 1923), or Mary Austin's *Earth Horizon, Autobiography* (Boston: Houghton Mifflin, 1932). Several journalists have written their versions of the Hoover years, including Robert Allen, *Washington Merry-Go-Round* (New York: Horace Liveright, 1931), and Bess Furman, *Washington By-Line: The Personal History of a Newspaperwoman* (New York: Alfred A. Knopf, 1949). There are also several useful, if biased, books detailing the experiences of some White House employees during the Hoover era: Irwin H. "Ike" Hoover, *Forty-two Years in the White House* (Boston: Houghton Mifflin, 1934); Lillian Rogers Parks, *My Thirty Years Backstairs at the White House* (New York: Fleet Publishing Corporation, 1961); and Mary Randolph, *Presidents and First Ladies* (New York: D. Appleton-Century, 1936). For more information on the Gann-Longworth feud, see Dolly Gann, *Dolly Gann's*

Book (Garden City, N.Y.: Doubleday, Doran and Company, 1933). Finally and most important, see the memoirs of the former president: *The Memoirs of Herbert Hoover: Years of Adventure, 1874–1920* (New York: Macmillan, 1951); *The Memoirs of Herbert Hoover: The Cabinet and the Presidency, 1920–1933* (New York: Macmillan, 1952); and *The Memoirs of Herbert Hoover: The Great Depression, 1929–1941* (New York: Macmillan, 1952).

The earliest published biography of Lou Henry Hoover is a hybrid between an analytical, objective treatment of her career and a memoir-driven account by a friend and colleague. Helen B. Pryor, who worked with Hoover on women's athletics at Stanford in the post–White House years, published a sympathetic biography in 1969 and a series of articles in one issue of *Palimpsest,* the journal of the State Historical Society of Iowa. See Helen B. Pryor, *Lou Henry Hoover: Gallant First Lady* (New York: Dodd, Mead, 1969), and "Girlhood in Waterloo," "A New Life in California," "Homemaker in Many Lands," "Lou Hoover: Gallant First Lady," and "The Years Following 1933," *Palimpsest* 52 (July 1971): 353–400.

Several secondary-source accounts of first ladies and of women's history provided a comparative and theoretical foundation for this book. The most important were Carl Sferrazza Anthony, *First Ladies: The Saga of the Presidents' Wives and Their Power, 1789–1961* (New York: William Morrow, 1990); Betty Boyd Caroli, *First Ladies,* expanded ed. (New York: Oxford University Press, 1995); Myra G. Gutin, *The President's Partner: The First Lady in the Twentieth Century* (Westport, Conn.: Greenwood Press, 1991); and Gil Troy, *Affairs of State: The Rise and Rejection of the Presidential Couple since World War II* (New York: Free Press, 1997). An edited collection by Sara Alpern, Joyce Antler, Elisabeth Israels Perry, and Ingrid Winther Scobie, *The Challenge of Feminist Biography: Writing the Lives of Modern American Women* (Urbana: University of Illinois Press, 1992), addresses the issues involved in writing feminist biography. For a continually updated bibliography of primary and secondary source material on first ladies, see the National First Ladies' Library website (maintained by Stacy A. Cordery) at *http://www.firstladies.org/.*

Works about the public activities of early-twentieth-century women also proved useful. Nancy F. Cott, J. Stanley Lemons, William L. O'Neill, and Rosalind Rosenberg all provide important treatments of feminism. See Cott, *The Grounding of Modern Feminism* (New Haven, Conn.: Yale

University Press, 1987); Lemons, *The Woman Citizen: Social Feminism in the 1920s* (Urbana: University of Illinois Press, 1973); O'Neill, *Everyone Was Brave: A History of Feminism in America* (Chicago: Quadrangle Books, 1971); and Rosenberg, *Beyond Separate Spheres: Intellectual Roots of Modern Feminism* (New Haven, Conn.: Yale University Press, 1982). A discussion of women's differing political styles can be found in Paula Baker, "The Domestication of Politics: Women and American Political Society, 1780–1920," *American Historical Review* 89 (June 1984): 620–47. Analysis of the relationship between women's voluntary associations and reform can be found in books by Karen J. Blair, *The Clubwoman as Feminist: True Womanhood Redefined, 1868–1914* (New York: Holmes and Meier, 1980), and Anne Firor Scott, *Making the Invisible Woman Visible* (Urbana: University of Illinois Press, 1984). Robyn Muncy, Lois Scharf, and Joan M. Jensen offer more general discussions of women's activism. See Muncy, *Creating a Female Dominion in American Reform, 1890–1935* (New York: Oxford University Press, 1991), and Scharf and Jensen, *Decades of Discontent: The Women's Movement, 1920–1940* (Boston: Northeastern University Press, 1987). Dorothy M. Brown, *Setting a Course: American Women in the 1920s* (Boston: Twayne Publishers, 1987), created a useful synthesis of women's lives in the 1920s, and Glenna Matthews, *The Rise of Public Woman: Woman's Power and Woman's Place in the United States, 1630–1970* (New York: Oxford University Press, 1992), constructed an account of how women emerged into the public sphere. See Barbara Young Welke, *Recasting American Liberty: Gender, Race, Law, and the Railroad Revolution, 1865–1920* (New York: Cambridge University Press, 2001), for a gendered analysis of Jim Crow policies in the South.

Scholars are beginning to recognize the importance of the Girl Scouts as a feminist organization. See Margaret Jennings Rogers, "From True to New Womanhood: The Rise of the Girl Scouts, 1912–1930" (Ph.D. diss., Stanford University, 1992); Mary Aickin Rothschild, "To Scout or to Guide? The Girl Scout–Boy Scout Controversy, 1912–1941," *Frontiers: A Journal of Women's Studies* 6 (August 1982): 115–21; and Wendy C. Sterne, "The Formation of the Scouting Movement and the Gendering of Citizenship" (Ph.D. diss., University of Wisconsin–Madison, 1993). An older but more useful study for understanding Scouting during Hoover's tenure with the organization is Ethel Mockler, *Citizens in Action: The Girl Scout Record, 1912–1947* (New York: Girl Scouts National Organization, 1947).

On the transition from nineteenth- to twentieth-century conceptions of womanhood, see Nancy F. Cott, *The Bonds of Womanhood:
"Woman's Sphere" in New England, 1780–1835* (New Haven, Conn.: Yale
University Press, 1977); Harvey Green, *The Light of the Home: An Intimate View of the Lives of Women in Victorian America* (New York:
Pantheon Books, 1983); Barbara Welter, "The Cult of True Womanhood: 1820–1860," *American Quarterly* 24 (Summer 1966): 151–74; Dorothy M. Brown, *Setting a Course: American Women in the 1920s* (Boston:
Twayne Publishers, 1987); Nancy F. Cott, "Marriage and Women's Citi-
zenship in the United States, 1830–1934," *American Historical Review* 103
(December 1998): 1440–74; and Steven Mintz and Susan Kellogg, *Domestic Revolutions: A Social History of American Family Life* (New York:
Free Press, 1988). A vast literature describes suffrage and temperance
politics. See, for example, Jean H. Baker, ed., *Votes for Women: The
Struggle for Suffrage Revisited* (New York: Oxford University Press,
2002), and Barbara Leslie Epstein, *The Politics of Domesticity: Women,
Evangelism, and Temperance in Nineteenth-Century America* (Middletown, Conn.: Wesleyan University Press, 1981). For women in higher education and scientific careers, see Barbara Miller Solomon, *In the Company of Educated Women: A History of Women and Higher Education in
America* (New Haven, Conn.: Yale University Press, 1985), and Margaret
W. Rossiter, *Women Scientists in America: Struggles and Strategies to
1940* (Baltimore: Johns Hopkins University Press, 1982).

For women, progressivism, and the Great War, see, for example, Karen
J. Blair, *The Clubwoman as Feminist: True Womanhood Redefined, 1868–
1914* (New York: Holmes and Meier, 1980); Allen F. Davis, *Spearheads for
Reform: The Social Settlements and the Progressive Movement, 1890–1914*
(New York: Oxford University Press, 1967); Ellen Carol DuBois, *Harriot
Stanton Blatch and the Winning of Woman Suffrage* (New Haven, Conn.:
Yale University Press, 1997); Sara Hunter Graham, *Woman Suffrage and
the New Democracy* (New Haven, Conn.: Yale University Press, 1996);
Maurine Weiner Greenwald, *Women, War, and Work: The Impact of
World War I on Women Workers in the United States* (Westport, Conn.:
Greenwood Press, 1980); Anne Firor Scott, *Natural Allies: Women's Asso-
ciations in American History* (Urbana: University of Illinois Press, 1991);
and Rosalyn Terborg-Penn, *African American Women in the Struggle for
the Vote, 1850–1920* (Bloomington: Indiana University Press, 1998).

Numerous volumes on Herbert Hoover's life and presidency depict
the context in which Lou Henry Hoover's life developed. The largest

differences between the early Herbert Hoover literature and more recent publications result from the availability of Lou Henry Hoover's papers and from the increased sympathy to women's history topics in the last quarter of the twentieth century. The first serious Herbert Hoover biographers lacked access to Lou Hoover's papers, which were not opened until 1985. David Burner's *Herbert Hoover: A Public Life* (New York: Alfred A. Knopf, 1979), is one of the best one-volume accounts of Herbert Hoover, but it does little to reveal the complexity of Lou Henry Hoover. An equally important one-volume survey of Herbert Hoover is Joan Hoff Wilson's *Herbert Hoover: Forgotten Progressive* (Boston: Little, Brown, 1975). It was the first Hoover biography to recognize the significance of Lou Henry Hoover's life. The most innovative one-volume Hoover biography to date is Kendrick A. Clements, *Hoover, Conservation, and Consumerism: Engineering the Good Life* (Lawrence: University Press of Kansas, 2000), for its attempt to understand Hoover's life through the lens of conservation, a cause that was important to both Bert and Lou.

For Herbert Hoover's life from birth through 1918, the definitive accounts are in the volumes by George H. Nash: *The Life of Herbert Hoover: The Engineer, 1874–1914; The Humanitarian, 1914–1917;* and *Master of Emergencies, 1917–1918* (New York: W. W. Norton, 1983, 1988, 1996). An additional benefit of the Nash books is the sympathetic treatment of Lou Henry Hoover. The best one-volume account of the Hoover presidency published to date is Martin L. Fausold, *The Presidency of Herbert C. Hoover* (Lawrence: University Press of Kansas, 1985). Richard Norton Smith and Gary Dean Best have written the best books on Herbert Hoover's life after the White House. Careful researchers will want to consult Smith, *An Uncommon Man: The Triumph of Herbert Hoover* (Worland, Wyo.: High Plains Publishing Company, 1984), and Best, *Herbert Hoover: The Postpresidential Years, 1933–1964,* 2 vols. (Stanford, Calif.: Hoover Institution Press, 1983).

The opening of Lou Hoover's papers for research in 1985 created a flurry of interest in her career. Dale Mayer's essay "Not One to Stay at Home: The Papers of Lou Henry Hoover," *Prologue* 19 (Summer 1987): 85–93, provides an excellent introduction to the possibilities for studying Hoover's career in biographical form. Mayer also wrote "An Uncommon Woman: The Quiet Leadership Style of Lou Henry Hoover," *Presidential Studies Quarterly* 20 (Fall 1990): 685–98, and *Dining with the Hoover Family* (West Branch, Iowa: Herbert Hoover Presidential

Library, 1991), and edited *Lou Henry Hoover: Essays on a Busy Life* (Worland, Wyo.: High Plains Publishing Company, 1994). This collection provides only an overview of the gold mine awaiting a patient and meticulous biographer of Hoover. A flavor for Hoover's White House correspondence style can be found in J. Keith Melville, "The First Lady and the Cowgirl," *Pacific Historical Review* 57 (February 1988): 73–76. For a strictly chronological account of Hoover's life, see Anne Beiser Allen, *An Independent Woman: The Life of Lou Henry Hoover* (Westport, Conn.: Greenwood Press, 2000). Juvenile readers will profit from an examination of Nancy A. Colbert, *Lou Henry Hoover: The Duty to Serve* (Greensboro, N.C.: Morgan Reynolds, 1998). The two best publications to date on Lou Henry Hoover are Martha H. Swain, "Prelude to the New Deal: Lou Henry Hoover and Women's Relief Work," in *Uncommon Americans: The Lives and Legacies of Herbert and Lou Henry Hoover,* ed. Timothy Walch (Westport, Conn.: Praeger/Greenwood, 2003), 151–66, and Kendrick A. Clements's article, "The New Era and the New Woman: Lou Henry Hoover and 'Feminism's Awkward Age,'" *Pacific Historical Review* 73 (August 2004).

Donald Lisio's *Hoover, Blacks, and Lily-Whites: A Study of Southern Strategies* (Chapel Hill: University of North Carolina Press, 1985) provides useful insights into the politics of race during the Hoover administration. For more specific accounts of the DePriest controversy, see David S. Day's "Herbert Hoover and Racial Politics: The DePriest Incident," *Journal of Negro History* 65 (Winter 1980): 6–17, and "A New Perspective on the 'DePriest Tea' Historiographic Controversy," *Journal of Negro History* 75 (Summer/Fall 1990): 120–24.

Several other secondary sources provided valuable background on specific aspects of Lou Henry Hoover's life and career. For more information on the Boxer Rebellion, see Diana Preston, *The Boxer Rebellion: The Dramatic Story of China's Civil War on Foreigners that Shook the World in the Summer of 1900* (New York: Walker and Company, 2000). For useful information on the various Hoover homes, see Ruth Dennis, *The Homes of the Hoovers* (West Branch, Iowa: Herbert Hoover Presidential Library, 1986). For details on women and sports in the 1920s and 1930s, see Alice Allene Sefton, *The Women's Division National Amateur Athletic Federation: Sixteen Years of Progress in Athletics for Girls and Women, 1923–1939* (Stanford, Calif.: Stanford University Press, 1941). For the crisis of modernity, see John William Ward, *Red, White, and*

Blue: Men, Books, and Ideas in American Culture (New York: Oxford University Press, 1969). For more information on Camp Rapidan, see Darwin Lambert, *Herbert Hoover's Hideaway* (Luray, Va.: Shenandoah Natural History Association, 1971). For background on Charles Curtis and the Gann controversy, see Marvin Ewy, *Charles Curtis of Kansas: Vice President of the United States, 1929–1933* (Emporia, Kans.: Emporia State Research Studies, 1961). The best accounts of the depression during the Hoover years are Albert U. Romasco, *The Poverty of Abundance: Hoover, the Nation, the Depression* (New York: Oxford University Press, 1965); Richard Vedder and Lowell Gallaway, *Out of Work: Unemployment and Government in Twentieth Century America* (New York: Holmes and Meier, 1993); and Robert S. McElvaine, *The Great Depression: America, 1929–1941* (New York: Times Books, 1984). For information on Appalachian culture and education, see David E. Whisnant, *All That Is Native and Fine: The Politics of Culture in an American Region* (Chapel Hill: University of North Carolina Press, 1983). Background on the creation of the Herbert Hoover National Historic Site is in Kevin Boatright, "A Simple Little Building," *Palimpsest* 68 (Summer 1987): 60–71. For more information on Pro-America, see June Melby Benowitz, *Days of Discontent: American Women and Right-Wing Politics, 1933–1945* (De Kalb: Northern Illinois University Press, 2002).

INDEX

Hagner, Belle, 60
Hall, Mildred. *See* Campbell, Mildred
Hall
Hampton Choir, 77
Hanley, Elizabeth, 173–74, 177
Harding, Florence Kling, 53, 92, 190;
and the media, 152
Harding, Warren G., 38
Harrison, Carolyn, 178
Hayes, Lucy Webb, 57
Heizer, Mabel, 104, 107, 108
Henriques, Alida, 162, 179
Henry, Charles D. (father), 6, 7, *7, 14,*
31
Henry, Florence Weed (mother), 6, 7,
14, 18, 21, 31
Henry, Jean (sister). *See* Large, Jean
Henry
Henry, Lou. *See* Hoover, Lou Henry
Herbert Hoover National Historic
Site, West Branch, Iowa, 186
Hoffman, Mira, 115–18, 133
Homemaking, 169; gender roles in,
147–48
Home-ownership program, 36
Hoover, Allan Henry (son), 19, *19,* 23,
24, 29, 31, 32, 41, 42, 144, 183
Hoover, Herbert, 2, *72;* and American
Relief Administration, 33, 115;
background and education of, 10–
11; and Bonus March, 157; business
career of, 15–19; in China, 15–16; fi-
nancial independence of, 19–20;
and Great Depression, 90, 91, 93,
105, 108; "Ike" Hoover's description
of, 173; inauguration of, 50; in Italy,
21; and LHH's activism, 3, 33; and
LHH's death, 185; LHH's first

meeting with, 10; LHH's support
and defense of, 141, 157–58; marriage of, 2, 3–4, 13–15, *14,* 80–81, 92–
93, 116, 132, 141, 188–89; and the
media, 152; and Navy Department
appropriations, 156; personality of,
79, 142; political ideology of, 3;
presidential campaigns and elections (1928) 37, 41–49 (1932) 154,
157, 160–63, *161;* and President's
Mountain School, 84; publications
of, 174–75, 181–82; public image of,
150; and public relations, 72; Eleanor Roosevelt's note to, 186; as
secretary of commerce, 29; South
American tour by, 48–49; southern
strategy of, 71; and U.S. Food Administration, 26–27, 100; and
White House decorations, 56; and
White House entertaining, 75–76;
world travels of, 18; in World War I,
3, 19, 22–27, 29; in World War II,
179, 183
Hoover, Herbert, Jr. (son), 18, *19,* 23,
24, 32, 42, 183; illness of, 100, 149–50
Hoover, Irwin H. "Ike" (White House
usher), 54, 77, 92, 171, 172–73
Hoover, Lou Henry, *184;* and African
Americans, 8, 54, 65–71, 169–70;
athleticism of, 7, 8; in Australia, 18;
in auto accident, 45–46; birth of, 6;
and Camp Rapidan, 58–59; charity
and generosity of, 17, 102, 104;
childhood and teenage years of, 6,
7, 8, 9; children's Christmas parties
(1929) 77, (1930) 143–44 (1931) 79–
80; in China, 15–16, *17;* at college,
9–12, *12;* conservatism of, 173–81;